LEADERSHIP AT THE CROSSROADS

LEADERSHIP AT THE CROSSROADS

Joanne B. Ciulla, Set Editor

Volume 3

Leadership and the Humanities

Edited by Joanne B. Ciulla

Praeger Perspectives

Westport, Connecticut
London

Library of Congress Cataloging-in-Publication Data

Leadership at the crossroads.
   v. cm.
  Includes bibliographical references and index.
  Contents: v. 1. Leadership and psychology / edited by Crystal L. Hoyt,
  George R. Goethals, and Donelson R. Forsyth – v. 2. Leadership and politics / edited by
  Michael A. Genovese and Lori Cox Han – v. 3. Leadership and the humanities /
  edited by Joanne B. Ciulla.
  ISBN 978-0-275-99760-1 ((set) : alk. paper) – ISBN 978-0-275-99762-5 ((vol. 1) :
  alk. paper) – ISBN 978-0-275-99764-9 ((vol. 2) : alk. paper) – ISBN 978-0-275-99766-3
  ((vol. 3) : alk. paper)
  1. Leadership. I. Forsyth, Donelson R., 1953-
  HM1261.L422 2008
  303.3'4—dc22   2008018976

British Library Cataloguing in Publication Data is available.

Library of Congress Catalog Card Number: 2008018976
ISBN: Set: 978-0-275-99760-1
    Vol. 1: 978-0-275-99762-5
    Vol. 2: 978-0-275-99764-9
    Vol. 3: 978-0-275-99766-3

First published in 2008

Praeger Publishers, 88 Post Road West, Westport, CT 06881
An imprint of Greenwood Publishing Group, Inc.
www.praeger.com

Printed in the United States of America

The paper used in this book complies with the
Permanent Paper Standard issued by the National
Information Standards Organization (Z39.48–1984).

10 9 8 7 6 5 4 3 2 1

In Memory of Our Fathers

Andrew Joseph Ciulla, 1926–2006
Marinus Johannes Kanters, 1929–2007

Contents

Preface

It is surprising that the field we now call "leadership studies" did not originate in the humanities because, as you will see, it has been there for a very long time. The humanities consist of disciplines that explain how we came to be what we are today. They tell us what people did in the past, how they felt, what they believed, and how they expressed themselves through language, literature, art, music, and dance. The subjects that make up the humanities peer into the depths of human nature and relationships. When we read a great piece of literature, history, or biography, we enter into a conversation that sometimes spans across place and time and connects us as human beings.

All too often in universities today, students, their parents, and some administrators write off humanity courses as nice luxuries that are not very useful, especially for getting a job. After all, except for history, biography, and anthropology, the rest of the humanities, such as art, music, literature, and philosophy, are not about *facts* or *real* things. They concern themselves with fictions—mere creations of human imagination. Yet when you think about it, perhaps leadership too is a creation of our collective imagination—an idea about human relationships forged from the hopes, fears, dreams, emotions, wants, needs, and collective experiences of humanity. This is not to disparage the social sciences and, in particular, the various fields of psychology that have long dominated leadership studies. Social scientists have done an excellent job of describing and explaining leadership. What the humanities offer that the social sciences cannot adequately provide is the backdrop or context for understanding leadership.

This book aims to do two things. First, it brings different areas of knowledge into leadership studies, and second, it demonstrates how to use this knowledge to learn about leadership. While most scholars believe that work in leadership studies should be interdisciplinary, that is easier said than done. Humanities scholars are typically not trained to do quantitative research and social scientists usually are not trained to interpret texts or works of art. The best way to develop an interdisciplinary field is by encouraging work on leadership from experts in their own disciplines. In doing so, we create a body of quality work from the social sciences and the humanities that can be used to do interdisciplinary research on leadership. The authors in this book draw from literature, autobiography, philosophy, classics, music, and art to deliver new perspectives on leadership.

The first three chapters of this book are stories about leaders who never existed—*Moby-Dick, Don Quixote,* and the *Gilgamesh Epic.* These chapters tease out different aspects of leadership and leaders. In all of the stories, we recognize some of the universal challenges that the leaders face. We find leaders with drive and vision who motivate and care for others, but we also witness the tragedy that befalls leaders and followers when leaders succumb to their own human frailty.

In the next chapters, the authors analyze real leaders. We first encounter the general, and then president, Ulysses S. Grant, through his autobiography. This chapter examines in detail Grant's description of the surrender of General Robert E. Lee to him at Appomattox. It scrutinizes what happened that day, how Grant felt, and what this episode teaches us about Grant as a leader and about leadership in general. We meet the second leader in this section in a different way. Chapter 5 draws from literature in philosophy and fiction to describe the powerful emotion of resentment (specifically the French concept of this emotion *ressentiment*). It then uses this description to explain how the controversial president, Hugo Chávez, has cultivated and exploited this emotion to gain and consolidate his power in Venezuela today.

The third section offers two papers by philosophers. In Chapter 6 we see how contemporary linguistic philosophy and Umberto Eco's work in semiotics offer a way of resolving the problem of defining leadership—a pervasive problem in the leadership literature. Through this linguistic analysis, we learn that it is followers who construct the meaning of the word "leader." Using examples of the Roman Emperor Nero and the former Russian president Vladimir Putin, the next chapter draws from the classics, literature, and philosophy to explain why followers expect leaders to be physically and mentally present in times of disaster. It assesses what this expectation means in terms of the normative aspects of leadership such as care, duty, and propriety.

The rest of the chapters in this book are about music and art. The arts contribute to the study of leadership in two general ways: first, leaders use the arts to lead, and second, artists and works of art can lead or initiate change in society and/or in the arts. Chapter 8 chronicles the ways in which music influences meaning, behavior, and morality. Leaders can and have used music to perform functions that are necessary to leadership. For example, music motivates us; it provides a way for people to come together, cooperate, and create community. In Chapter 9, we have a look at a composer as a leader. This chapter describes how the English composer Henry Carey used satire to bring English opera back to the English stage. Carey exercises leadership among other artists and uses his art to help change the artistic preferences of English society in his time.

The last two chapters are about the visual arts. In Chapter 10 we look at leadership through the lens of art history. It begins by focusing on how leaders used art during Renaissance and the Reformation. The chapter then goes on to examine how artists such as Honoré Daumier acted as powerful social critics in the eighteenth and nineteenth centuries. The final chapter looks at how art and design sell the ideas of leaders and consumer products. Leaders take advantage of art to create symbols that represent their values, ideologies, and perceptions of truth and reality. In particular, the chapter examines some of the poster art that was used in Nazi propaganda and in the service of the Bolshevik Revolution. We learn how the artist Ludwig Hohlwein provided Adolf Hitler with images that promoted Hitler's Aryan ideology. We also encounter artists who banded together in small groups to challenge leaders and the status quo.

As I hope the reader will discover, this volume offers new insights and unique approaches to the study of leadership. I am very grateful to all of the authors of this book for their time, wisdom, scholarship, creative energy, and willingness to do something different. I also owe a debt of thanks to the Keck Foundation for funding a project that encouraged academics from disciplines that are typically outside of leadership studies to develop courses on leadership. Many of the authors in this book either taught such courses and/or took part in the conferences supported by this grant. Last, but not least, books are not born without editors. I also want to thank our editor, Jeff Olson, for shepherding us through the process of turning our ideas into a book.

Joanne B. Ciulla

PART I

WHAT FICTITIOUS LEADERS TELL US ABOUT LEADERSHIP

1

Of "Gods and Commodores": Leadership in Melville's *Moby-Dick*

NICHOLAS O. WARNER

Given its concern with all forms of human conflict and cooperation, it is not surprising that literature has abundant ramifications for the study of leadership. Literary works offer compelling depictions of the ways that leadership can succeed or fail, of the emotional relationship between leaders and followers, and of the ethical complexities and challenges that that relationship so often entails. This discussion focuses on a masterpiece both of American literature and of the artistic depiction of leadership: Herman Melville's *Moby-Dick*, first published in 1851. The action of the novel, of course, takes place largely on a nineteenth-century whaling vessel, the *Pequod*, but its relevance to leadership goes far beyond its immediate period and setting. Relying on all of the artistic resources available to him as an author, rather than on scholarly discourse or quantitative research, Melville presents, in effect, a qualitative examination of the insidious ways that an inspiring, imaginative leader can mold followers to do his will, even against their better judgment; of the competing claims that exert their force on followers; and of the tensions between ethical and pragmatic considerations in leadership. Through precise language, evocative imagery, an eventful plot, and rich characterization, *Moby-Dick* delves into the nature of leaders, followers, and the forces that both bind them and drive them apart. In addition to clarifying one particular novel's take on leadership, an analysis of these issues can testify to the broader importance of leadership as a theme in literature, and to the importance of literature for understanding leadership.

From his earliest adventure narratives, *Typee* and *Omoo,* to his last prose fiction, "Billy Budd," Melville's work shows a persistent concern with such leadership-related topics as official versus unofficial authority, justice in the treatment of subordinates, the hierarchies of rank and power, and a love of democracy combined with a fear of social disorder.[1] The primary literary locus of these issues is a world that Melville knew well—that of his own youthful experiences as a sailor on ships both military and commercial. Thus the bulk of Melville's fiction gives us a nineteenth-century world, an American world, a male world, a seaman's world. Nevertheless, though bound by nation and period, and often located within the microcosm of a ship with its officers and crew, Melville's depictions of power relations between leaders and followers have applicability beyond the confines of any one profession or context. Melville himself understood his works to have broad moral and philosophical implications. This is apparent in his frequent metaphorical use of nautical imagery and in the explicit comparisons his fiction makes between its particular settings, American society, and the human condition in general. In the last chapter of *White Jacket,* for instance—a novel dealing with naval life and published a year before *Moby-Dick*—Melville makes his analogical approach plain. Specifically addressing his readers as "shipmates and world-mates," Melville writes, "As a man-of-war that sails through the sea, so this earth that sails through the air. We mortals are all on board a fast-sailing, never-sinking, world-frigate, of which God was the shipwright."[2] Clearly, this is a writer for whom life and leadership at sea exist in significant parallel with life and leadership on shore.

Like many of his other writings, *Moby-Dick* depicts matters of shipboard hierarchy, rank, and protocol, reflecting Melville's interest in leadership and the organizational structures within which it occurs. But *Moby-Dick* goes further than any of Melville's other works to explore the relation between institutional and personal authority as a basis for leadership; the moral dimensions of means and ends in leadership; the powers and perils of charisma; and above all, the emotional intertwining of followers and leaders, whether for good or ill. A full account of these issues in *Moby-Dick* could easily threaten to reach the length of a novel itself. This discussion, instead, will focus on several salient examples of the topics mentioned above, with emphasis on the infamous Captain Ahab, and on the important role played in the book by Ahab's followers.

At this point, I should make it clear that my use of the term "leader" extends to moral and immoral leaders alike. James MacGregor Burns has argued that a tyrannical or unethical authority figure should be called by some other term than leader, such as "power-wielder," a phrase that certainly fits the dictatorial Captain Ahab.[3] But Ahab is also an undeniably brilliant influencer, motivator, and persuader—in a word, a leader. In this regard, I follow Robert C. Solomon's view that it is possible "to distinguish between effective but evil leadership and ethical leadership." [4] The work of Jean Lipman-Blumen is also apposite here, as she has painstakingly analyzed the damage wrought by people in power who, though alluring and at times even inspiring, are "toxic" in their effects; pernicious as their leadership is, it seems artificial not to call them leaders. [5] Similarly, Barbara Kellerman argues that "To deny bad leadership equivalence in the conversation . . . is misguided, tantamount to a medical school that would claim to teach health while ignoring disease." Drawing on Adolf Hitler as "the most extreme example" of evil leadership, Kellerman points out that "not only was his impact on twentieth-century history arguably greater than anyone else's but also he was brilliantly skilled at inspiring, mobilizing, and directing followers." [6] One of the most significant things about *Moby-Dick* is that, while fully revealing the dangers of his leadership, "the book neither justifies nor condemns Ahab." [7] Instead—and more interestingly—through the character of Ahab, Melville invites his readers to contemplate the intricacies of the leader-follower dynamic, and of the ways that people assess both leadership ethics and effectiveness.

Central as Captain Ahab is to *Moby-Dick,* he is neither the only nor the first leader we meet in the novel. By beginning with the various leader-figures and themes introduced in the book's opening chapters, we can follow Melville's own creative process, as he gradually develops the issues identified in the preceding paragraphs. As we will see, although Ahab is the "supreme lord and dictator" [8] on an isolated ship thousands of miles from shore, his leadership, like that of all leaders, takes place in a context where other influences—whether of religion, ideology, past experience, the examples of other models of leadership, and even personal temperament—exist in the minds and memories of his followers. That context is carefully established by Melville early in the novel.

"Who ain't a slave? Tell me that." With this striking rhetorical question in the book's very first chapter (*Moby-Dick,* 28), Melville's narrator, Ishmael, alerts us to his view of the universality of servitude and obedience in some form or other, and to the ubiquitous need to accept the presence of authority, if not of leadership. Everyone in life is buffeted, whether by crotchety sea captains or others in positions of power—a truth to which Ishmael submits with ironically resigned good humor. In fact, Ishmael prefers to go to sea as a common sailor rather than as an officer. Explaining that the power of leaders is not as great or enviable a thing as it seems, Ishmael slyly jokes that "for the most part the Commodore on the quarter-deck gets his atmosphere from the sailors on the forecastle. He thinks he breathes it first; but not so." The text then shifts to leaders in general: "In much the same way do the commonalty lead their leaders in many other things, at the same time that the leaders little suspect it" (*Moby-Dick,* 28–29). Of course, this generalization only partially applies to Ahab; while he is highly sensitive to his followers' reactions to him, in his overall goal of wreaking vengeance on the great white whale, Moby-Dick, and in specific decisions in the pursuit of that goal, Ahab is the prime initiator and controller. But what is especially noteworthy here is that Melville himself includes this comment about leaders being led by their followers—a comment that ties in with much recent thinking on the reciprocity of the leader-follower dynamic, and that points to Melville's concern with leadership already in the book's earliest pages.[9]

The leadership theme in *Moby-Dick* expands with the introduction of several other figures whose depiction provides a background against which the novel's chief leader, the mysterious Captain Ahab, will appear all the more powerfully when he makes his theatrical entry on the *Pequod*'s upper deck in Chapter 28. Long before Ahab, however, we meet the enigmatic clergyman known as Father Mapple, a popular spiritual leader among the whalemen, who preaches a powerful sermon about the Biblical Jonah (himself swallowed by a whale). I do not attempt here to resolve or even to join the critical debate over Melville's attitudes toward Father Mapple's Calvinistic sermon in Chapter 9. While earlier critics tended to take Mapple's sermon "straight," as a reflection of Melville's own views, scholars since Lawrance Thompson's controversial *Melville's Quarrel with God* have inclined toward a far darker, satirical reading of both Mapple and his sermon. My own sense is that Father Mapple's sermon is at least partly a send-up of the fire-and-brimstone sermons familiar to Melville from youth; irony, whether facetious or bitter, is always close at hand in Melville's work.[10] Be that as it may, my emphasis here is not on Melville's theological views, but on the relevance of Mapple and his sermon to the larger theme of leadership in *Moby-Dick.*

Father Mapple's personal vigor, his thunderous oratory, his employment of a ship's rope for a ladder with which to climb into his prow-shaped pulpit—all of these facts speak to his leaderly ability to communicate with his congregation. It is intriguing, as well, that his stern and suffering persona, as well as the fierceness of his message, actually foreshadow the demonic Captain Ahab. But the actual content of Father Mapple's sermon is also important to leadership in two basic ways. First, Father Mapple stresses the importance of following the commands of God, the leader above all others. To follow such commands is not easy, Father Mapple asserts, for "if we obey God, we must disobey ourselves; and it is in this disobeying ourselves, wherein the hardness of obeying God consists" (*Moby-Dick,* 72). Second, Father Mapple explains the need to disobey not only ourselves but our earthly leaders when they conflict with the commands of God. "Delight is to him," Father Mapple promises, "a far, far upward, and inward, delight—who against the proud gods and commodores of this earth ever stands forth his own inexorable self" (*Moby-Dick*, 80). Both of these issues—the need to obey God and to disobey earthly "gods and commodores," including our own selfish desires—implicitly appear later in the novel. Examples include Ahab's refusal to respect the natural order that seems a reflection of God's order, his monomaniacal pursuit of the whale that bit off his leg, his blasphemous "baptism" of his harpoon "in nomine diaboli" (in the name of the devil), and his first mate Starbuck's agonized internal struggle between loyalty and mutiny. Ahab, indeed, will come to seem a Father Mapple in reverse as he indeed insists on being his "own inexorable self," but a self that seeks to obey not God or the laws of God's creation, but rather its own willful desire to destroy Moby-Dick.

Through Father Mapple's sermon, Melville introduces a web of ideas—obedience, acceptance, pride, humility, defiance, self-assertion, and the choice between conscience and expedience, between the "God of heaven" and "the gods and commodores of this earth." It is possible that Father Mapple also comes off as a self-appointed "god" or "commodore"; Melville's wonderfully ironic juxtaposition of the power and divinity of "gods" combined with the far less significant, but still dignified, almost pompous image of those who would set themselves up as "commodores," redounds to Father Mapple himself. He is, after all, very ready to tell everyone else what to do, even as he tells them not to listen to what *others* tell them to do! In this way, Father Mapple suggests the "noisy" quality that Robert Solomon, drawing on Voltaire, detects in leadership: "Too many leaders, as Voltaire complained of heroes, 'are so noisy.'" Solomon goes on to say, "So much of what I have noticed about leadership is the noise." [11] In any event, Father Mapple's persona, the ideas raised in his sermon, and even, perhaps, his "noise," form part of the ethical backdrop for the leader-follower relationship that unfolds on the *Pequod* over the course of the book's remaining several hundred pages.

From Father Mapple, Melville turns to more secular authority figures—two of the owners of the *Pequod,* Captains Peleg and Bildad, and then to the *Pequod's* first, second, and third mates. The blustering Peleg and the taciturn Bildad are really more managers than leaders—their focus is on such necessary but mundane things as efficiency, profit, and competence. Of the two, Bildad especially is singled out for his hypocrisy. Just after reading aloud the passage from Matthew beginning "Lay not up for yourselves treasures upon earth," he obsesses about the slightest costs of materials and fussily orders the crew to be sparing in their use of cheese and especially butter, at "twenty cents the pound" (*Moby-Dick*, 147). (The character of Bildad is, in fact, on a spectrum with a whole subset of hypocritical or sanctimonious authority figures whom Melville exposes throughout his work, e.g., the pietistic missionaries in *Typee*, the two-faced Captain Riga in *Redburn*, and, of course, the sinister, Iago-like mate, Claggart, in "Billy Budd.") What is notably lacking in both Bildad and Peleg is any sense of something larger than their own immediate pecuniary concerns; it is clear that neither will ever rise to the kind of intense relation with followers or articulation of a vision that is usually associated with leadership. These two men also form part of the larger background for the development of leadership in this novel.

Once aboard the *Pequod*, Ishmael gives us a detailed description, in two successive chapters both entitled "Knights and Squires" (Chapters 26 and 27), of the subleaders of the ship: the three mates Starbuck, Stubb, and Flask, each with his own particular strengths and failings. All are skilled at their tasks, yet each is a distinct individual. Starbuck is the most thoughtful and serious of the three; Stubb is the happy-go-lucky second mate whose abilities are limited by what he himself calls his eleventh commandment: "think not" (*Moby-Dick*, 174). The third mate is the mediocre, unimaginative Flask, a man of "ignorant, unconscious fearlessness" (*Moby-Dick*, 163). Each mate is accompanied by his own "squire" or harpooner—the South Sea islander Queequeg for Starbuck, the American Indian Tashtego for Stubb, and the African Daggoo for Flask. Through his description of officers and harpooners, of the owner-captains Bildad and Peleg, and the figure of Father Mapple, Melville has on one level merely created suspense about the mysterious, much talked about but as yet invisible Captain Ahab. But at the same time, Melville has achieved something more important: he has unobtrusively set up the hierarchical, cultural, religious, multiracial, and commercial organizational structure of the *Pequod*, thereby creating a realistic context within which we can see Ahab's own leadership and the interrelations of those around him.

To understand Ahab's leadership, we must understand the profound irony at its heart: Ahab embodies what many today consider to be positive, admirable leadership skills, but he deploys those skills toward a disastrous end, resulting in the destruction of his ship, himself, and his crew—save the "one [who] did survive the wreck," the narrator Ishmael (*Moby-Dick*, 723). Quite apart from his rank as Captain, which in nineteenth-century American law gave him powers on shipboard far in excess of what most leaders on land would have,[12] Ahab's personal qualities read like a recipe for successful leadership. These include charisma, social and emotional intelligence, oratorical skills, imagination, professional competence, courage, and the ability to exert both transformational and transactional leadership.

As the above suggests, dictatorial though he often is, Ahab relies far less on coercion than on inspiration, motivation, and theatrics to bond his followers to his own dark vision—the destruction of the great white whale, Moby-Dick. Ahab well understands what Ishmael tells us about the importance of theater in leadership: "For be a man's intellectual superiority what it will, it can never assume the practical, available supremacy over other men, without the aid of some sort of external arts and entrenchments, always, in themselves, more or less paltry and base" (*Moby-Dick*, 98). Such "external arts and entrenchments" appear throughout the book, but most vividly in "The Quarter-Deck" (Chapter 36), especially the scene where Ahab first reveals to the crew his own secret agenda of pursuing Moby-Dick. If, as Edwin Hollander points out, Peter Drucker was correct in noting that "leadership *is* performance," it could also be said that leadership is *a* performance.[13] And performance, in this theatrical sense, rather than the evaluative sense that Drucker and Hollander mean, is certainly what we see in Ahab's carefully managed use of language and gesture throughout the novel, but especially in "The Quarter-Deck." As he speaks to his assembled mariners, Ahab uses the institutional aura of his captaincy as a stepping stone to something more emotionally compelling—to the noninstitutional, personally charismatic authority whereby Ahab convinces the sailors to make his goal of slaying Moby-Dick their own.[14] But to accomplish this, Ahab needs to evoke the kind of fervor and personal loyalty that will allow him to transform the ostensible, legitimate task of the *Pequod* into the illegitimate task of his own purely personal vendetta.

"The Quarter-Deck" chapter reveals just how Ahab evokes such fervor and loyalty. Far more than the authority of his institutional rank as captain, Ahab uses such devices as his potent oratory (reminiscent of the eloquence of Milton's Satan in *Paradise Lost*); his personal interaction with crew members (e.g., affectionately calling the harpooner Tashtego "Tash," calling the rest of the crew "my hearties" as he gathers them around to hear him speak of the white whale, and exchanging tales with them of Moby-Dick); his offer of the golden doubloon that he nails to the mast as a trophy for the sailor who first spots Moby-Dick; and his communion-like ritual of drinking with his crew. In a shrewd, daring manipulation of metaphor, Ahab turns his three mates into, as he calls them, "cardinals" (by which logic, of course, he himself is the Pope); Ahab also makes them "cup-bearers" to the three harpooners— the men who will be most instrumental in slaughtering Moby-Dick. Intoxicated by his rhetoric no less than by the grog he has them drink from the caps of their own harpoons, the harpooners Queequeg, Tashtego, and Daggoo join Ahab in swearing "Death to Moby-Dick," whereupon the celebratory drink, with its traditional symbolism of sealing a pledge, is passed round to the entire crew in Ahab's masterful manipulation of ritual to his own purposes: "The long, barbed steel goblets were lifted; and to cries and maledictions against the white whale, the spirits were simultaneously quaffed down with a hiss" (*Moby-Dick*, 225).

As ship's captain, Ahab has the official authority to dispense or withhold grog; but in turning the grog drinking into a eucharistic ritual of brotherhood and solemn oath-taking, Ahab charismatically forges an emotional bond with his followers more intense than that between mere employer and employee,

or between superior officer and common sailor. The full flavor of this bond—
and its perilousness—can only be conveyed by Melville's own prose:

> Receiving the brimming pewter, and turning to the harpooneers, he ordered
> them to produce their weapons. Then ranging them before him near the capstan,
> with their harpoons in their hands, while his three mates stood at his side with
> their lances, and the rest of the ship's company formed a circle round the group;
> he stood for an instance searchingly eyeing every man of his crew. But those
> wild eyes met his, as the bloodshot eyes of the prairie wolves meet the eye of
> their leader, ere he rushes on at their head in the trail of the bison; but, alas! only
> to fall into the hidden snare of the Indian (*Moby-Dick*, 223).

One important feature of the episodes with the doubloon and the communal drink is Ahab's seeming empowerment of his followers, as he extends prestige and a semblance of power to carefully selected subordinates. This is apparent in Ahab having Starbuck provide the hammer with which to nail up the doubloon, thus involving the first mate in this act that symbolizes the *Pequod's* new mission of finding Moby-Dick. Empowerment also appears in Ahab's making the three mates "cup-bearers" and "cardinals" during the ceremonial toast, and in his elevation of the harpooners to the role of virtual communicants. Ahab's treatment of the three nonwhite harpooners as elites is all the more significant and symbolically potent a gesture when one remembers that when *Moby-Dick* was published (1851), slavery still existed in the United States, and nonwhite mariners were paid at a lower rate than whites.[15] Thus Ahab's leadership here transcends even the racial boundaries of his day as he unifies all of his followers into a single, controllable unit.

Through the doubloon itself, Ahab cleverly sets up a perpetual emblem and reminder of the crew's new mission; at the same time, he democratically offers status and monetary incentive to any sailor, however humble, who first spots the white whale. In truth, however, all of Ahab's elevations and inclusions amount to no more than a nineteenth-century version of what Joanne Ciulla, in a more contemporary business context, has called "bogus empowerment."[16] Ahab's empowerment of his followers is temporary and shallow—such things as having men provide hammers and share in symbolic drinking rituals give them no genuine or lasting authority, and serve only to involve the crew more deeply in Ahab's own personal agenda.

In "The Quarter Deck," first mate Starbuck alone remonstrates against Ahab's quest, recalling the *Pequod's* proper mission—to hunt whales and provide whale oil for the crew's (and Ahab's) employers. But the ever adroit Ahab turns his subleader's legitimate objection into an opportunity to manipulate what Burns, in his well-known discussion of transforming and transactional leadership, would call higher level and lower level needs. For Burns, transactional leadership is associated with more material, "lower-level needs"; thus transactional leaders "approach followers with an eye to exchanging one thing for another: jobs for votes, or subsidies for campaign contributions." Transforming leadership, on the other hand, "seeks to satisfy higher needs"; the transforming leader "taps the needs and raises the aspirations and helps shape the values—and hence mobilizes the potential—of followers." [17] The pragmatic, honest Starbuck tries to recall Ahab to his basic transactional contract with the *Pequod's* owners: "I came here to hunt whales," Starbuck coolly informs Ahab, "not my commander's vengeance. How many barrels will thy vengeance yield thee even if thou gettest it, Captain Ahab? It will not fetch thee much in our Nantucket market." Belittling such prudential considerations, Ahab contemptuously cries, "Nantucket market! Hoot!" Telling Starbuck, and by implication the entire crew that looks on, that "thou requirest a little lower layer"—i.e., a layer of deeper insight and meaning—Ahab goes on to emphasize the more intangible, emotional, and even spiritual dimensions of his quest as he strikes his chest and declares, "my vengeance will fetch a great premium *here!*" (*Moby-Dick*, 220).

Ahab's leadership in this scene typifies the charismatic leader's bold departure from the confinements of the routine and the rational. As Sonja Hunt puts it in her analysis of Max Weber's famous conceptualization of charisma, the charismatic leader opposes the "routinizing process by rejecting rational, economic objectives and redressing the balance toward more 'irrational,' but more essentially human pursuits." [18] This helps to explain the futility of Starbuck's rational, economic arguments to Ahab—the first mate will never get past Ahab's visionary monomania through such appeals. Starbuck is, after all, not addressing two other captains whom we, like the sailors on the *Pequod,* have already met: and if ever two men embodied the "routinizing process" that Hunt describes, it would be Peleg and Bildad. Their earlier appearance helps to explain how, in contrast with such uninspiring, petty figures, Ahab's color, daring, and contempt for narrow monetary considerations can only make his leadership all the more dangerously appealing to his crew.

Not content with just dismissing the objections of his first mate, Ahab, in one of the most famous passages in nineteenth-century American literature, calls on his sailors to transform themselves into heroes, if they but "strike through the mask!"—the "pasteboard" mask of mundane reality (*Moby-Dick*, 220). In so doing, they will then reach some transcendent truth beyond the world of mere appearances, including the "Nantucket Market" that the conventionally dutiful Starbuck invokes. Ahab here seems to epitomize transformational leadership—he calls on his men to rise above merely mercantile considerations so as to pursue a nobler, more heroic quest; to repeat Burns's language above, Ahab "taps the needs and raises the aspirations and helps shape the values—and hence mobilizes the potential—of followers." At the same time, through the very tangible gold doubloon that he has nailed to the mast, Ahab addresses the crew's natural interest in lower level, material needs. Thus both transforming and transactional leadership, with their attendant higher and lower level needs, become tools that Ahab cunningly deploys in his successful manipulation of the crew to his disastrous enterprise. As Ahab himself says, in the pithiest commentary I have yet seen on his blend of effective technique with unethical ends, "my means are sane; my method and my object mad" (*Moby-Dick*, 250).

Ahab's awareness of the more mundane side of his followers—and of the importance of keeping this side satisfied while challenging the crew to rise to the heroic, if misguided opportunity he offers them in chasing down Moby-Dick—clearly emerges later in the book, when Ahab worries about maintaining control over the crew as their voyage continues:

> In times of strong emotion mankind disdain all base considerations; but such times are evanescent. . . . Granting that the White Whale fully incites the hearts of this my savage crew, and playing round their savageness even breeds a certain generous knight-errantism in them, still, while for the love of it they give chase to Moby-Dick, they must also have food for their more common, daily appetites.

Reasoning thus, Ahab does not forget the uninspiring but ineluctable lower level needs of human beings: "I will not strip these men, thought Ahab, of all hopes of cash—aye cash" (*Moby-Dick*, 286). Cynical as Ahab's thinking is here, it has important implications about the insufficiency of purely inspirational or higher-level appeals to one's followers; given the realities of human nature as Melville presents them, both the lower and higher level needs require satisfaction for leadership to succeed.

Of course, part of what makes Ahab's approach to his men so seductive is that the pursuit of Moby-Dick is not that far removed from the ship's official mission—to hunt, capture, and kill whales. It is not as if Ahab has proposed some task unrelated or antithetical to the ship's original assignment; in fact, the very closeness of Ahab's goal—the pursuit of a single particular whale—to that assignment helps to assure the crew's acquiescence. Consequently, Ahab's violation of his own duty to the ship's owners is less immediately and flagrantly obvious than it might otherwise have been; as we have seen, his first mate publicly upbraids him for this violation, but following Ahab's fiery response, lapses into tacit submission to the captain's will. Precisely because whale hunting is already the purpose of everybody on board the *Pequod*, it is easier for Ahab to divert his followers toward his personal, vengeful goal of slaying Moby-Dick—and indeed, to fill those followers with enthusiasm for this goal. Through Ahab, Melville illuminates the insidiousness with which a deceptive leader, whatever the context, can substitute his own wrongful agenda for the rightful, original agenda to which both he and his followers were bound.

That Ahab's relation to his crew can be called seductive points to its chief defect: the inspiring visions that Ahab offers his men are counterfeit, exemplifying what Bernard Bass calls "pseudotransformational leadership." [19] Just as with his ostensible empowerment of his followers, so too the transforming nature of Ahab's leadership is ultimately illusory, since Ahab is quite willing to destroy not only himself but the ship and the entire crew in the service of his proud, courageous, but suicidal quest for Moby-Dick. As the novel shows, Ahab's charismatic persona, his skill with symbolic gestures (such as the nailing of the doubloon or, later in the book, his "baptism" of his harpoon with the blood of Queequeg, Tashtego, and Daggoo), and his tireless ability to invoke "higher-level" ideas and motivations make it hard, on the surface, to distinguish his pseudotransformational leadership from the genuine article.

Prominent as Ahab is in *Moby-Dick,* the novel's treatment of leadership is far from being leader-centric. A brief consideration of just three passages (out of many) will clarify Melville's insight into the role of followers—especially the interplay of psychological, ethical, and pragmatic factors in that role. The first of these passages recounts Ishmael's own response to Ahab's impassioned quarterdeck scene with the doubloon; the second reflects on the consequences of a particular conjunction of followers and leader; the third deals with the dilemmas confronting a follower who tries to stop a deluded or evil leader.

The emotional bond that a follower can feel for a leader is nowhere more strongly expressed than at the beginning of Chapter 41, where Ishmael recounts his reaction to Ahab: "I, Ishmael, was one of that crew; my shouts had gone up with the rest; my oath had been welded with theirs and stronger I shouted, and more did I hammer and clinch my oath, because of the dread in my soul. A wild, mystical, sympathetical feeling was in me; Ahab's quenchless feud seemed mine" (*Moby-Dick,* 239). That by this point in the novel we have gotten to know Ishmael well, as a tolerant, peaceable character, makes the violence of his attachment to Ahab all the more disturbing. Both the intensity and the lyricism of Ishmael's language here reveal, as only a work of art can, the infectious nature of Ahab's leadership; indeed, the passage supports Andrew Delbanco's claim that "some eighty years before it emerged as the central political fact of the twentieth century, Melville had described in *Moby-Dick* the reciprocal love between a demagogue and his adoring followers." [20] But the love Ishmael feels is not just that of a follower for a leader, but of a follower for his fellows. Ishmael experiences a heightened sense of self-identity not just through devotion to the figure in command, but through fusion with the group around him. The first thing Ishmael tells us here is that he "was one of that crew"; it is with the crew that

he first expresses his sense of belonging, and the term he uses here is telling—
"welded." This passage with Ishmael exemplifies part of Melville's genius in
exploring leadership; rather than deal only with the obvious, and admittedly
important figure of the leader, Melville probes—or, as he liked to say, *dives*—
into the deepest parts of a follower's response to the leader. Going even
beyond the leader-follower connection, Melville recognizes an undeniably
important but relatively little-studied aspect of leadership: the relationship
among the followers themselves, and the potent role that this relationship
can play in the entire process of leadership.

The interconnectedness of leaders and followers, and the potential of such
interconnectedness for disaster, emerges explicitly in a passage where Ishmael becomes more aware of his own and his fellow followers' contributions
to the tragedy of the *Pequod*. What Melville paints here is largely a failure of
followership—or, to be more precise, a failure of a leadership situation in
which a particular leader was matched with particular followers in a particular set of circumstances that proved fatal:

> Here, then, was this grey-headed, ungodly old man, chasing with curses a Job's
> whale round the world, at the head of a crew, too, chiefly made up of mongrel
> renegades, and castaways, and cannibals—morally enfeebled also, by the
> incompetence of mere unaided virtue or right-mindedness in Starbuck, the
> invulnerable jollity of indifference and recklessness in Stubb, and the pervading
> mediocrity in Flask. Such a crew, so officered, seemed specially picked and
> packed by some infernal fatality to help him to his monomaniac revenge. How
> it was that they so aboundingly responded to the old man's ire—by what evil
> magic their souls were possessed, that at times his hate seemed almost theirs . . .
> all this to explain, would be to dive deeper than Ishmael can go (*Moby-Dick,* 251).

For Melville, as this passage suggests, leadership can entail elements so
deeply, mysteriously, and unpredictably interconnected as to defy generalization. Such a conclusion may seem fatalistic, and indeed, there is a streak of
fatalism in Melville's work, including *Moby-Dick*. Ahab himself asks, "Is
Ahab, Ahab? Is it I, God, or who, that lifts this arm?" (*Moby-Dick,* 685), and
during the actual encounter with Moby-Dick, Ahab declares, "This whole
act's immutably decreed. . . . I am the Fates' lieutenant; I act under orders"
(*Moby-Dick,* 707). But Melville's reference to the seeming "fatality" by which
leaders, followers, and circumstances come together does not mean that good
or bad leadership depends merely on the luck of the draw. Yes, Melville's text
acknowledges, even emphasizes, the uncontrollable factors that come into
play with leadership. But far from encouraging a hopeless or passive fatalism,
this acknowledgement can be seen as constituting a realistic understanding of
just how elusive the nature of leadership is—and thus how difficult it can be
to withstand leadership that goes awry, however necessary such an effort
must be.

Of the *Pequod's* crew, the only member who seriously tries to withstand Ahab's leadership gone awry is Starbuck. In addition to the quarterdeck scene discussed above, Starbuck challenges Ahab several more times in the book. The struggle between the two even assumes a briefly comic cast when, in Chapter 119, that dependable man of affairs, Starbuck, informs Ahab that they must repair an oil leak in the ship's hold. Dismayed by Ahab's refusal to expend time on anything other than his quest for Moby-Dick, Starbuck asks, helplessly, "What will the owners say, sir?" Despite the grim context, Ahab's response is truly amusing:

> Let the owners stand on Nantucket beach and outyell the Typhoons. What cares Ahab? Owners, owners? Thou art always prating to me, Starbuck, about those miserly owners, as if the owners were my conscience. But look ye, the only real owner of anything is its commander, and hark ye, my conscience is in this ship's keel.—On deck! (*Moby-Dick,* 604)

One cannot help feeling that poor Starbuck is out of his depth here, and that he does, in fact, "prate." The eminently sane but limited, protocol-observing first mate is right, of course, in trying to stop Ahab. But how do you stop a man who, in a King-Lear-like rage at the universe, demands that his sailors "strike through the mask," and who at the moment of his death still cries out to the white whale that destroys him, "from hell's heart I stab at thee" (*Moby-Dick,* 721)? Not, in any event, by asking him what the owners will say.

Starbuck's plight takes a more somber turn in Chapter 123, significantly entitled, as we will see, "The Musket." By presenting Starbuck's thoughts in the form of an interior monologue that anticipates modernist stream of consciousness techniques, Melville dramatizes with great pathos the turmoil of a follower who knows that his leader is going in the wrong direction.[21] Aptly summarizing all autocratic leadership as he watches Ahab asleep in his cabin, Starbuck says, under his breath, "Not reasoning; not remonstrance; not entreaty wilt thou hearken to; all this thou scornest. Flat obedience to thy own flat commands, this is all thou breathest" (*Moby-Dick,* 651). Desperately seeking a "lawful way" to prevent Ahab from going on, Starbuck considers arresting his captain, but realizes that his own emotions could not endure for long the sight and sound of a caged, bound Ahab. Thus the practical facts of his situation, and the toll that an imprisoned Ahab would make on him personally, hinder Starbuck's ability to stop, or even to decide how to stop Ahab.

If only land were closer, then perhaps the option of arrest would work, thinks Starbuck, but he knows that the closest land where he could turn Ahab over to the law would not be America, but the unfamiliar Japan—and that is still "hundreds of leagues away" (*Moby-Dick,* 651). Even murder occurs to Starbuck, an option all the more extreme for this pious Quaker, loyal first

mate, and friend to Ahab, at whom Starbuck will still gaze with tearful affection in the *Pequod's* final moments. But if he does not kill Ahab, "shall this
crazed old man be tamely suffered to drag a whole ship's company down to
doom with him?" (*Moby-Dick,* 651). Starbuck wonders if he would really be
a murderer when, by killing Ahab he could save himself and his crew, as well
as prevent his wife and son from becoming his widow and his orphan.

As so often with Melville concerning such questions, no answer comes.
Starbuck goes so far as to point a loaded musket at the sleeping Ahab's
head—hence the chapter's title—but the mate remains adrift, unable to
resolve either his moral dilemma or the practical one of what to do next.
"Great God, where art thou? Shall I? shall I?" says Starbuck, only to put the
musket away and leave for the deck (*Moby-Dick,* 652). It is as if Starbuck has
been torn asunder and rendered powerless by the many images, ideals, and
persons competing for his allegiance here, like so many different "gods and
commodores." Chief among these are his basic sense of duty to his superior
officer, whoever that officer might be; the "ungodly, god-like" figure of Ahab
himself (*Moby-Dick,* 119), who even in sleep exerts a powerful hold on Starbuck; the moral injunction against murder; Starbuck's duty to the ship's owners; the memories of Starbuck's wife and child, whom he fears he will never
see again if Ahab continues unchecked; Starbuck's sense of self-preservation
and fear of death; his compassion for his endangered crew; his reverence for
legal procedure.

Through the intimate, detailed, and realistic rendering of what goes on in
Starbuck's mind, Melville puts us, the readers, into Starbuck's. In this
way, Melville is the leader here, and we, the readers, are his followers. But
we are followers who, even as we follow, participate actively in interpreting
the text, reacting to it, and entering into the consciousness of the characters
at the same time that we retain our own consciousness. We become, as
Georges Poulet has written of the reading experience, "on loan to another,
and this other thinks, feels, suffers, and acts within [us]." Then, as readers,
we "start having a common consciousness" with the text that we read.[22] In
a situation such as Starbuck's in the cabin, where the action unfolds chiefly
on the inner stage of the character's mind as he struggles with various ethical
and pragmatic options, such a merging of consciousness between reader and
character is all the more effective a means of deepening our experience of the
text. The word experience is important, for what takes place here is not simply a cognitive *understanding* of the text, but an emotional *experience* of it, leading us to an imaginative empathy with the character and the moral issues at
stake. This empathy includes but also goes beyond a cognitive apprehension
of the text's "meaning" to a deeper level of intellectual, emotional, aesthetic,
and vicariously experiential engagement with the text.

In just a few short pages, Melville has recreated the moral anguish endured by Starbuck, and shown what it *feels* like to be a follower, pulled upon by so many competing ethical and practical considerations, yet feeling stymied at every turn. And by ending the chapter with no resolution, Melville throws the ball into the reader's court: *should* Starbuck have killed Ahab? *should* he have arrested him? and what would we, from the comfort of our position as readers and outsiders gazing on the situation, have done?

In one of his letters about Russian literature, Anton Chekhov famously wrote that "There is not a single question answered in *Anna Karenina* or *Eugene Onegin*, but they are still fully satisfying works because the questions they raise are all formulated correctly."[23] Similarly, *Moby-Dick* provides few, if any, answers about leadership, even as it raises many hard questions. The character of Ahab himself, for all of his clearly evil *misleadership*, eludes attempts to pin him down with a single label or to find an easy answer to the mystery of his power. Indeed, as Alfred Kazin warned long ago, we should avoid the temptation to "construe *Moby-Dick* into a condemnation of mad, bad Ahab"[24]—like the book in which he appears, Ahab's complexity is too great for any such reductive categorization. So too, in Melville's rendering, the issues of leadership are of a complexity that cannot be finally categorized or fully explained. But in representing that complexity with such vividness and emotional resonance, Melville's novel still breathes life into our understanding of leadership in theory and practice alike.

NOTES

1. Although there has been no full-scale analysis of leadership in Melville, several studies make valuable contributions to aspects of leadership or related matters in his work. These include C. L. R. James, *Mariners, Renegades, and Castaways: The Story of Herman Melville and the World We Live In* (Hanover, NH: Dartmouth College Press, 2001, originally published 1953); Nicholas Canaday Jr., *Melville and Authority* (Gainesville: University of Florida Press, 1968); Michael Davitt Bell, "Melville's *Redburn*: Initiation and Authority," *New England Quarterly* 46 (1973): 558–572; Richard E. Ray, " 'Benito Cereno': Babo as Leader," *American Transcendental Quarterly* 7 (1975): 18–23; Mark R. Patterson, "Democratic Leadership and Narrative Authority in *Moby-Dick*," *Studies in the Novel* 16 (1984); Christopher S. Durer, "*Moby-Dick* and Nazi Germany," *Melville Society Extracts* 66 (1986): 8; Larry J. Reynolds, "*Moby-Dick*, Napoleon, and Workers of the World," *Melville Society Extracts* 6 (1986): 6–7; Catherine H. Zuckert, "Leadership—Natural and Conventional—in Melville's 'Benito Cereno,' " *Interpretation* 26 (1999): 239–255. Although more oblique in its treatment of leadership than these studies, a thought-provoking discussion of politics, power, and literary interpretation in connection to *Moby-Dick* appears in Denis Donoghue's "*Moby-Dick* After September 11th," *Law and Literature* 15 (2003): 161–188. On the tension in Melville between rebelliousness and a conservative veneration for legal order, see Milton R. Stern,

"Introduction," in Herman Melville, *Billy Budd*, ed. Milton R. Stern (Indianapolis, IN: Bobbs-Merrill, 1975), vii–xliv.

2. Herman Melville, *White Jacket or, The World in a Man-of-War* (London: Purnell & Sons, 1952), 374.

3. James MacGregor Burns, *Leadership* (New York: Harper & Row, 1978), 18–19.

4. Robert C. Solomon, "Ethical Leadership, Emotions, and Trust: Beyond 'Charisma', in *Ethics, the Heart of Leadership*, ed. Joanne B. Ciulla (Westport, CT: Quorum Books, 1998), 93.

5. Jean Lipman-Blumen, *The Allure of Toxic Leaders* (Oxford: Oxford University Press, 2005).

6. Barbara Kellerman, *Bad Leadership* (Boston: Harvard Business School Press, 2004), 11. Also helpful with regard to the confusion surrounding "leadership" as a value-free or value-laden term is Ronald A. Heifetz, *Leadership without Easy Answers* (Cambridge, MA: Harvard University Press, 1994), 13–14.

7. Richard B. Sewall, "*Moby-Dick* as Tragedy," in Herman Melville, *Moby-Dick*, ed. Harrison Hayford and Hershel Parker (New York: Norton, 1967), 700.

8. Herman Melville, *Moby-Dick*, ed. Charles Feidelson Jr. (Indianapolis: Bobbs-Merrill, 1964), 167. All further quotations from *Moby-Dick* are from this edition and will appear in the text.

9. John W. Gardner notes that such reciprocity was pointed out long ago by the sociologist Georg Simmel; see Gardner, "Leaders and Followers," in *The Leader's Companion*, ed. J. Thomas Wren (New York: The Free Press, 1995), 186. On leader-follower reciprocity of influence, see also Burns, *Leadership*, 425; Martin Chemers, "The Social, Organizational, and Cultural Context of Effective Leadership," in *Leadership: Multidisciplinary Perspectives*, ed. Barbara Kellerman (Englewood Cliffs, NJ: Prentice-Hall, 1984), 91–112; and Joseph C. Rost, *Leadership for the Twenty-First Century* (Westport, CT: Greenwood, 1991), 107–108. A recent scholarly conference entirely focused on such reciprocity, with particular emphasis on followers, was the Kravis–de Roulet Conference, "Rethinking Followership," held in February 2006 at Claremont McKenna College, Claremont, California.

10. For a summary of, and rebuttal to, positive views of Mapple's sermon, see Lawrance Thompson, who interprets the sermon as a "mousetrap" for the naïve reader in his *Melville's Quarrel with God* (Princeton: Princeton University Press, 1952), 9–11, 153–155, 427–429; another highly critical discussion of the sermon is William V. Spanos, *The Errant Art of "Moby-Dick"* (Durham and London: Duke University Press, 1995), 87–114; for a cogent, up-to-date commentary on recent views of the sermon, see " 'Chiefly Known by His Rod': The Book of Jonah, Mapple, and Scapegoating," in *"Ungraspable Phantom": Essays on "Moby-Dick,"* ed. John Bryant, Mary K. Bercaw Edwards, and Timothy Marr (Kent, OH: Kent State University Press, 2006), 37–57.

11. Solomon, "Ethical Leadership, Emotions, and Trust," in *Ethics*, ed. Ciulla, 87.

12. Kathryn Mudgett, " 'I Stand Alone Here upon an Open Sea': Starbuck and the Limits of Positive Law," in *"Ungraspable Phantom,"* ed. Bryant, Edwards, and Marr, 132.

13. Edwin Hollander, "Ethical Challenges in the Leader-Follower Relationship," in *Ethics*, ed. Ciulla, 56.

14. My analysis builds on Mark Patterson's excellent discussion of *Moby-Dick*, in which he observes that Ahab's authority undergoes a transformation "from legitimate and institutional to charismatic," and that Ahab succeeds in "blurring the distinction between the two"; see Patterson, "Democratic Leadership and Narrative Authority in *Moby-Dick*," *Studies in the Novel* 16 (1984): 292. Obviously relevant here is Max Weber's analysis of authority in terms of rational and traditional categories, both of which Ahab possesses by virtue of his officially sanctioned and traditionally respected position; the third and most famous type of authority that Weber discusses, the charismatic, is fostered by Ahab partly through his rank but mainly through his skillful dramatic self-presentation—aka his demagoguery. For Weber's categories, see his *On Charisma and Institution Building*, ed. S. N. Eisenstadt (Chicago: University of Chicago Press, 1968), 46–48. For an insightful discussion of Weber, and an extension of his notions of institutional versus noninstitutional forms of charisma, see James V. Downton Jr., *Rebel Leadership: Commitment and Charisma in the Revolutionary Process* (New York: Free Press, 1973). A helpful overview of theories of charisma appears in Jay A. Conger, "Theoretical Foundations of Charismatic Leadership," in *Charismatic Leadership: The Elusive Factor in Organizational Effectiveness*, ed. Jay A. Conger and Rabindra N. Kanungo (San Francisco and Oxford: Jossey-Bass, 1989), 12–39.

15. Fred V. Barnard, "The Question of Race in *Moby-Dick*," *Massachusetts Review* 43 (2002): 385.

16. Joanne B. Ciulla, "Leadership and the Problem of Bogus Empowerment," in *Ethics, the Heart of Leadership*, ed. Ciulla, 63–86.

17. Burns, *Leadership*, 4, 455.

18. Sonja M. Hunt, "The Role of Leadership in the Construction of Reality," in *Leadership*, ed. Kellerman, 157–178.

19. Bernard M. Bass and Ronald E. Riggio, *Transformational Leadership*, 2nd ed. (Mahwah, NJ: Lawrence Erlbaum Associates, 2006), viii, 12–16.

20. Andrew Delbanco, *Melville, His World and Work* (New York: Knopf, 2005), 143.

21. "Interior monologue," as I use it here, refers to "the technique of recording the continuum of impressions, thoughts, and impulses either prompted by conscious experience or arising from the well of the subconscious," as defined in J. A. Cuddon, *A Dictionary of Literary Terms and Literary Theory* (Oxford: Blackwell, 1998), 422.

22. Georges Poulet, "Phenomenology of Reading," in *Critical Theory Since Plato*, ed. Hazard Adams (New York: Harcourt Brace Jovanovich, 1992), 1149–1150.

23. Anton Chekhov to Alexei Suvorin, October 27, 1888, trans. Kate Jenkins, http//:www.minimumfax.com/video/2003/3cechov.pdf (accessed July 18, 2007).

24. Alfred Kazin, " 'Introduction' to *Moby-Dick*," in *Melville: Twentieth-Century Views*, ed. Richard Chase (Englewood Cliffs, NJ: Prentice-Hall, 1962), 45.

2

The Relevance of *Don Quixote* to Leadership Studies: Nostalgia, Cynicism, and Ambivalence

AURORA HERMIDA-RUIZ

Miguel de Cervantes is one of the great authors of the European Renaissance, one of the most prominent authors of the Western canon, and one of the most important figures in the history of human culture. With the recent worldwide celebration in 2005 of the 400th anniversary of the publication of *Don Quixote*, there should be no doubt that Cervantes continues to be one of the most effective and charismatic "leaders" of contemporary literary culture.[1] An interesting manifestation of the magnitude of *Don Quixote*'s influence and vitality has recently been made by way of a poll of leading world cultural figures. Winning by a landslide, *Don Quixote* was chosen as the "most meaningful book of all time."[2] Salman Rushdie, one of the authors queried, considers it "the unifying novel between the literatures of the East and the West," and categorically affirms: "the history of the whole literature of the world comes out of this single novel."[3] At such a level, it is not surprising to see the Bible appearing often as the only other "key" text of the Western tradition worthy of its company. For Saint-Beuve, *Don Quixote* was "the Bible of humanity";[4] for Miguel de Unamuno, "the true Spanish Bible."[5] Harold Bloom, confessing to be overwhelmed by it, considers it a "vast scripture."[6] Dismissing with Cervantine irony this lofty reading of *Don Quixote*, Nabokov said: "let us not fall under the spell of these enchanters."[7] Indeed, though religion and faith are fundamental topics of debate among readers and critics of *Don Quixote*, one needs not interpret the analogy with the Bible *religioso modo*.[8] In a broader sense, they both are what Matei Calinescu calls "rereadable" texts, that is, texts that are impossible to consume or dispose of on a first and single reading.[9] Certainly, the more *Don Quixote* is reread and suggested for repeated reflective (re)reading, inspiration, and imitation, the more *Don Quixote* becomes the exemplary never-ending text: whether as an icon of the "inexhaustible genre," as Robert Alter put it in his seminal study of *Don Quixote*;[10] or as "an endless pleasure," as it has been described by Bloom.[11] By virtue of becoming one of the best-known, if most reviled, readers and commentators of *Don Quixote*, Nabokov himself seems to have fallen heavily under the spell of Cervantes's fiction. As is the case with the Bible, the power of *Don Quixote* is also extended to those who, like Nabokov, need to proclaim their cynicism or disbelief about its power or its authority. Whether in reverence or irreverence, hyperbole has become the standard mode among Cervantes's readers.

Certainly, much of the power and authority of Cervantes today comes from this ongoing tradition of (re)reading *Don Quixote* as a difficult riddle still to be solved or as a worthy quest for meaning. The struggle attached to the quest is perhaps best exemplified by Harold Bloom, who begins his introduction to Edith Grossman's recent translation of *Don Quixote* with little critical *decorum*: "What is the true object of Don Quixote's quest? I find that unanswerable" (xxi).[12] Considering the object of don Quixote's desire, Diana de Armas Wilson, a leading Cervantes critic, asks the same question, albeit with more drama: "(D)ear God, what *does* he want?"[13] There are many answers. The list of important readers and readings of *Don Quixote* is so immense that name-dropping seems more superfluous than usual. As Harry Levin, a highly reputed expert on the theme of Cervantes's posterity, put it: "no book has had more spectacular fortune" than *Don Quixote*.[14] For Levin, it was nothing short of a paradox that "a book about literary influence, and indeed against it, should have enjoyed so wide and pervasive a literary influence."[15] Paradox, to be sure, does seem to be a particularly fitting figure of speech as far as readings and readers go. This is a book that is easy to read and difficult to grasp. It has been considered the most comic and the most tragic of books, the cruelest and the most humane; a celebration of life, of freedom and faith as well as the testament of a pessimist and nihilist. *Don Quixote* seems to make possible and plausible the opposite of any single interpretation. In the words of Harold Bloom, the reading history of *Don Quixote* proves that the book "will sustain any theory you bring to it, as well or as badly as any other."[16]

READERS, AND (MIS)READINGS

... investigating what people have made of canonical texts is as important as reading those texts themselves. It is the misreadings that have often been historically effective.

—Hillis J. Miller[17]

The instability of *Don Quixote*'s meaning is particularly intense as a result not only of history and culture, but of the profound differences between part I—*El ingenioso hidalgo don Quijote de la Mancha* (*The ingenious gentleman Don Quixote of La Mancha*), published in 1605—and part II—*Segunda parte del ingenioso caballero don Quijote de la Mancha* (*Second part of the ingenious gentleman Don Quixote of la Mancha*), published in 1615. Further complicating matters is the multiplicity of narrators, stories, and characters as well as the novel's parodic and ironic openness. In the dilemma over what we are to take literally and what we are to take ironically lies much of the meaning of the book. As John J. Allen explains, the most common approach has been to identify a particular meaning of the book and interpret any contradictory statements as meant ironically.[18] The range of interpretations of *Don Quixote* has hence become a major focus of Cervantine scholarship, as it is considered not only a continued gloss to Cervantes's text, but also an important key to cultural history.[19] Confronting the sheer variety of interpretations, experts on the historical reception of *Don Quixote* have come to approach its canonical status not just as a particularly deceiving form of permanence but, perhaps more importantly, as a kind of guarantee that freshly minted interpretations are to be expected in the future. Wondering about the next meaning or metamorphoses of *Don Quixote*, Margaret Atwood recently asked: "What will Don Quixote become next? It's hard to say, but he will become something, for he is a figure of many lives, always transforming."[20] This mixture of confidence and anticipation is extensive in *Quixote* scholarship, where a new "trend-setting–'ism'" is not simply expected but almost eagerly anticipated.[21] However active they may be in their search for clues, and while perhaps too focused on the most likely places or the most usual suspects, Cervantes's literary critics remain mostly unaware of what could possibly be the most effective or influential reading of *Don Quixote* being made today: the Leadership approach to *Don Quixote*, that is, a reading of Cervantes's novel that is mainly concerned with the evaluation of its hero as leader, and the related notion of leadership as a "quixotic" endeavor. This new approach is a highly idealistic take on *Don Quixote* born in the unexpected context of business education in the United States, and it is rapidly gaining adepts in programs of leadership and business management around the globe. It is a reading meant to add a new category to the already long list of "quixotic" descendants of Don Quixote, a list that comfortably includes and mixes historical figures from Mohandas Gandhi or Martin Luther King Jr.—whose "I have a dream" speech has become the paradigmatic American "quixotic"—to successful entrepreneurs like Bill Gates, Steve Jobs, or David Packard and William Hewlett: versions of the legendary rags-to-riches story that often starts in the quintessentially American garage. *Don Quixote*, it appears, has arrived through the gates of the "impossible dream" of *Man of la Mancha* to the canon of the "American dream."

The shift is certainly meaningful. The mix of social idealists and successful businessmen has the interesting effect of comparison and correspondence: the dreamers and the "movers and shakers" of society are no longer, or at least not necessarily, of the venerably stoic type. Leadership, from the perspective and the example of Don Quixote, may be considered a romantic and visionary endeavor but, from the perspective and example of Bill Gates, needs no longer be an "impossible" dream or yield a sacrificial victim. As Joe Badaracco, Harvard Business School professor of ethics, so clearly puts it, leaders "are the kinds of people who make a difference in the world, not just the saints." [22] The shift is starting to be noticeable even in the use of the term "quixotic." As an adjective, "quixotic" has traditionally identified a lofty pursuit of impractical idealism and, as such, has often been used to qualify nouns like "quest," "vision," "dream," "fight," or "battle." Lately, nonetheless, the results of a Google search of the word brings in "proposal" and "campaign" as very frequent companions, proof that the newest vogue in the quixotic imaginary is leaving behind the realm of the unique and extraordinary. In this sense, the interest and the study of "quixotic" leadership not only foresees a new kind of hero or a new hierarchy of heroism but, for our purposes, a redefinition as well of the "quixotic" itself; a new reading indeed.

Don Quixote is the story of an extremely avid, enthusiastic, and gullible reader who, at the age of 50, loses his mind, decides to revive knight errantry and imitate one his favorite heroes of chivalry books: the brave, young, handsome, and chaste Amad's of Gaul, the first chivalric hero of Spanish literature (1508). Briefly and somewhat pessimistically put, this decision sets him on a journey that will be plagued with ridicule, deception, and failure. In the end, vanquished and having achieved nothing tangible—no princess for himself and no kingdom for his squire Sancho Panza (no Dulcinea and no Insula Barataria)—Don Quixote returns home "vencedor de sí mismo" ("conqueror of himself") in Sancho's words (II, LVXXII, 928), and dies deeply aware and deeply repentant of his past madness and ignorance.[23] Is *Don Quixote* an incongruence in the curriculum of leadership studies and business management? Can it be "right" to approach Don Quixote as a role model for leadership or a success story? Does *Don Quixote* have "lessons" for the exercise of leadership? To start answering these questions, let me first approach briefly the wider context of leadership studies in the United States. By connecting the redefinition of the quixotic, the recent emphasis on quixotic leadership and the vogue of leadership studies, I hope to emphasize the role of context in the reception history of *Don Quixote*. My ultimate goal is to prove that, considering the current discourse of crisis in the humanities and the move towards its reappraisal in higher and professional education, the best way to honor Cervantes and the humanist tradition that he represents is through acknowledging not the time-lessness of quixotic leadership, but the "timeliness" of leadership studies and its nostalgic rereading of the humanist tradition.

THE CASE OF LITERATURE IN LEADERSHIP STUDIES

> ... (L)iberal arts colleges have allowed moral and civic education to be divorced from the curriculum, thereby compromising one of their defining qualities.
>
> —Dr. Kenneth Ruscio, President, Washington and Lee University[24]

The notion of a "divorce" between higher education and moral and civic values, the "divorce" of the liberal arts from the professional schools, and the parallel notion of neglect in the teaching of ethics in professional schools have become some of the most debated topics in American higher education today. There is a strong sense among critics and analysts of American higher education that this divorce has, regrettably, already happened and been detrimental to society, as it has exclusively served individual and competitive interests at the expense of the common good. According to many of its critics, American higher education itself has become an individual interest in dire need of reform or correction. Finding the usefulness of scholarship in the world outside the university, or finding the purpose and immediate use of research, is equivalent to making a sound public investment.[25] There is, in other words, a strong tendency to correlate the crisis of values in contemporary society, or the strong sense of moral bankruptcy, with a failure in higher and professional education.[26] And there is, ultimately, a profound fear about the future: the future of the American democracy, the future of the market economy, the future of the planet, etc.[27] As Tom Piper put it, referring to Harvard Business School's initiative to create what later became the *Program in Leadership, Ethics and Corporate Responsibility*, the "call to rebalance the educational trilogy of values, knowledge and skills" has become by now ubiquitous in higher education.[28] Leadership studies have evolved from this context of crisis as a conscious attempt to "send students into the world with the knowledge and conviction to change the world for the better—to be good citizens and live lives of consequence."[29] If leadership can be taught or, in other words, if conviction in the power of leadership can be restored, it is assumed that John Gardner's concerns about the "social disintegration, the moral disorientation, and the spinning compass needle of our time" will no longer be on the horizon of expectations.

According to many, the first step towards change is a curricular reform that brings back the "solid grounding of the humanities" in higher learning, a return, as it were, to the "original" role and spirit of the humanities.[30] If a liberal education does what it is supposed to do—that is, improving the individual by enriching the mind and the spirit—then society, as a result, can only improve.[31] In contrast to divorce as a figure of crisis, the prevalent figure of hope implies companionship, reunion, inclusion, combination, common ground, interdisciplinarity, balance, and so on. The figure, in other words, is that of a new marriage, a marriage that immediately recalls Martianus Capella's foundational assemblage of the seven liberal arts, *De nuptiis Philologiae et Mercurii* (*The Marriage of Philology and Mercury*), in the very midst of the barbarian invasions. The emphasis on the humanities as a necessary grounds for leadership is, therefore, set in motion by different degrees of apocalyptic scenarios, and guided by a very pragmatic as well as optimistic approach to education.[32] Hence the way out of the crisis requires not only an intensified focus on the moral and social responsibility of higher and professional education, but a complete reassessment of the function and values of the humanities in the hierarchy of knowledge. How this blissful "marriage" may actually work is indeed the main question facing leadership studies and its future in American institutions of higher education.

It is in this context of perceived crisis and advocated reform that leadership programs have approached literature and its didactic usefulness. It is a recent incorporation and, to a certain degree, almost a working project, but its main premises are fairly clear.[33] The general approach is that literature, both as a tool for critical thinking or as a source of moral reasoning or moral energy, does have an important role to play in the ethical formation of future leaders. This explains how the original leadership program designed by the Harvard Business School can present the course *The Business World—Moral and Social Inquiry through Fiction* as a platform to approach "the ethical and existential aspects of life and work." [34] In the words of James March, Professor Emeritus of Business Management, Sociology, Political Science, and Education at Stanford University and a figure widely recognized for his leading role in the integration of literature in business courses, "the critical concerns of leadership are not technical questions of management or power, they are fundamental issues of life." [35] For March, great literature not only addresses these fundamental issues of leadership, but provides an insight into them that is far superior to any research on the topic: "Look at great literature—Shakespeare's *Othello*, Cervantes' *Don Quixote*, Tolstoy's *War and Peace*—and try to learn lessons from them." [36]

Joe Badaracco, author of *Questions of Character: Illuminating the Heart of Leadership through Literature* (2006) and a key figure as well in the current trend of incorporating literature into the MBA curriculum, is unequivocal about what he considers to be the usefulness of literature. For him, literature is a universal value that can provide the "raw material" of universal leadership.[37] What literature offers to leadership education are particular cases, examples, or lessons that are considered to be more "illuminating" or "richer and more realistic" than those in research articles or textbooks on leadership.[38] Together with the emphasis on universality, the pragmatism of the "case studies" approach also explains the literary choices being made.[39] Reading lists are assembled without any cultural, historical, or chronological boundaries and with a tendency to include short texts—short stories, short novels, and plays—as a way to cover a wide array of topics.[40]

As it seems from the examples available, the standard application of literature is also regulated by certain parameters of productivity. When Diane Coutu of the *Harvard Business Review,* for example, asks literary critic Harold Bloom, "Who has time for literature anymore?" or "Who has time to pick up a 400-page novel?" the questions seem far from rhetorical.[41] Literary criticism and literary history are thus fully and emphatically dismissed on grounds of productivity or ethical inefficiency. The search for the "right" meaning of a work—the very logic, one might add, behind the philological method of the humanities—is considered to be an impractical pursuit of knowledge.[42] The intense emphasis on the universality, timelessness, and, indeed, usefulness of poetic truth tacitly and strongly infer literary criticism to be the kind of irrelevant scholarship that is now set in the "ivory tower." The case of *Don Quixote* is, to a certain extent, an exception within the general pattern, and this in turn makes the example of Stanford Business School Professor James March's reading of *Don Quixote* an interesting exception that deserves the in-depth evaluation I will give it later on in this chapter. Still, even in the case of the *Quixote,* the main tendency of business and leadership analyses to date has been that of a short "lesson," and even that of a short manual of very useful and unambiguous leadership principles for succeeding in business and life.[43] With apparent optimism, *Don Quixote* is read and advised for reading in the world of leadership development and business management as timeless evidence that conviction and belief in one's own hopes and dreams is the key to any achievement, any enterprise, and, of course, any progress. As a kind of slogan of this rather optimistic and individualistic lesson for leadership, one could simply recall the words of Purdue University President Martin C. Jischke in his 2004 commencement ceremony speech: "Dream the impossible dream and then make it come true." [44] According to Jischke, "progress is built on impossible dreams," and *Don Quixote*'s "lessons are as old as time." [45]

LINEAGES OF READING: LEADERSHIP STUDIES AND THE "ROMANTIC" APPROACH TO *DON QUIXOTE*

Interestingly enough, although the dominant approach to literature in the context of leadership studies is explicitly nonliterary, most literary critics of

Don Quixote would immediately recognize it as a natural offspring of the so-called "romantic approach" to *Don Quixote*. According to Anthony Close, around 1800 the German romantics initiated a watershed in the historical reception of Cervantes's text that has come to be known as the romantic approach. Although its history is by now long, its main legacy, according to Close, is fairly clear: the rejection of the book as a comic parody of chivalry novels, and its subsequent interpretation as a symbolic representation of the human condition in its struggle to transcend reality.[46] As the romantic approach to *Don Quixote* broadly defines a tendency to read *Don Quixote* as a source of knowledge fully unrelated to its original context—literary, cultural, historical—it has often been dismissed as simply erroneous, subjective, or ideologically misguided. Erich Auerbach, a leading voice in the 1940s against the romantic approach, saw the association of Don Quixote with ideal greatness or heroic idealism as nothing short of a violent act of overinterpretation that became universal in spite of enduring philological criticism.[47] Nowadays, the verdict is less harsh. The romantic approach is mostly understood not only as a sign of cultural contingency or "quixotic" dialogism between text and context or past and present, but also as a clear sign of the relevance of literary and cultural studies.[48] Indeed, if the contexts of Cervantes's texts were not meaningful at all, what we would be left with would be complete arbitrariness, not universality. A corollary to this idea is that cultural knowledge is the best guarantee against the kind of manipulations *Don Quixote* has been exposed to throughout its history. Certainly, there is a high dose of ambiguity that one can taste here. The deep meanings that the Romantics discovered in *Don Quixote* have certainly given Cervantes the cultural relevance that he has today. On the other hand, one can easily see this relevance "as having been purchased too dear," as John J. Allen put it, referring precisely to a number of ideological reconstructions "in which scarcely one stone of the original structure is left upon another."[49]

Historically, the "most influential reader" of the romantic approach is Miguel de Unamuno (1864–1936) who searched *Don Quixote* for answers to overcome the angst of *fin de sicle* Europe and, closer to home, the profound sense of crisis and decadence that followed Spain's defeat in the war of 1898 (the Spanish-American War).[50] For Unamuno, as much as for the other members of the so-called Generation of 1898 in Spanish literary historiography, the *Quixote* became a guide for the regeneration of Spain's spiritual values. Moral degeneration and *abulia*—paralysis of the will to act—were considered to be the ultimate cause for the military disaster against the United States, the widespread corruption of government, the apathy of citizens, the lack of national cohesion, and the decadence of Spain's international power. Thanks to the tremendous zeal that Unamuno infused in his reading of the *Quixote*, its hero became widely revered as the best representative of Spain's core national values and, as such, as its best possible redeemer. In Unamuno's case, these unifying values happened to be Catholicism, antiliberalism, and antieuropeism, In the case of his opponents—most prominently, Américo Castro in his equally influential *El pensamiento de Cervantes* (*The Thought of Cervantes*) of 1925—Spain's values as represented by Don Quixote were those of liberalism, laicism, republicanism, and all the progressive values associated with modern European culture. In either case, it was a doctrinaire reading of *Don Quixote* that had as much to do with history, life, and the context and circumstances of pre–Civil War Spain as it had to do with the interpretation of literature. Historically, it was Unamuno's view of Spain's rebirth that Francisco Franco's military dictatorship elevated to dogma.[51] In a particularly strong use of the legacy and lineage of quixotic leadership, the dictatorship sought to legitimize the military rebellion against the democratic government of Spain's Second Republic in July 1936 and its victory in the Civil War.[52] Considering this brutal history of quixotic leadership, the move since the 1940s to debunk the romantic or idealist approach to *Don Quixote* needs to be properly understood as a form of skeptical cynicism born in the context of fascist ideologies, great wars, and totalitarian regimes.[53]

For the purpose of leadership studies, it is important to stress that the "romantic" lineage of *Don Quixote* has gone in sharply different ideological directions. In fact, it has often been claimed and purportedly been reenacted by an interesting array of self-proclaimed visionary leaders and crusaders, Che Guevara and Mexico's Subcomandante Marcos among them. In the case of Spain, from dictator Francisco Franco to socialist José Luis Rodríguez Zapatero—Spain's president since 2004—there is hardly a political figure that has escaped the temptation to see his leadership image in the mirror of *Don Quixote*. An illustrative recent example is that of Venezuelan President Hugo Chávez, who used the occasion of *Don Quixote*'s 400th anniversary to launch a massive "Operation Dulcinea" destined to distribute 350,000 free copies of Cervantes's classic to poor Venezuelans. Playing with the classical conflict of arms versus letters, Chávez rationale for this civic gesture was to inspire and unite the citizens of Venezuela in the fight against the United States. The motto of the campaign, "we are still oppressed by giants," needs little explanation.[54] His romantic approach to Don Quixote was at once idealistic and ideological.

The popular expression of the romantic approach is "quixotism": a belief that is not substantiated by empirical reality or a supreme form of idealism and visionary power. In the realm of literature, the antagonist most often used as a contrast to the romantic idealism of Don Quixote has been Hamlet, specifically, a romantically demonized Hamlet. Basically, as the romantic approach goes, what Don Quixote would be to faith, hope, action, and companionship, Hamlet would be to reason, doubt, solitude, and unproductive skepticism. In his well-known essay "Hamlet and Don Quixote," Ivan Turgenev applied this contrast to better illuminate his idea of popular and inspirational leadership. For him, Don Quixote is a leader because he represents faith and altruistic service.[55] If Quixotes are natural "leaders of men," it is because they are "essentially useful to humanity."[56] Hamlet, by contrast, is "of no service to the masses."[57] Hamlets are "thoughtful, discriminating ... but useless and doomed to practical inaction."[58] As for the nature of followers, Turgenev sees in Sancho Panza a representative of the "finest characteristic of the masses" in his quite unselfish, altruistic, or "blind" followership. If Quixotes represent the leaders, saviors, or redeemers of humanity, Sanchos romantically represent humanity in need and in search of salvation.[59]

Harry Levin approached Turgenev's polar opposition between Hamlet and Don Quixote as a "simplistic dichotomy," which has more to say about Russian nineteenth-century culture than the intentions of either Shakespeare or Cervantes.[60] Harold Bloom, who could be considered the most influential representative today of the romantic approach to *Don Quixote*—and the most "quixotic," perhaps—has also seen Shakespeare as an "illuminating analogue" to Cervantes.[61] Asked in a *Harvard Business Review* interview what literary readings would he recommend to Bill Gates—the antonomasia, as it were, of American CEOs—Bloom chose and stressed the transcendence of both authors.[62] Interestingly enough, Harold Bloom does not follow Turgenev in his all too easy dichotomy of leadership. What he finds, instead, is a shocking similarity: Hamlet and Don Quixote are equally reckless in their pursuit of knowledge; Shakespeare and Cervantes are, deep down, equally nihilistic.[63] Although Bloom, the old cynic, avoids telling *Harvard Business Review* and Bill Gates his dirty little secret about the ultimate meaning of life and the ultimate irrelevance of knowledge, the fact that he evokes the traditional pairing of Shakespeare and Cervantes in the context of a business journal and to the intended audience of corporate America is good proof of the strong hold that the romantic opposition between Hamlet and Don Quixote has on the contemporary imaginary of leadership. As was the case for Turgenev, behind the fear that selfish, doubtful Hamlets are not only "numerous" but on the "increase," and that Don Quixotes are not only scarce but about to "disappear from among us," the real question is the loyalty and the strength of Sancho's followership;[64] in this case, the trust of voters and investors, and the strong perception that a fast growing cynicism is severely damaging the American way of life. As John Gardner put it, "fragmentation and divisiveness have proceeded so far in American life that we can no longer lend ourselves to any worthy common purpose."[65] The renewed interest, not on *Don Quixote,* but on the most "romantic" version possible of *Don Quixote*— the one supposedly representing unshakable faith and conviction, and capable of leading by unshakable trust—can only be explained in reference to a series of apocalyptic disasters directly related to the context of contemporary American culture.

Harold Bloom, for his part, plays the role of the idealistic Quixote living in the demonized world of cultural materialism. In an extreme answer to what he considers to be an extreme commodification of literature as a "useful" document for culture and ideology, he has become the romantic champion of the timeless Western canon. For him, as is the case for so many other critics of American higher education today, the humanities are directly responsible for the decline of the humanities. The end result of "so-called feminism, Marxism, and French fanciness" is a disaster that will lead to nothing but the destruction of the study of literature.[66] As a cultural critic himself, Bloom has turned out to be particularly effective at demonstrating the uselessness of Gender studies, for example. Recalling a dissertation by a "young lady" on representations of the female breast as "the Victoria's Secret vision of English literature," he sounds both witty and incisive.[67] But the anecdote is also meant to be ironic in reference to Bill Gates and the culture of corporate America. For Bloom, high literature is by definition useless and uncontaminated. When Diane Coutu, the Harvard Business Review interviewer, asks him whether there is "anything" literature can offer business, he directly rejects the notion that "literature will make business people more moral," and confesses to be "very unhappy with any attempt to put the humanities, and literature in particular, in the service of social change."[68]

Quixotic idealism is becoming to the business world what the literary canon is to Bloom: an extremist form of compensation in a culture driven by materialism and increasingly perceived as excessive, demonic, or dehumanizing. The intensity that romantic quixotism has achieved in the unlikely world of business management and leadership development can be best illuminated by the example of James March and his seminal reading of *Don Quixote*. I refer to *Passion and Discipline: Don Quixote's Lessons for Leadership*, an unconventional documentary on the theme of "quixotic" leadership that deserves to be analyzed in depth as the best example, to my knowledge, of the relevance that the romantic approach to *Don Quixote* has achieved in the context of leadership studies.[69]

Passion and Discipline is based on *Organizational Leadership*, a course that James March taught from 1980 to 1994 at Stanford Business School. Readings for the original course included Shakespeare's *Othello*, George Bernard Shaw's *Saint Joan*, Tolstoy's *War and Piece*, and Cervantes's *Don Quixote*—in March's view, a "primordial source of learning" about the major issues of leadership.[70] The influence of March's reading of *Don Quixote* is, in itself, an important phenomenon, indeed one that very few readers of *Don Quixote* could actually rival today. The pervasiveness of March's influence in the social sciences has been compared to that of Miles Davis in jazz.[71] In the field of management theory, he is considered a "gurus's guru" whose influence, according to a *Harvard Business Review* survey of 2003, is more often recognized than that of Nobel laureate economists Herbert Simon, Ronald Coase, or Kenneth Arrow.[72] All in all, he is revered as "a rigorous scholar and a deep source of wisdom."[73] According to *Stanford Business Magazine*, March's "landmark" course *Organizational Leadership* became "legendary" as some 300 to 400 students—approximately 100 from the Business School—took it each year.[74] In documentary form, it has appeared on PBS stations across the country, as well as on cable TV, and it is readily available as a *Films for the Humanities* production for other courses and public showings. In this sense, James March's views on leadership certainly qualify as a particularly "influential" contemporary reading of the *Quixote*. As evidence of March's global reach, one needs only mention the case of the Indian Institute of Management in Ahmedabad, reputed to be the premier business school of India, which has for years offered a course on corporate leadership—the actual title of the course is *Leadership, Vision, Meaning and Reality*—directly inspired by the example, the celebrity, and the reading list of March's course in Stanford.[75] Interestingly enough, it was the possibility of reproducing the influence of March's "lessons" indefinitely that gave a university administrator, Deborah J. Stipek, dean of Stanford's School of Education, the idea and the stamina to convince March to make the film.[76]

March's indebtedness to the romantic approach to the *Quixote* is evident from the very beginning of the documentary, when he introduces Don Quixote as that "romantic knight" from la Mancha who has captured our imagination. His reading is, in fact, directly inspired by Miguel de Unamuno, whose version of the romantic approach is often regarded, in addition to being one of the most influential and idealistic, as among the most individualistic as well.[77] Unamuno's reading of *Don Quixote* is a particularly anguished take on the individual quest for eternal meaning, directly influenced in turn by Kierkegaard's idea of religious faith. Although James March has often acknowledged the influence of both Unamuno and Kierkegaard on his thought, *Passion and Discipline* does not mention them; instead, March's documentary does a good job of erasing the extreme existential *fin de sicle* angst that inspired his forebears.[78] In place of any darkness or agony in Don Quixote's landscape, what this documentary gives us is the full sun of Spain shining on the grapes of a vineyard, the bright colors and sensuality of gypsy dancers, and the lively sound of a flamenco guitar. Granted that while March always appears fully dressed in black, more often than not he has a glass of Spanish wine in his hand and a blissful smile on his face. All in all, instead of any romantic despair, what March gives us is romantic exoticism; instead of existential angst, all the pleasures and the gusto of Mediterranean *joie de vivre.* One can hardly imagine a more charming and hedonistic package for *Don Quixote*'s lessons.

What March does keep from Unamuno's reading is its extreme form of idealism and individualism. March presents *Don Quixote* as a "teacher" in possession of what seems to be a very simple teaching lesson: "Yo sé quien soy" (I know who I am): the last words Don Quixote says before coming back home at the end of his first sally (I, V), and, indeed, among the most quoted ones in the book. What these words mean for March becomes clear by mere repetition. "Yo sé quien soy" is the logic of self that the "romantic," "visionary" Quixote follows and teaches us to follow regardless of the consequences. This lesson, according to March, manifests in a trilogy of *sine qua non* leadership characteristics: passion, discipline, and joy.[79] All of them come "from inside, from Quixote's sense of himself," and do not "depend in any way on expectations about the world." Quixote's legacy can hence be resumed in the dictum "Yo sé quien soy" taken as a religious principle or an article of faith about one's own identity: always be who you are, and believe in your own logic of self, however arbitrary, whatever it takes, and wherever it takes you, regardless of the consequences.[80] As March sees it, it is the absence of any consequential justification for one's actions that raises identity—the commitment to one's identity—to the dignity of a religion.[81]

Organized around the three features of leadership, the film mixes scenes from different cinematic adaptations of *Don Quixote*, footage of iconic figures of popular culture and history who would need no introduction to an average educated audience (Lyndon B. Johnson, Bill Gates, Robert McNamara, Dennis Green, Martin Luther King, Richard Nixon, Ronald Reagan, Robert Kennedy, Ted Kennedy, Franklin D. Roosevelt, Albert Einstein, Charlie Chaplin, Mohandas Gandhi, Louis Armstrong, Laurel and Hardy, Hewlett and Packard, Carly Fiorina, etc.), and a series of interviews with his own friends and pupils about their own experiences as leaders, and the wisdom that they have gained in the process.[82] This later group includes: John Gardner, founder of Common Cause; Robert Koski, CEO, Sun Hydraulics; Cory Booker, City Councilman, Newark; Jerry L. Beasley, President of Concord College, West Virginia; Anne Kreiner, a CEO famous in Denmark and the only female and only non-American of the group; and Rod Beckström, CEO of C-ATS Software, later turned environmentalist. The pick is in itself revealing, as the group of successful business entrepreneurs is perfectly balanced by an equal number of public servants. The resulting leadership cocktail has the very democratic effect of *egalité:* they all are leaders in some way or at some level. Perhaps better put, they are all followers of the romantic tradition of "quixotic" dreamers. The movie makes an emphatic parallelism between the famous "dream" speeches of Martin Luther King and Robert Kennedy, and a few memorable "dream" aphorisms particularly endeared to his own interviewees.[83] One of these is Cory Booker's "your dream is the promise of all you can become," an obvious trace of the highly successful discourse of self-improvement in American culture. Although the resulting cocktail is also a clear attempt to mix reality and fiction, past and present, and the United States and the rest of the world, there is, nonetheless, an obvious imbalance between them. Aside from scenes from different movie recreations of *Don Quixote*, Hayao Miyazaki's *My Neighbor Totoro* (1993), and Jean-Jacques Beineix's *Betty Blue* (1986), everyone appearing in documentary footage is a leader from fairly recent history, mostly American, and mostly from the very iconic 1960s. The inconsequential gospel of the self that March considers so "quixotic" and so vital for modern leadership seems to be not only a very American creed, but one that March, as well as John Gardner, seems to preach with no more faith than nostalgia. What March tells us through the example of *Don Quixote* could hence be summarized thus: (1) that leadership is a leap of faith that cannot depend on consequences and guarantees, and (2) that this leap of faith is perhaps indicative of our universal human condition, but is, most definitely, the best of American tradition, and therefore, the most American thing to do. In this respect, *Passion and Discipline* is a documentary as much about the relevance of *Don Quixote* today as it is about the relevance of the "dreaming," inspired, or romantic 1960s for contemporary American culture.

One could argue that March's quixotic gospel of the self is, in its easy-to-remember list of three ingredients, dangerously close to the message of a good number of self-help gurus whose recipes of individual success tend to come packaged in equally easy to remember lists of numbered commands: the "x" number of steps, the "x" number of habits, the "x" number of principles, the "x" number of rules . . . , to success, to leadership, to power, to happiness, etc. Many of the contemporary gurus preaching the gospel of the self have, together with the secret of life they claim to possess, a wealthy bank account that certainly helps them appear to be the living proof of the power of their recipe. And some are in themselves a leadership phenomenon, as they truly have, thanks to mass media, legions of devoted followers. As such, their inspirational speeches, their stories, and their mass success may speak volumes about the power of positive thinking or, for that matter, the ambivalent power of the American dream, but they have very little to say about the empowerment values of the humanities or the cathartic effect of reading great works of literature like *Don Quixote*. In March's case, the power of quixotic dreaming is no less ambivalent, since it is hardly distinguishable from blind faith, childish fantasies, utopic mythologies, manic schizophrenia, or religious fanaticism. March knows this very well, and certainly insists on referring to leadership neither as a recipe for success nor as an academic discipline. In fact, he has often emphasized the futility of any pedagogical effort to manufacture leadership,[84] and refers to it condescendingly as a "my-thology" by no means capable of even telling the difference between a leader and a lunatic "until after the fact." [85] Still, he considers it to be a "vitally important" mythology and makes a clear effort in this documentary to keep it alive.[86] However careful March is to avoid any direct link between quixotic dreaming and leadership achievement, and however many clues he gives us about his general skepticism of leadership studies, his emphasis on joy is nei-ther hesitant nor ambivalent. The blissful smile on his own face and those of his interviewees and the many pleasures promised by the exotic landscape of Spain—all that music, dance, women, wine, and sun—make it particularly hard to even consider the possibility of a negative outcome. There is, in other words, a significant lack of balance between the cynical content of some of March's statements about leadership in *Passion and Discipline* and the won-derful images used to convey the idea that, as he puts it: "After 400 years, Quixote lives!" [87] And certainly, as a result of March's reading of *Don Quixote* or as a simultaneous event, the truth is that *Don Quixote*'s lessons for leader-ship have already been packaged from West to East as a product that, erasing all ambivalence, promises immediate success in both life and career.[88] Martin C. Jischke's "dream the impossible dream and then make it come true" is a good indication of this tendency. It is in this sense that March's reading of *Don Quixote* can be considered particularly influential for the discourse of leadership studies without being representative of the mainstream. His repu-tation, after all, is not that of a guru, but of a "gurus's guru."

March's academic reputation is serious enough to not dismiss his reading of *Don Quixote* as that of a snake-oil salesman. He is a poet and a very highly reputed scholar from a very reputable university. He is, in other words, as close as anyone can be to what we consider to be a humanist. How then can he celebrate such reckless and irrational quixotism? What inconsequential logic of self is he himself following? What is, indeed, the meaning of his romantic nostalgia? Unfortunately, his reading of *Don Quixote* avoids answer-ing all these questions. *Passion and Discipline* comes purposely orphaned of his intended audience and his original context, the absence of both of which may give us the idea that there is an unquestionable sense of truth and time-lessness in his message.[89] The presence of a university professor among those interviewed in *Passion and Discipline* is perhaps the strongest trace left of that context and that audience, and it is a thread for us to read March reading *Don Quixote*.[90] The gusto of his romanticism is that of a business professor who has fought the pervasiveness of modern consequentialist thought within the business world since the early stages of his career.[91] In the midst of the extreme commodification of higher learning, he has also defended that a uni-versity education and scholarship are "worthy of their names when they are embraced as arbitrary matters of faith, not as matters of usefulness." [92] In this sense, March's case recalls that of Harold Bloom: they both play with reckless gusto the role of maverick Quixotes living in the demonized world of materialism and pragmatism. The extreme idealism of March's quixotic nonconsequentialism is but a form of extreme compensation during "a time of disappointment," to put it in the words that he himself uses to refer to Cervantes's times.[93] For March, our society critically needs "more Quixote vision" to restore its lost vigor and balance but, as it was for Turgenev, Quixotes seem to belong to a species always in danger of extinction.[94] And, as was also the case with Turgenev, the universality of this claim happens to have a very direct impact in a context that is, to say the least, completely alien to that of Cervantes: the culture of corporate America and the development of leadership studies in American higher and professional education. Within this particular "time of disappointment," *Passion and Discipline* is, at best, a testament of James March's own need to find a "compromised" solution to a very present predicament. At worst, it is a testament of his own betrayal of the alleged uselessness and reckless independence of scholarly research. After all, he does find a very good use and a very good market for *Don Quixote*. Undoubtedly, the current vogue of "idea practitioners" in the world of leadership and business management is directly linked to the current vogue of the romantic quixotic.[95] The same could be said about the increasing presence of literature courses in professional education.

The story that March tells us draws on not one but rather two powerful mythologies. One is the American dream; the other is the quixotic dream. One stands as a core value of the American identity; the other as a core value of humanity. One is heavily endowed with material success; the other with poetic and spiritual success. Their combination in the contemporary imaginary of leadership is indeed very attractive, as it promises fulfillment and joy in the final resolution of several dilemmas of human existence: body and soul, reason and faith, individual and society, now and always . . . . But what these two mythologies have in common is not only a sense of hope and optimism, but a problematic relationship with reality. As many would say today, what America needs to safeguard its future is not myth, but truth; not dreams, but facts; not fiction, but reality; not beautifully tailored stories, but conclusive statistics and scientific veracity. Al Gore, for example, is arguing in precisely this way to talk about global warming or the war in Iraq. But, of course, he is also telling a very compelling story for us to follow—here the happy and reckless inconsequentialists happen to be smokers who actually die of cancer—and he is far from free of the allure of romantic, quixotic leadership.[96] Ironically, this is but an aspect of our quixotic or modern condition: the interaction between fiction and reality, and the possibility and, indeed, the responsibility of telling them apart.

THE CASE OF LEADERSHIP STUDIES AND THE QUESTION OF POETIC TRUTH: (MIS)READING *DON QUIXOTE* WITH A PURPOSE

The case of the leadership studies approach to literature in general and to the *Quixote* in particular makes the question of reading and ethical responsibility unavoidable. Insofar as the leadership approach to literature can be described as reading with a purpose, reading to make a difference, reading for action, or reading for practical implications, the choice of reading *Don Quixote* comes doubly charged with ethical responsibilities. The notion of the ultimate irrelevance of interpretation that John Jay Allen, a leading scholar of Cervantes, once pondered as a possible horizon for literary criticism in its cult of contingency and relativity is clearly absent from the discourse of leadership studies.[97] To leadership studies, rather, the question of reading contingency seems both irrelevant and settled: it is the timeless value of literature that makes it so undeniably relevant to life. As I see it, this premise marks not only the very antipodes of contemporary *Quixote* criticism, but a significant gap as well in the logic of ethical responsibility.

In this respect, perhaps the main question about leadership's approach to *Don Quixote* is its tendency to read literature as if the interaction of reader and text, literature and life, or fiction and history could be fully avoided by simply stating the absolute universality of leadership and literature. And, as most reputed literary critics of Cervantes would immediately admit, one of the most important lessons of Cervantes may be lost by doing just that: approaching literature as a simple one-way affair, reading literature as if one were not fully implicated in the act of reading it. Don Quixote's madness as much as Don Quixote's identity are the ambivalent results of such an approach to literature as the best mirror of life, of such a confusion, in Harry Levin's words, "between literary artifice and that real thing which is life itself." [98] As E. C. Riley so succinctly put it, "the interaction of literature and life is a fundamental theme of *Don Quixote*." [99] Whatever else he may be as a modern fictional hero, *Don Quixote* is a reader who cannot tell the difference anymore between life and "the most impossibly fabulous form of fiction that could be imagined." [100] If Levin and Riley are right, this confusion is embarrassing not only for *Don Quixote* as reader—the most gullible reader in literary history—but also for all the fictional genres that were popular at the time of Cervantes, from the most romantic and allegedly entertaining (chivalric romance) to the most realistic and allegedly didactic (the picaresque novel).

Inextricably related to the first question, another important issue concerning the dominant leadership approach to *Don Quixote* is that, even as it attempts to make Cervantes's fiction readily applicable to contemporary life, it tends to neglect the fact that *Don Quixote* does also have a life: a literary lineage, a birthplace, and a long and very diverse posterity. Here too are, in my opinion, important lessons for leadership studies. Over 400 years of reading *Don Quixote* have yielded a bountiful harvest of readings that can speak volumes about readers' creativity, cultural contingency, and the historical realities and even brutalities of quixotic fiction. Relativity, as Harry Levin once put it, does not mean relativism.[101] As we have seen, to leading experts in the historical reception of Cervantes, like Anthony Close, the romantic approach to *Don Quixote* is emphatically not a timeless tradition that one can see seamlessly continuing from origin to present. Today, however, and apparently still unbeknownst to most *Quixote* experts, there is an unmistakable interest in renewing or reviving this tradition as if it were one to proudly reclaim and to which joyfully to belong. What seems more important, there is an unmistakable interest in making the revival of this tradition somehow equivalent to the very survival of the humanist tradition.

It could be argued that the approach to literature as a source of timeless and universal didactic value is, in fact, a reenactment of classical Aristotelian poetics in its two basic tenets: *Mimesis*—the idea that poetry differs from history in its depiction of universal truth—and *Catharsis*—the idea that poetry produces a purging of the spirit. Interestingly enough, as Giuseppe Toffanin already pointed out in 1920, Aristotle's *Poetics* and the intense neo-Aristotelianism of the Counter Reformation is at the very origin of the creation of *Don Quixote,* which, as has been said countless times, also marks the historical birth of the modern novel.[102] Since the 1920s, *Quixote* criticism has tried to explain exactly how *Don Quixote,* in more ways than one, is Cervantes's direct participation in the contemporary debate on literary theory. It has shown it to be his individual response, not only to the profound ethical questions concerning artistic *Mimesis,* but to all the fictional genres that happened to be popular at his time, and to the actual didactic needs of Counter Reformation Spain. In many respects, Cervantes's formula for the novel—the new realist novel or the new quixotic fiction—is considered to be his genuine contribution to a debate that can only be properly understood considering the fact that, as the prologue of *Don Quixote* clearly states, Aristotle had no clear authority over any of the modern literary genres that were popular at Cervantes's time, including, very prominently, the very novel that he was creating.[103] Considering that literary critics have given Cervantes's commitment to the principles of truth in fiction sharply opposed interpretations—from total respect to didacticism and Counter Reformation values, to the most rebellious questioning of authority—the parodic and ironic openness of *Don Quixote* may very well be its most important ethical lesson. To many of his critics, Cervantes's focus on the active interaction of texts and readers, fiction and life, amounts to be a severe blow to the extreme dogmatism of the Counter Reformation and, in this sense, is proof of Cervantes's defiant place in the humanist tradition of the early Renaissance: the tradition of the *dignitas homini*, a tradition that is predicated on free will, choice, and responsibility. Literary historiography has given credit to Cervantes's uniqueness by pulling him conspicuously out of the context of the Counter Reformation and the company of his very contemporaries; by trying to understand, in other words, "that he was in so many ways something of an outsider." [104] At the beginning of the seventeenth century, Imperial Spain was mostly defined by dogma, intolerance, violence, genocide, exile, poverty, and deeply rooted double standards regarding spirituality and social prestige. Cervantes was a humanist—a committed humanist according to most critics—when humanism was not simply out of vogue in Spain, but mostly out of the question. To keep alive the tradition of the *studia humanitatis* and the *dignitas homini* in 1605 was perhaps an act of individual heroism and proof of genius and wisdom, but also a significant attempt to confront at once his own nostalgia and his own cynicism.[105]

LEADERSHIP STUDIES AND THE RELEVANCE OF *DON QUIXOTE:* NOSTALGIA, CYNICISM, AND AMBIVALENCE

The contemporary nostalgia for visionary leadership represents a fundamental question for leadership studies. In its extreme reaction to anything that can represent cynicism—considered unhealthy, unproductive, nihilistic, hopeless, and doomed—there is a danger that needs to be very carefully pondered. March's "I know who I am" is a very good example of the dangers of an indirect dogmatic reading and, indeed, the relevance of keeping alive the humanities in its most basic method of returning to the text. For once, March avoids quoting Don Quixote's statement in full, which says: "Yo sé quien soy y sé que puedo ser . . ." (I know who I am and I know I can be . . .).[106] Be-ers know who they are and their stories hold no surprises. Don Quixote, unlike Amad's of Gaul, is constantly surprised by a reality that does not seem to be functioning as properly as it does in the fiction he loves to read. According to Spanish novelist Antonio Muñoz Molina: "Becoming, not being is what the novel is all about. And that is why we regard *Don Quixote* as the first fictional hero." [107] As the exact opposite of James March, Muñoz Molina considers that *Don Quixote* is relevant nowadays because it tells us to confront all the mantras of identity of our own time—sexual, cultural, national, religious . . . —that keep promising us comfort, contentment, and success. For him, if this "is a time for be-ers, not becomers," *Don Quixote* must be "relevant, especially to those who are not willing to abide to any fixed laws of identity" or "proudly proclaim what we already are." [108]

Don Quixote deserves to be at the very center of the canon of leadership studies not just because Cervantes is a major artistic leader, which is true, and definitely not so that we can show Don Quixote as the exemplary "leader," the exemplary "positive thinker," or the exemplary "idea practitioner." The main reasons, as I see them, are others: nostalgia, cynicism, and ambivalence. At the heart of Renaissance humanism lies a question about the nature and values of the human and about the power of learning and education as agents of change, progress, freedom, happiness, and perfection. For many, the Renaissance was mainly a time of crisis and of transition to what we now call modernity, a time of conflict and change that made possible the very debate on change, history, and progress.[109] Leadership studies represents a renewed interest in proving that the liberal arts education—the old tradition of the *studia humanitatis*—continues to have a transforming role in our present life and in the shape of our future—the old tradition of the *dignitas homini*. As such, the Renaissance should rightly appear in the field of leadership studies as the origin of an ongoing tradition and as a continued source of knowledge and inspiration. But it could also be considered, from the more cynical point of view of postmodernity, as a nostalgic or romantic search for the ideal "human" or the ideal "individual" and, in this sense, as a reaction against history, culture, discourse, ideology, and context. As we know, the Renaissance has also been deemed responsible for an eternal, universal, or absolutist definition of the human that, ironically, happens to be Western, white, male, and Judeo-Christian, a definition that is key to the exercise of much violence, much injustice, and much "inhumanity." The legacy of the Renaissance is then a very ambivalent tradition to which to belong. And leadership studies will have to ultimately prove, in the selection and the interpretation of its canon, the meaning of its own nostalgia.

NOTES

These pages are, in part, my personal expression of gratitude and nostalgia for the inspiring humanity and humanities of Kenneth Ruscio, the new president of Washington and Lee University and former dean of the University of Richmond's Jepson School of Leadership Studies whose example I have often pondered while writing these pages. If it were not for Dr. Ruscio, I would have never even considered the relevance of *Don Quixote* for leadership studies. My gratitude also extends to Joanne Ciulla, whose invitation to write these pages has given me the opportunity to find the vitality of *Don Quixote* in a context as unexpected and unfamiliar to me as that of leadership studies.

1. Throughout this chapter, the presence or absence of italics in the name of Don Quixote is meant to distinguish between book (*Don Quixote*) and character (Don Quixote).

2. The poll was conducted in May 2002 and it was reported worldwide. As reported in *The Guardian*, the poll of some 100 of the world's leading authors from 54 countries was organized by the Norwegian Nobel Institute. *Don Quixote*, with more than

50 percent of the votes, was a clear runaway winner. "*Don Quixote* is the World's Best Book Say the World's Top Authors," *Guardian Unlimited,* May 8, 2002, Book news, http://books.guardian.co.uk/news/articles/0,6109,711688,00.html

3. Salman Rushdie, "*Quixote* at 400: A Tribute," *Pen America: A Journal for Writers and Readers,* no. 7, *World Voices* (2005): 137.

4. As translated by Vladimir Nabokov, *Lectures on "Don Quixote,"* ed. Fredson Bowers, foreword by Guy Davenport (San Diego: Harcourt Brace Jovanovich, 1983), 7.

5. As translated by Harold Bloom in "Miguel de Cervantes: *Don Quixote,"* in *How to Read and Why* (New York: Scribner, 2000), 145. The original can be found in *Vida de Don Quijote y Sancho* (*Life of Don Quixote and Sancho*), originally published in 1905.

6. Harold Bloom, "Don Quixote, Sancho Panza, and Miguel de Cervantes Saavedra," introduction to *Don Quixote,* by Miguel de Cervantes Saavedra, trans. Edith Grossman (New York: Ecco, 2003), xxxiv.

7. Ibid., 7.

8. Don Quixote has been considered a Christ-like figure by many, including Miguel de Unamuno, Fyodor Dostoevsky, and Graham Green. By the same token, in an almost Borgesian twist, Jesus too has been read as a "quixotic" figure. Illustrative is the example of Pope Benedict XVI who, while still Cardinal Ratzinger, used the "Gospel" of Don Quixote in the epilogue to his *Principles of Catholic Theology:* "What a noble foolishness Don Quixote chooses as his vocation: 'To be pure in his thoughts, modest in his words, sincere in his actions, patient in adversity, merciful toward those in need and, finally, a crusader for truth even if the defense of it should cost him his life.' " Benedict, *Principles of Catholic Theology: Building Stones for a Fundamental Theology* (San Francisco: Ignatius Press, 1987), 392.

9. Matei Calinescu, *Rereading* (New Haven, CT: Yale University Press, 1993), 78.

10. Alter chose "The Inexhaustible Genre" as the title for the conclusion of *Partial Magic: The Novel as a Self-conscious Genre* (Berkeley: University of California Press, 1975). The first chapter of the book, "The Mirror of Knighthood and the World of Mirrors" is Alter's influential analysis of *Don Quixote* as the origin of metafiction. Interestingly enough, the last author that Alter analyzes as belonging in the same metafictional or "quixotic" tradition is Vladimir Nabokov.

11. Bloom, trans., "Miguel de Cervantes: *Don Quixote,"* 150.

12. Bloom, "Don Quixote, Sancho Panza, and Miguel de Cervantes Saavedra," xxi.

13. Diana de Armas Wilson, "Cervantes and the Night Visitors: Dream Work in the Cave of Montesinos," in *Quixotic Desire: Psychoanalytic Perspectives on Cervantes,* ed. Ruth Anthony El Saffar and Diana de Armas Wilson (Ithaca, NY: Cornell University Press, 1993), 71.

14. "The Quixotic Principle: Cervantes and Other Novelists," in *The Interpretation of Narrative: Theory and Practice,* ed. Morton Bloomfield, Harvard English Studies, 1, (Cambridge, MA: Harvard University Press, 1970), 57. Levin's contributions also include "Don Quixote and Moby Dick" and "The Example of Cervantes," both of them included in *Contexts of Criticism,* 2nd ed. (1957; Cambridge, MA: Harvard University Press, 1958), 79–109. For a bibliographic panorama on the topic of Cervantes's literary influence, see J. B. Avalle-Arce and E. C. Riley's seminal anthology *Suma cervantina* (London: Tamesis, 1973), 440–441.

15. Levin, "The Quixotic Principle," 45.

16. Ibid., xxvii.

17. Hillis J. Miller, *Reading Narrative*, Oklahoma Project for Discourse and Theory, v. 18 (Norman: University of Oklahoma Press, 1998), 3–4.

18. "A common approach is to set the text against one's interpretation of it and then identify as ironic those passages which run counter to the interpretation." John J. Allen, *"Don Quixote," Hero or Fool?; Part II, University of Florida Humanities Monographs, no. 46* (Gainesville: University Press of Florida, 1979), 41.

19. Aside from Harry Levin, among the most important studies in this respect are the following: Erich Auerbach, "The Enchanted Dulcinea," in *Mimesis: The Representation of Reality in Western Literature*, trans. Willard Trask (Princeton, NJ: Princeton University Press, 1953; New York: Anchor Books, 1957; first published in 1946), 293–315; John J. Allen, *Don Quixote: Hero or Fool?* (Gainesville: University of Florida Press, 1969); P. E. Russell, *"Don Quixote as a Funny Book," Modern Language Review* 64 (1969): 312–326; Anthony Close, *The Romantic Approach to "Don Quixote"* (Cambridge: Cambridge University Press, 1978); José Montero Reguera, *El Quijote y la cr'tica contemporánea*, Biblioteca de Estudios Cervantinos (Alcalá de Henares: Centro de Estudios Cervantinos, 1996); José Montero Reguera, *El Quijote durante cuatro siglos: lecturas y lectores*, Colección "Acceso al saber," 3 (Valladolid: Secretariado de Publicaciones e Intercambio Editorial, Universidad de Valladolid, 2005).

20. "In his multiplicity—continues Atwood—is the secret of his inmortality." Margaret Atwood, *"Quixote at 400: A Tribute," Pen America: A Journal for Writers and Readers*, no. 7, *World Voices* (2005): 143.

21. Anthony Close's contribution to the recent *Cambridge History of Spanish Literature* concludes thus: "Since (*Quijote* criticism) has traditionally taken its cue from novelists, philosophers, artists, and aestheticians, it is doubtless awaiting a new trend-setting '-ism' to give it a fresh impulse forward. As we have seen, *Don Quixote* and its readers have never failed to respond to that kind of prompting." Anthony Close, "Miguel de Cervantes," in *Cambridge History of Spanish Literature*, ed. David T. Gies (Cambridge: Cambridge University Press, 2004), 221.

22. In an interview with Martha Lagage, "Why Leaders Need Great Books," *Harvard Business School Working Knowledge*, June 18, 2001, http://hbswk.hbs.edu/item/2327.html

23. "My judgment is restored, free and clear of the dark shadows of ignorance imposed on it by my grievous and constant reading of detestable books of chivalry. I now recognize their absurdities and deceptions, and my sole regret is that this realization has come so late it does not leave me time to compensate by reading other books that can be a light to the soul." (II, LXXIV, 935). All quotations are from Edith Grossman's translation of *Don Quixote* (New York: Ecco, 2003).

24. From his inaugural address as president of Washington and Lee University in October 2006. Go to http://inauguration.wlu.edu, and, for the video, to http://mswms1.wlu.edu/RuscioInaug.wmv

25. The argument is that society has been seriously shortchanged by "ivory tower" scholarship. See, for example, Warren Bennis and James O'Toole, "How Business Schools Lost Their Way," *Harvard Business Review* 83, no. 5 (May 2005): 96–104.

26. Harvard President Derek C. Bok has been a leading and influential voice against the moral vacuum of higher education. Of particular interest are the following: *Beyond the Ivory Tower: Social Responsibilities of the Modern University* (Cambridge, MA: Harvard University Press, 1982); *Higher Learning* (Cambridge, MA: Harvard University Press, 1986), and *Our Underachieving Colleges: A Candid Look at How Much Students Learn and Why They Should Be Learning More* (Princeton, NJ: Princeton University Press, 2006). See also Peter Smith, *The Quiet Crisis: How Higher Education is Failing America* (Boston: Anker Publishing Co., 2004).

27. Indeed, the urgency of leadership is often correlated not to one but to many ominous futures. According to John Gardner, "we are faced with immensely threatening problems—terrorism, AIDS, drugs, depletion of the ozone layer, the threat of nuclear conflict, toxic waste, the real possibility of economic disaster. Even moderately informed citizens could extend the list. Yet on none of the items listed does our response acknowledge the manifest urgency of the problem." *On Leadership* (New York: The Free Press, 1990), xii.

28. Thomas R. Piper, Mary C. Gentile, and Sharon Daloz Parks, *Can Ethics Be Taught? Perspectives, Challenges, and Approaches at Harvard Business School* (Boston: Harvard Business School, 1993), 10. In the words of Kenneth Ruscio: "it would be worth thinking how best to prepare students for a world in which most problems require ethical insight and moral reasoning, as well as technical and analytical skills." Available at http://inauguration.wlu.edu, and, for the video, http://mswms1.wlu.edu/RuscioInaug.wmv

29. I quote from the main Web page of the University of Richmond Jepson School of Leadership Studies, founded in 1992 as the first degree granting School of Leadership studies in the United States. Available at http://jepson.richmond.edu/

30. Following Warren Bennis and James O'Toole: "Traditionally, business schools have lacked offerings in the humanities. That is a serious shortcoming. As teachers of leadership, we doubt that our topic can be understood properly without solid grounding in the humanities." Bennis and O'Toole, "How Business Schools Lost Their Way," 104.

31. Kenneth Ruscio directly relates higher education to the well-being of democracy: "I am not an alarmist about the state of democracy . . . . The opportunity of higher education, indeed our obligation, is to model a democratic culture of mutual respect and trust." Available at http://inauguration.wlu.edu, and, for the video, http://mswms1.wlu.edu/RuscioInaug.wmv

32. This is John Gardner on the subject: "Many dismiss the subject with the confident assertion that 'leaders are born, not made.' Nonsense! Most of what leaders have that enables them to lead is learned. Leadership is not a mysterious activity." Gardner, *On Leadership*, 15. See also J. Thomas Wren, "Teaching Leadership: The Art of the Possible," *Journal of Leadership Studies* 1 (1994): 73–93, and the already mentioned Piper, Gentile, and Daloz Parks, *Can Ethics Be Taught?, Perspectives, Challenges, and Approaches at Harvard Business School.*

33. For the history of leadership studies as an emergent discipline and the development of a higher education curriculum, see Ronald E. Riggio, Joanne B. Ciulla, and Georgia Sorenson, "Leadership Education at the Undergraduate Level: A Liberal Arts

Approach to Leadership Development," in *The Future of Leadership Development*, ed. Susan E. Murphy and Ronald E. Riggio (Mahwah: Lawrence Erlbaum Associates, 2003), 223–236.

34. Thomas R. Piper, "A program to integrate leadership, ethics and corporate responsibility into management education," in Piper, Gentile, and Daloz Parks, *Can Ethics Be Taught?* 144. As rationale for the course, Piper tells us that "Fiction is employed as an instrument of social and cultural observation and a source of moral energy" (144–145). In relation to this particular course, see also Pamela Troyer, "Ethics in the MBA Curriculum (Part II)," *HBS Bulletin* (February 1992): 26–3.

35. I transcribe March's words from his documentary on the topic of quixotic leadership. Steven Schecter and James G. March, *Passion and Discipline "Don Quixote"'s Lessons for Leadership* (Princeton: Films for the Humanities & Sciences, 2003).

36. I quote from the online transcription of the Q&A period that followed the first public showing in 2003 of March's documentary. Available at www.wisdomportal .com/Stanford/JamesMarch.html

37. Joseph Badaracco Jr. is sufficiently clear on this point: "The basic challenges of leaders appear so widely perhaps even universally, because they reflect two fundamental, enduring aspects of leadership. One is the humanity of leaders—the hopes and fears, traits and instincts of the human nature we all share. The other is the unchanging agenda of leadership, in all times and places" (6). In *Questions of Character: Illuminating the Heart of Leadership through Literature* (Boston: Harvard Business School, 2006). Badaracco, a professor of Business Ethics at Harvard Business School has taught for over 10 years an "unusual MBA course" based on these assumptions (5). In an *NPR* interview about the book, Badaracco adds: "I think that the basic thing literature does is give students some very compelling raw material to think about their own lives, their goals, how they work with other people." *Weekend Edition Saturday, NPR,* May 6, 2006, http://www.npr.org/templates/story/story.php?storyId=5388057

38. As Badaracco puts it: "Think of Shakespeare's *Julius Caesar*. You could learn as much about leadership from that play as you would from reading any business book or academic journal." In Joseph L. Badaracco Jr. and Diane Coutu, "Leadership in Literature: A Conversation with Business Ethicist Joseph L. Badaracco Jr.," *Harvard Business Review* 84, no. 3 (March 2006): 48. Warren Bennis and James O'Toole emphasize the leading example of James March at Stanford and his use of "imaginative literature to exemplify and explain the behaviour of people in business organizations in a way that was richer and more realistic than any journal article or textbook." Bennis and O'Toole, "How Business Schools Lost Their Way," 104. In the introduction to James March and Thierry Weil's *On Leadership,* we can also read the following statement: "The fundamental issues of leadership—the complications involved in becoming, being, confronting, and evaluating leaders—are not unique to leadership. They are echoes of critical issues of life more generally. As a result, they are characteristically illuminated more by great literature than by modern essays on research and leadership." James G. March and Thierry Weil, *On Leadership* (Malden, MA: Blackwell Publishing, 2005), 1.

39. The approach to literature as a "case study" is the direct influence of law and business schools practice. The Olsson Center at University of Virginia's Darden

Business School, for example, presents the course *Business Ethics Through Literature* as "a Second Year elective that addresses the definition of success in business, race, gender, the role of culture, the privileged place of the executive, and new understandings or models of human beings. The course is taught Socratically with fiction, both novels and short stories, as case studies." Available at http://www.darden.edu/html/standard.aspx?menu_id=35&styleid=3&id=600

40. Badaracco's cases in *Questions of Character: Illuminating the Heart of Leadership through Literature* are the following: Arthur Miller's play *Death of a Salesman*; Chinua Achebe's novel *Things Fall Apart*; Allan Gurganus's story "Blessed Assurance"; F. Scott Fitzgerald's novel *The Love of the Last Tycoon*; Joseph Conrad's story "The Secret Sharer"; Louis Auchincloss's novel *I Come as a Thief*; Robert Bolt's play *Man for All Seasons*; and Sophocles's play *Antigone*. In terms of multiplicity, it is a very uneven mix of contemporary English works and one Greek classic.

41. Harold Bloom and Diane Coutu. "A Reading List for Bill Gates—and You. A Conversation with Literary Critic Harold Bloom," *Harvard Business Review* 79, no. 5 (May 2001): 63.

42. Joseph Badaracco says something very powerful to this effect in reference to his course *The Moral Leader*, from which *Questions of Character* evolved: "this is not a course in literary criticism, and students aren't looking for the 'right' interpretation of these works." In *Questions of Character*, 5. He repeats the same idea in his conversation to Diane Coutu: "I have found that many business people associate literary discussions with abstruse academic talk and Freudian imagery. But this wasn't a class in literary criticism, and I wasn't looking for the 'right' interpretation." In "Leadership in Literature," 48. Warren Bennis and James O'Toole are also unequivocal in their pragmatic approval of literature and their parallel refutation of literary studies as a field of knowledge fully unnecessary for business students. When they single out the example of James March and his influential course at Stanford, they do it by making clear that "he emphatically was not teaching a literature course." Ibid., 104.

43. See, for example: Michael K. Green, *"Don Quixote" Teaching Notes*, Hartwick Classic Leadership Cases (Oneonta, NY: Hartwick Humanities in Management Institute, 2001); Luis Cremades, *"Don Quijote" para triunfar: guía práctica para emprendedores, l'deres y directivos (Don Quixote to Triumph: a Practical Guide for Entrepreneurs, Leaders, and Executives) MR Prácticos* (Madrid: Ediciones Martínez Roca; and Pablo Molina. "IT Leadership Principles from *Don Quixote*," *EDUCAUSE Review* (May–June 2005): 8–9.

44. I am using the title that Jischke gave to his inspirational speech. Although Jischke grants that Don Quixote was ultimately unsuccessful in his quest, he quotes the famous song from *Man of la Mancha*—to him, "among the most soul-stirring ever written"—and advises the students to continue the legacy of quixotic dreamers and transformational leaders: "You are the ones who will carry the seemingly impossible dreams of today into the realities of tomorrow. Your dreams will power this exciting 21st century . . . . I believe in the promise of tomorrow because I believe in the beauty of your dreams." Available at http://news.uns.purdue.edu/UNS/html3month/2004/040515.SP.Jischke.commence.html

45. Ibid.

46. The substance of this approach to *Don Quixote,* according to Close, can be summarized thus: "a) the idealization of the hero and the denial of the novel's satiric purpose; b) the belief that the novel is symbolical . . . about the human's spirit relation to reality." *The Romantic Approach to "Don Quixote"* (Cambridge: Cambridge University Press, 1978), 1.

47. "There are probably few lovers of literature who do not associate the concept of ideal greatness with *Don Quixote.* It may be absurd, fantastic, grotesque; but it is still ideal, unconditional, heroic. It is especially since the Romantic period that this conception has become almost universal, and it withstands all attempts on the part of philological criticism to show that Cervantes intention was not to produce such an impression." "The Enchanted Dulcinea," in *Mimesis: The Representation of Reality in Western Literature,* trans. Willard Trask (Princeton, NJ: Princeton University Press, 1953; New York: Anchor Books, 1957; first published in 1946), 302. Auerbach based his interpretation on a single passage from *Don Quixote* (II, 10): the moment when Sancho tricks the gentleman by making him believe that an ugly peasant woman on a donkey is Dulcinea enchanted. According to Auerbach, "to find anything serious, or a concealed deeper meaning in this scene, one must violently over interpret it." Auerbach, "The Enchanted Dulcinea," 303.

48. Close himself dismissed it as "misguided" and "subjective" for being so unconcerned with the original reception of Cervantes "as a comic artist—satirist, ironist, parodist, or whatever—." Close, *The Romantic Approach to "Don Quixote,"* 1–2. More recently, Close has toned down his assessment to stress only on the "incongruity" between original and subsequent receptions of the book. See his "Miguel de Cervantes," in *The Cambridge History of Spanish Literature,* 203.

49. Allen, *Don Quixote, Hero or Fool? Part II,* 36.

50. "The most perfect and (with Menéndez Pidal) the most influential," says Miguel Herrero. In "Dulcinea and her Critics," *Cervantes: Bulletin of the Cervantes Society of America* 2, no. 1 (1982): 25.

51. Following Miguel Herrero: "Dulcinea, as the personification of Don Quijote's dream, represented the great ideal of virginal Spain, the country which through unparalleled generosity and utter disregard for material gain ruined itself defending selflessly the true Catholic faith, serving the Church with missionary zeal in remote lands and inclement climates, oblivious to danger and hardship. Don Quijote, in short, was the incarnation of Spain, and his virtues were hers. Dulcinea, of course, was the object and source of the love that guided its arms in innumerable adventures. The romantic approach became the official position of Spanish culture through the Restoration (especially so with the Generation of '98) and, of course, achieved the status of dogma in post-civil war Spain." Ibid., 25. For a full account of Unamuno's views of the *Quixote,* see Close's *The Romantic Approach* (134–158).

52. I have analyzed the purpose of political legitimization of the Francoist reading of *Don Quixote* in "Secreta Palinodia: La 'Contrautopía' de José Antonio Maravall como descargo de conciencia," *Bulletin of Hispanic Studies* 78, no. 4 (2001): 504–516.

53. Well known is the story of Erich Auerbach, who wrote *Mimesis* in Istanbul between 1942 and 1945, while in exile from Nazi Germany.

54. "Free Quixotes Big Pull in Caracas," *BBC News,* April 24, 2005. Available at http://news.bbc.co.uk/2/hi/americas/4478007.stm

55. "Let us begin with Don Quixote. What does the character of Don Quixote convey to us? First of all, faith; faith in something eternal, in something immutable, in truth— in short, in that truth which exists outside of an individual . . . , and accessible only through long constancy in service and devotion . . . . What does the character of Hamlet represent? Preeminently, introspection and egoism, and therefore a complete absence of faith . . . . He is an skeptic, constantly preoccupied with himself." "*Hamlet* and *Don Quixote*," trans. William A. Drake, in *The Anatomy of "Don Quixote,"* ed. M. J. Bernadete and Angel Flores (Ithaca, NY: Dragon Press, 1932; New York: Kennikat Press, 1969), 100–102.

56. Ibid., 112.

57. Ibid., 107.

58. Ibid., 112.

59. "He thrice abandons country, home, wife, and daughter, to follow this lunatic. He follows him everywhere, submits to all manners of hardships and affronts, is faithful to him to his very death, believes in him, is proud of him, and sobs on his knees at the bedside of his dying master. His devotion cannot be explained by the expectation of reward or any personal advantage . . . . It originates in what is perhaps the finest characteristic of the masses, in, if we may so express ourselves, their capacity to abandoning themselves to a happy and honest blindness in their devotion to a cause . . . . This is a characteristic of tremendous and universal importance." Ibid., 107–108.

60. "However this simplistic dichotomy may deviate from the intentions of either Shakespeare or Cervantes, it could be related to the physiognomies of Russian literature . . . . In the broad typology of Russian nineteenth century culture, the so-called Westerners—like Turgenev—were the Hamlets, while the Slavophils were the Quixotes—especially Dostoevsky, who found Cervantes a recurrent source of inspiration." In Bloomfield, ed., "The Quixotic Principle," 56. As stressed by Turgenev, the polar opposition between Hamlets and Quixotes was not a Russian matter, but the essence of human nature: "It seems to me that all humanity belongs to one or the other of these two types." Turgenev, "*Hamlet* and *Don Quixote*," trans. William A. Drake, in *The Anatomy of "Don Quixote,"* ed. Bernadete and Flores, 99.

61. Bloom, "Don Quixote, Sancho Panza, and Miguel de Cervantes Saavedra," xxii.

62. "Well, I have never met Bill Gates, and I'm not likely ever to do so. So at the risk of sounding too predictable, I would have to start by recommending the works of William Shakespeare . . . . Shakespeare's only possible rival in imaginative literature of the past four centuries is Miguel de Cervantes, who wrote the classic, *Don Quixote.* Cervantes remains the best of all novelists, just as Shakespeare remains the best of all dramatists." Harold Bloom and Diane Coutu, "A Reading List for Bill Gates—and You. A conversation with literary critic Harold Bloom," *Harvard Business Review* 79, no. 5 (May 2001): 64.

63. According to Bloom, the Knight and Hamlet represent forms of knowing that are "reckless beyond belief." Sancho and Falstaff, on the other hand, represent a "delighted" form of "being." "Don Quixote, Sancho Panza, and Miguel de Cervantes Saavedra," xxxv.

64. Ibid., 99 and 118. Turgenev ultimately defends the need and the usefulness of Hamlets, but repeats the idea that the lack of proportion between Hamlets and Quixotes is the sign of the degeneration of a "troubled epoch." Turgenev. "*Hamlet and Don Quixote*," 119.

65. March and Weil, *On Leadership*, xii.

66. Ibid., 65.

67. Ibid., 65.

68. Ibid., 65.

69. See note 35.

70. March and Weil, *On Leadership*, xi. *On Leadership* is a clear reference to the late John Gardner's influential book of the same title. In a way that many readers of *Don Quixote* will find amusing and cannot possibly be unintended, *On Leadership* is based, according to March, on his own course notes as interpreted originally in French by Thierry Weil and later translated into English by Matthew Clark (xii). For reasons of accuracy, I have chosen to focus, whenever possible, on direct statements by March.

71. James G. March and Diane Coutu, "Ideas as Art: A Conversation with James March," *Harvard Business Review* 84, no. 10 (October 2006): 82.

72. In fact, only Peter Drucker was considered more influential. For the complete rank of gurus' gurus, see Laurence Prusak and Thomas H. Davenport, "Who Are the Gurus' Gurus?" *Harvard Business Review* 81, no. 12 (December 2003): 14–16.

73. March and Coutu, "Ideas as Art," 82.

74. Janet Zich, "Don Quixote's Lessons for Leadership," *Stanford Business Magazine,* May 2003. Available at http://www.gsb.stanford.edu/news/bmag/sbsm0305/leadership.shtml

75. See "Literary Influences Combine in Indian Institute of Management," *Financial Times*, February 5, 1999, Business Line. The chronology of the course can be found at http://www.iimahd.ernet.in/~manikuti/smkcourses.htm

76. As is clear from the introductory remarks to the presentation of the film in February 2003, Stipek's role is as important as March's sense of gratitude to Stanford University. In his words: "This is a rare institution. Stanford University sustains our imagination. This film is a valentine for Stanford." Available at www.wisdomportal.com/Stanford/JamesMarch.html

77. The core of Unamuno's interpretation, according to Close, is the "idea of the hero as a man of Faith, Poetry, the Ideal." *The Romantic Approach*, 156.

78. In the introduction to *On Leadership*, March singles out Unamuno together with Kierkegaard as one of those "great geniuses" of philosophy whose insight is particularly valuable to the appreciation of leadership (6). Not coincidentally, Kierkegaard happens to be a main influence on Unamuno's reading of *Don Quixote*. March has often acknowledged Kierkegaard as a main influence on his scholarly career. See, for example, March and Coutu, "Ideas as Art: A Conversation with James March," 83–89; and "A scholar Quest," *Stanford Business School Magazine* 64, no. 4 (June 1996). Available at http://www.gsb.stanford.edu/community/bmag/sbsm0696/ascholar.htm

79. "We follow Don Quixote, not because we think he's a model leader, but for the light he has on three vital issues of modern Leadership and modern life. First, the role

of imagination and fantasy; second, the sources of persistence and commitment; and third, the possibility of Joy." Ibid.

80. "Don Quixote's legacy . . . is a moral message about creating a life that ennobles the human spirit, a life of commitment that does not depend on consequences. Quixote shows that life and leadership require passion and discipline, being able to say 'Yo sé quien soy' (I know who I am). After 400 years, Quixote lives!" Ibid.

81. Clearly, it is an existential religion based in Kant, Kierkegaard, and Unamuno. In "A Scholar Quest" March says: "Søren Kierkegaard said that any religion that could be justified by its consequences was hardly a religion." See also March and Coutu, "Ideas as Art" (85).

82. Among the leadership figures from documentary footage, the only unfamiliar leader to an American audience—and the only one actually explained by March— would be General Gutiérrez Mellado, whose courage during the frustrated 1981 *coup d'état* by Lieutenant-Colonel Tejero made him become, together with King Juan Carlos, a hero of Spain's transition to democracy.

83. The featured ones are Martin Luther King's "I have a dream," and Bobby Kennedy quoting George Bernard Shaw: "Some men see things as they are, and say 'Why?' I dream of things that never were and say, 'Why not?'"

84. "I doubt that 'leadership' is a useful concept for serious scholarship. The idea of leadership is imposed on our interpretation of history by our human myths, or by the way we think that history is supposed to be described. As a result, the fact that people talk about leaders and attribute importance to them is neither surprising nor informative. Although there is good work on several aspects of asymmetric relations in life, broad assertions about leadership are more characteristic of amateurs than of professionals. Unless and until a link to significant scholarship can be made, the thinking on leadership will produce more articles in popular journals than in professional ones, more homilies and tautologies than powerful ideas." In March and Coutu, "Ideas as Art," 85. See also March's statements in the preface of *On Leadership*, where he refers to his skepticism of leadership studies as a "tolerant" form of inquiry (xi).

85. In *Passion and Discipline*, March tells us: "We portrayed a world in which visionaries turn out to be right. Such stories are not typical of the history of imagination but they are vitally important to leadership and, even more, to our mythology of leadership." In the Q&A session after the first showing of the film in 2003, he gives this answer to the question of how to tell a leader from a lunatic: "You can't tell the difference until after the fact."

86. See previous note.

87. Ibid.

88. See notes 43 and 75.

89. In the Q&A session referred to in note 85, March warns: "Don't ask who is the intended audience. This is a rare institution. Stanford University sustains our imagination. This film is a valentine for Stanford."

90. In the same Q&A session, Jerry L. Beasley, president of Concord College, says: "I'm not a leader. I'm a disciple of Jim March. As President of Concord College, I'm a living experience of Jim's ideas."

91. In 1996, March wrote: "Modern portrayals of human action are overwhelmingly in a calculative and consequentialist tradition . . . . It is no surprise that schools of applied economics (or business) teach such a consequentialist theology as a sacred doctrine. The opposite of this tradition is *Don Quixote:* a second grand tradition for understanding, motivating, and justifying action. This tradition sees action based not on anticipation or consequences but on attempts to fulfill the obligations of personal and social identities and senses of self . . . . This second vision has become somewhat obscured in contemporary life, and in particularly, in the halls of business schools." "A Scholar Quest."

92. Again from "A Scholar Quest": "A university is only incidentally a market. It is more essentially a temple—a temple dedicated to knowledge and a human spirit of inquiry. It is a place where learning and scholarship are revered, not primarily for what they contribute to personal or social well-being but for the vision of humanity that they symbolize, sustain, and pass on. Søren Kierkegaard said that any religion that could be justified by its consequences was hardly a religion. We can say a similar thing about university education and scholarship. They only become truly worthy of their names when they are embraced as arbitrary matters of faith, not as matters of usefulness. Higher education is a vision, not a calculation. It is a commitment, not a choice. Students are not customers; they are acolytes. Teaching is not a job; it is a sacrament. Research is not an investment; it is a testament."

93. From *Passion and Discipline.*

94. In the Q&A session at Stanford University referred to in note 85, he is fairly clear about the fading nature of Don Quixote: "If a society is all Quixote, then we have to teach a different method. But as it is, this society needs more Quixote vision."

95. See Thomas H. Davenport and Laurence Prusak with H. James Wilson, *What's the Big Idea? Creating and Capitalizing on the Best Management Thinking* (Boston: HBS Press, 2003).

96. In the documentary *An Inconvenient Truth,* Gore tells us the story of his sister, who died of lung cancer, as evidence of what he considers to be a much graver disease in contemporary American culture: the avoidance of reality. In *An Inconvenient Truth, a Global Warning,* presented by Al Gore, directed by Davis Guggenheim, produced by Lawrence Bender and Laurie David (Hollywood: Paramount, 2006). Talking about his book *The Assault on Reason,* Al Gore said in an interview on *NPR:* "I don't think it's naive or quixotic to believe that the truth still matters. I have heard millions of people around this country in one way or another ask the same question that I ask myself. What is it that's gone basically wrong in the way America is operating? This book is my effort to . . . say exactly what it is and how we can fix it." Al Gore, interview by Michele Norris, *All Things Considered, NPR,* May 25, 2007. Available at http://www.npr.org/templates/story/story.php?storyId=10440121

97. "Our respective accounts of how things are have a dismaying relativity to them, a relativity that one cannot read *Don Quixote* without acknowledging. But the relativity is never total for Cervantes, nor can it be for us. . . . There is something vital at stake here and I, for one, cannot be comfortable knowing that an important and influential chunk of our theoretical vanguard can only be tolerated, forgiven, simply because we are all of us irrelevant to real life." In "Generational Conflicts within Hispanism: Notes

from the Comedia Wars," in *Cervantes and His Postmodern Constituencies*, ed. Anne J. Cruz and Carroll B. Johnson (New York: Garland, 1999), 76–77.

98. Levin, "The Example of Cervantes," in *Contexts of Criticism*, 2nd ed. (1957; Cambridge, MA: Harvard University Press, 1958), 81.

99. "Literature and Life in *Don Quixote*," in *Cervantes; a Collection of Critical Essays*, ed. Morton Bloomfield, Twentieth century views (Englewood Cliffs, NJ: Prentice-Hall, 1969), 123.

100. Riley, *Suma cervantina*, 125.

101. Preface to Levin, *Contexts of Criticism*, x.

102. See Giuseppe Toffanin, *La fine dell' umanesimo* (Milano: Fratelli Bocca, 1920). Harry Levin, who called Cervantes the "exemplary" novelist, added: "It is a truism, of course, that he sets the example for all other novelists to follow." Levin, "The Quixotic Principle," 79. To Harold Bloom, *Don Quixote* "stands forever as the birth of the novel out of the prose romance, and is still the best of all novels." In "Don Quixote, Sancho Panza, and Miguel de Cervantes Saavedra," xxiii.

103. "Besides, if I understand it correctly, this book of yours has no need for any of the things you say it lacks, because all of it is an invective against books of chivalry, which Aristotle never thought of, and St Basil never mentioned, and Cicero never saw, and whose unbelievable absurdities do not enter into the calculations of factual truth . . . ." (I, Prologue, 8).

104. E. C. Riley, "Cervantes and the Cynics (*El licenciado Vidriera* and *El coloquio de los perros*)," *Bulletin of Hispanic Studies* 53 (1976): 198.

105. To enter any deeper into the related questions of nostalgia and cynicism in Cervantes is basically tantamount to opening Pandora's box. Among the many insightful analyses and interpretations, E. C. Riley's previously mentioned "Cervantes and the Cynics" stands, in my view, as one of the best.

106. " 'I know who I am,' replied Don Quixote, 'and I know I can be not only those I have mentioned but the Twelve Peers of France as well, and even all the nine paragons of Fame, for my deeds will surpass all those they performed, together or singly' " (I, V, 43).

107. Antonio Muñoz Molina, "*Quixote* at 400: A Tribute," *Pen America: A Journal for Writers and Readers*, no. 7, *World Voices*: 140–142. Muñoz Molina continues his argument thus: "That is why the heroes of so many modern novels are liars, deceivers, fugitives, impersonators, impostors, vocational becomers, perpetually unsatisfied . . . , forever trying not to be what other people have agreed or decided they are but something else, somebody else" (140).

108. Ibid., 141.

109. I am referring very generally to post-Burckhardtian views on the Renaissance.

3

Against the Heroic: Gilgamesh and His City

MICHAEL HARVEY

Study the brickwork, study the fortification;
climb the great ancient staircase to the terrace;
study how it is made; from the terrace see
the planted and fallow fields, the ponds and orchards.
This is Uruk, the city of Gilgamesh. . .[1]

When the *Gilgamesh* epic was rediscovered in November 1872—"I am the first man to read that after more than two thousand years of oblivion," cried its translator, the heroically self-educated Londoner George Smith, leaping up from the Babylonian tablets before him in the British Museum and, according to one recollection, stripping off his clothes in frantic ecstasy[2,3]—what immediately struck readers with wonder were the text's astonishing echoes of the Biblical story of the flood: the account by an old man of how, with a god's assistance, he built an ark, filled it with animals, and survived the deluge that obliterated his city.[4]

In the decades after George Smith's electric discovery, as more cuneiform fragments were pieced together and as more versions of the story were discovered from different ancient Near Eastern cultures, the flood story came to be seen as a "digression," not the central story.[5] Critical attention shifted to the figure of Gilgamesh himself, the hero-king in search of immortality. Rivkah Schärf-Kluger, for instance, sees Gilgamesh as an archetype, a "modern ancient hero" struggling to make sense of his mortality.[6] The epic's most influential recent student, Jeffrey Tigay, approvingly quotes the Cambridge classics scholar G. S. Kirk that it "exemplifies through a single legendary figure, the various attitudes to death that humans tend to adopt."[7]

In recent years scholars have sensibly started paying attention to a long neglected aspect of the story, its treatment of gender relations and of women in particular—for instance, the figure of Shamhat, the temple prostitute who tames the wild man Enkidu; or Ishtar, the highly sexualized goddess whose advances Gilgamesh rejects; or Siduri, the tavern keeper he meets in the wilderness, who guides him on his way.[8] Sex, erotic power, and gender identity—as well as friendship and love—are central elements of the poem; perceiving this helps recenter our reading, so that the poem becomes much more than the story of a solitary, supermasculine hero-archetype.[9]

All of these ways of making sense of the story—the city-destroying flood, the hero's search for immortality, gender, and sex—provide useful perspectives. Indeed, the epic of *Gilgamesh* has a stolidly unheroic hero who serves to connect these perspectives, as well as the story's people—men and women, kings and commoners, dead and living. That "hero" is the city. Uruk, the city of Gilgamesh, with its assertion of the good life within the city walls, and its patient insistence on community as the enduring measure of human things is, from the opening to the closing lines, the thematic heart of the poem. As we shall see, even seeming digressions like the story of Utnapishtim, the ancient survivor of the ruined city of Shuruppak, serve to develop the thematic importance of the city as the preserver and teacher of human understanding and civility. (It is something more than idle coincidence that three cities—third-millennium BCE Uruk, seventh-century BCE Nineveh, and nineteenth-century London, each in its day the world's most populous city—are responsible for bringing forth, preserving, and rediscovering the epic of *Gilgamesh,* the story of how a city tamed and taught its ruler.[10]

* * *

To read *Gilgamesh* is to enter a world at once ancient and modern, magic and real. When we read it, we feel both very old and newly risen on the earth, seeing with fresh eyes our own world and our own lives: the everyday magic of life and death, friendship and loss, terrible grief and painfully gained knowledge—self-knowledge, but also knowledge of others and of the fragile but vital threads that weave our lives together. The story explores fundamental questions about leadership that scholars—and all of us, to some degree— wrestle with. I want to draw attention, in particular, to four questions the poem poses about leadership. First, it gives us a vivid portrait of a strong, fierce, indomitable leader—"the perfect, the terror"—but no sooner does the poem set up this image than it undermines it, by asking, *But what about the followers?* Second, the poem explores the loneliness of heroic leadership, asking if the heroic ideal is not a trap for individuals and communities. Against the heroic, the poem argues for the transforming power of friendship, love, and empathy that can turn a hero into something even more precious: a man. Third, the poem suggests that the deepest and most enduring kind of leadership is not conquest but discovery, and that the leader's most difficult journey is the one he must undertake to discover his own heart. And, finally, the fourth question the poem poses about leadership concerns this inward journey of discovery. The poem suggests that this almost Socratic self-examination is not its own end, its own *telos*, but is embedded in a social and indeed a civic identity, and actually contributes to and strengthens the life of the community. The city, in short, is the only immortal hero of the poem, and Gilgamesh's greatest accomplishment is to sustain his city and to recognize himself in it. Let us see how the poem explores these four questions—about followers, heroes, the quest, and the city.

The poem begins with a description of Gilgamesh as a journeyer, a discoverer, a sufferer, and a possessor of "secret" knowledge:

THE STORY

> *of him who knew the most of all men know;*
> *who made the journey; heartbroken; reconciled;*
> *who knew the way things were before the Flood,*
> *the secret things, the mystery: who went*
> *to the end of the earth, and over; who returned,*
> *and wrote the story on a tablet of stone.*[11]

Immediately establishing Gilgamesh as having a special claim to experience and understanding, the poem turns to his actions as a city builder:

> *He built Uruk. He built the keeping place*
> *of Anu and Ishtar. The outer wall*
> *shines in the sun like brightest copper; the inner*
> *wall is beyond the imagining of kings.*
> *Study the brickwork, study the fortification;*
> *climb the great ancient staircase to the terrace;*
> *study how it is made; from the terrace see*
> *the planted and fallow fields, the ponds and orchards.*[12]

These lines merge past and present, linking what Gilgamesh wrought with a present-tense address bidding the reader or listener to experience and "study" the city's extent.

First Gilgamesh is a discoverer, then a builder. Now the third early portrayal of Gilgamesh follows, as a powerful, overwhelming physical force:

> the Wild Ox, son of Lugulbanda, son
> of the Lady Wildcow Ninsun, Gilgamesh
> the vanguard and the rear guard of the army,
> Shadow of Darkness over the enemy field,
> the Web, the Flood that rises to wash away
> the walls of alien cities, Gilgamesh
> the strongest one of all, the perfect, the terror. . . .[13]

Prefiguring Utnapishtim's story of the flood at the end of the epic, Gilgamesh is likened to the deluge that destroys cities.

Now Gilgamesh's three faces—discoverer, builder, and master of force—are brought together in a portrayal of a godlike maker:

> It is he who opened passes through the mountains;
> and he who dug deep wells on the mountainsides;
> who measured the world; and sought out Utnapishtim
> beyond the world; it is he who restored the shrines;
> two-thirds a god, one-third a man, the king.[14]

Such power, however, comes at a high price. Gilgamesh's people pay dearly for his mastery:

> There was no withstanding the aura or power of the Wild
> Ox Gilgamesh. Neither the father's son
> nor the wife of the noble; neither the mother's daughter
> nor the warrior's bride was safe. The old men said:
> "Is this the wise shepherd of the people? Is this
> the wise shepherd, protector of the people?"[15]

So the people ask the gods for protection against their own king. Tigay, the epic's most celebrated scholar, calls this a "stock pattern" of oppression, complaint, and divine response often appearing in ancient Near Eastern texts:[16]

> The gods of heaven listened to their complaint.
> "Aruru is the maker of this king.
> Neither the father's son nor the wife of the noble
> is safe in Uruk; neither the mother's daughter
> nor the warrior's bride is safe. The old men say:
> 'Is this the shepherd of the people? Is this
> the wise shepherd, protector of the people?
> There is no withstanding the desire of the Wild Ox.' "[17]

The poem, thus, introduces a hero as a leader only to question that image almost immediately, by asking, *What about the followers?*

* * *

The second question the poem poses is about the loneliness and isolation of the heroic leader. The people complain about Gilgamesh because he does not consider them, and does not treat them, as moral equals. He sees his kingdom as his personal property, to use as he wishes. So how do the gods decide to solve this problem? By giving Gilgamesh, who towers over ordinary people, an equal. They create Enkidu, "the stormy-hearted other." [18] The gods go to the goddess Aruru:

> *"You made this man. Now create another.*
> *Create his double and let the two contend.*
> *Let stormy heart contend with stormy heart*
> *that peace may come to Uruk once again." [19]*

The story of Enkidu is astonishing. Once created, he lives on the grasslands, with the wild animals. A hunter spies him in the fields and reports the discovery to Gilgamesh. The plan to snare Enkidu is simple: He is lured by sex and beer, the temple prostitute Shamhat ("who showed him the things a woman knows how to do"), and seven jugs of beer that, the poem says, make Enkidu "suddenly joyful." [20] Captivated by the luxuries of city life, Enkidu remains outside Uruk for a time. But eventually he comes to the city, angered by the *jus primae noctis*—Gilgamesh's custom of raping the bride as his contribution to the marriage ceremony:

> *Enkidu stood, guardian on the threshold*
> *of the marital chamber, to block the way of the king,*
> *the aura and power of the Wild Ox Gilgamesh,*
> *who was coming to the chamber to take the bride.*
> *Stormy heart struggled with stormy heart*
> *as Gilgamesh met Enkidu in his rage.*
> *At the marital threshold they wrestled, bulls contending;*
> *the doorposts shook and shattered; the wrestling staggered,*
> *wild bulls locked-horned and staggering staggered wrestling*
> *through the city streets; the city walls and lintels*
> *shuddered and swayed, the gates of the city trembled*
> *as Gilgamesh, the strongest of all, the terror,*
> *wrestled the wild man Enkidu to his knees.*
> *And then the rage of Gilgamesh subsided.[21]*

Enkidu's anger is worth remarking on: here in his natural, unschooled reaction is a suggestion of a sense of natural ethics, that ordinary people have some reasonable expectation to live their lives undisturbed by arbitrary power.

The contest with Enkidu is a first turning point for Gilgamesh. Matched in strength for the first time in his life, he now has, also for the first time, a friend:

> *Then Enkidu and Gilgamesh embraced,*
> *and kissed, and took each other by the hand.*[22]

In a remarkable passage, Gilgamesh takes Enkidu to meet his mother, the goddess Wild-Cow Ninsun (represented in the poem as a human queen living in Uruk). The mother's perceptive grasp of Enkidu's lonely childhood creates a scene of charged emotional intimacy. (The cuneiform text here, Tablet II, is highly damaged and David Ferry's generally excellent translation falters, so we turn to a version of A. R. George's authoritative translation.) Ninsun speaks to the two men:

> *"Enkidu possesses no [kith or kin.]*
> *Shaggy hair hanging loose . . .*
> *he was born in the wild and [has] no [brother.]"*
> *Standing there, Enkidu heard [what she said,]*
> *and thinking it over, he sat [down weeping.]*
> *His eyes brimmed with [tears,]*
> *his arms fell limp, [his] strength [ebbed away.]*
> *They took hold of each other and . . . ,*
> *they [linked] their hands like. . . .*[23]

Gilgamesh asks Enkidu why he weeps:

> *"Why, my friend, [did your eyes] brim [with tears,]*
> *your arms fall limp, [your strength ebb away?]"*
> *Said Enkidu to him, [to Gilgamesh:]*
> *"My friend, my heart was made to ache . . ."*
> *"Through sobbing [my legs do] tremble,*
> *terror has entered my heart."*[24]

Intimacy makes friendship possible, but it also brings the experience of intense self-awareness, wonderfully felt by Enkidu as "terror." The poem suggests that understanding others must begin with an understanding of oneself. For Enkidu, the "wild man" who grew up with beasts, this dawning of feeling self-knowledge is another critical developmental step, after his discovery of the joy of prolonged physical intimacy (not just brief coupling) with Shamhat the temple prostitute.

As if to gird themselves against such uncomfortable feelings by turning to what they know, the two friends decide to venture into the fearsome cedar forest. There, they will counter Enkidu's "terror" by taking on and defeating the "terror of the people" that lurks there—the monster Huwawa:[25]

> *Huwawa's breath is fire; his roar is the floodwater;*
> *his breath is death.*[26]

The two men visit the armorers to obtain weapons and tell Ninsun of their quest. Making an offering to the sun-god Shamash, Gilgamesh's mother cries,

> *"Why have you given my son a restless heart?*
> *No one has ever undergone the journey*
> *that he will undergo."* [27]

Ninsun's last act before the young men venture into the forest is to formally adopt Enkidu as her son: "Though not my son, here I adopt you son." [28]

Gilgamesh and Enkidu enter the terrible cedar forest. Again, the text here (Tablet V) is quite damaged, but Ferry's conjectural translation (faithful to the extant fragments) captures the spirit of how the friendship between Gilgamesh and Enkidu heartens them: "Two people, companions," they tell each other, "they can prevail against the terror." [29]

Working together and encouraging each other, the two strong men manage to kill Huwawa. At this point the poem reads like a buddy movie, or like a scene from the classic Western novel *Shane*, with the farmer Joe Starrett and the cowboy Shane straining their muscles, fighting the bad guys, and glorying in their manly strength together.

Back in Uruk, the cleaned-up Gilgamesh catches the attention of the goddess Ishtar, who now finds him irresistible. But all of his erotic energy is sublimated into his friendship with Enkidu, and he dismisses Ishtar contemptuously:

> *"You are the fire that goes out. . . .*
> *. . .*
> *You are the house that falls down. You are the shoe*
> *that pinches the foot of the wearer."* [30]

The enraged goddess sends the bull of heaven to destroy Gilgamesh. But he and Enkidu, fighting together, overcome even this monster. Boisterously triumphant, Gilgamesh, to dip into modern idiom, "parties like a rockstar":

> *Gilgamesh spoke a word to the serving girls* [of his palace:]
> *"Who is the finest among men?*
> *Who the most glorious of fellows?"*
> *"Gilgamesh is the finest among men!*

[Gilgamesh the most] glorious of fellows!"
* * *
Gilgamesh made merry in his palace.[31]

As skillfully as any movie, however, the scene of revels cuts to an ominous dream of Enkidu's: "Why is it that the gods are meeting in council?"

The gods, now alarmed by the two friends' sheer power, cut them short by killing Enkidu, and so they send sickness upon him:

And so it was that Enkidu fell sick.
Gilgamesh looked at him and weeping said:
"Why am I left to live while my brother dies?
Why should he die and I be spared to live?" [32]

Enkidu's death scene occupies all of Tablet VII of the Babylonian text. At first Enkidu dreams and despairs and throws curses at those who brought him into civilization, including the hunter who found him and Shamhat, the temple harlot who tamed him. Reproached by the god Shamash, who reminds him of the good things that the prostitute has let him experience— bread, beer, clothing, and sex—Enkidu relents, and blesses Shamhat instead:

"May [governors] and noblemen love you,
may he [that is one league (distant)], slap his thigh!
May he that is two leagues (distant) shake out his hair,
may no soldier [be slow] to undo his belt for you!
May he [give you] obsidian, lapis lazuli and gold,
multiple-ear-[rings] shall be your gift!" [33]

Gilgamesh tries to hearten his dying friend:

"Do not forget how we,
two people together, prevailed against the terror." [34]

But it is no help, and Enkidu dies: "Gilgamesh heard the death rattle."[35]

* * *

Enkidu's death plunges Gilgamesh into grief, a new emotion for him. It also introduces the poem's third great question about leadership: *What is the leader's most difficult journey?* Gilgamesh's earlier journey had been into the cedar forest, where he and Enkidu killed the fearful Huwawa. (The poem's first translator, George Smith, interpreting as he discovered new fragments, incorrectly believed that this clash in the forest was the poem's central episode and constituted a metaphoric overthrow of a tyrant.)[36] But now Gilgamesh has no interest in hunting monsters. He undertakes a new journey, to find the secret of immortality. This quest, which takes up the rest of the poem, proves far more difficult and consequential than the episode in the cedar forest. And it will end, apparently, in failure or, at best, a lesson in humility even for kings. Gilgamesh sets out to find a man named Utnapishtim,

> *by means of whom*
> *he might find out how death could be avoided.*[37]

Who is Utnapishtim? He is a precursor of the Old Testament's Noah—a survivor, the only man still alive from the ancient city, Shuruppak, that was destroyed by a flood. This was the part of the story that first attracted headlines in the 1870s.

To find Utnapishtim, Gilgamesh treks to the eastern mountains. His first act reminds us of the old Gilgamesh: he kills several lions blocking his way through a mountain pass. After this, he is done fighting. At each stage of his journey he encounters beings—some human and some not—with whom he talks, and from whom he learns. He finds strange creatures guarding the mountain—two scorpion beings, male and female, who guard a pass through which the sun travels at night. They tell him that no mortal has ever come through this path, and that no mortal can do so. But they allow him to pass through. After a long passage of darkness and terror, he comes out the other side and finds himself in a lovely garden at the edge of the ocean. Here he meets Siduri, "an ale-wife who lived by the sea-shore."[38] At first she is frightened by this strange, hairy-bodied, martial man; she bars her gate and retreats to the roof of her tavern. Gilgamesh threatens to smash her gate in if she tries to keep him out. But then, in a striking change of tone, he tells her about Enkidu, "my friend, whom I love so deeply."[39] She is struck by his suffering and helps him on his way.

The pattern continues with Urshànabi the boatman, who takes Gilgamesh across the "waters of death,"[40] and it continues when they reach the far shore, where an old man stands waiting. The old man—Utnapishtim himself, though Gilgamesh does not know it yet—cannot understand why a hero so mighty and celebrated would look so sad:

> *"[Why are] your cheeks [hollow, your face] sunken,*
> *[your mood] wretched, [your features] wasted?*
> *(Why) is there sorrow in [your heart,]*
> *[and your face like] one who has traveled a distant road?*
> *[Why is it your face is burnt] by frost and sunshine,*
> *and [you roam the wild] got up like a lion?"*[41]
> *"I look like one whose grief lives in his heart,"* Gilgamesh answers,
> *"because of the death of Enkidu the companion."*[42]

Utnapishtim, still unrecognized, speaks to Gilgamesh about grief and mortality. His words link nature and human life, especially civic life, and emphasize the transience of all things:

> *How long does a building stand before it falls?*
> *How long does a contract last? How long will brothers*
> *share the inheritance before they quarrel?*
> *How long does hatred, for that matter, last?*
> *Time after time the river has risen and flooded.*
> *The insect leaves the cocoon to live but a minute.*
> *How long is the eye able to look at the sun?*
> *From the very beginning nothing at all has lasted.*
> *See how the dead and the sleeping resemble each other.*
> *Seen together, they are the image of death.*[43]

Hearing these words, Gilgamesh realizes that he has reached his goal—Utnapishtim. Now the old man tells Gilgamesh his story: the warning, the ark, the flood, the gods' shock that he had lived, Enlil's judgment that Utnapishtim and his wife become immortal and live apart from mortals. Utnapishtim sets Gilgamesh a test, to stay awake for one week, and promises the secret of immortality if he can do it. But Gilgamesh cannot. He falls asleep, and his quest suddenly is at an end. Solemn, stunned, he sets out on his return to his city.

All that he has gained, besides the journey itself, are Utnapishtim's words, in effect handed down from the ancient lost city of Shurrupak. This is what Gilgamesh's quest to find immortality really gives him: a sense of the fragility of human things, and the recognition that all men and women, from the mightiest to the humblest, share a common human identity. Both live, both will die, and both wrest meaning from the slender margin of life.

* * *

The contemplation of death brings us to the poem's fourth and final question about leadership: *What is the leader's legacy?* The leader's quest, and his discoveries, turn out not be ends in themselves. They are embedded in a civic identity—the city or community that the leader serves as well as leads.

As he is leaving, however, it appears he will take something tangible after all. Utnapishtim's wife urges her husband to give Gilgamesh something to recompense some of his suffering, and the old man yields up one more secret of immortality: a plant that grows beneath the water—"How-the-Old-Man-Once-Again-Becomes-a-Young-Man."[44] (Today's version of the plant is found in a variety of pharmaceuticals and cosmetic procedures.) Gilgamesh dives into the water and plucks the plant from the river bottom. But on his journey back to the city with the boatman Urshànabi a serpent steals it away:

> *he sat down weeping by the pool of water.*
> *He took Urshànabi by the hand and said:*
> *"What shall I do? The journey has gone for nothing.*
> *For whom has my heart's blood been spent? For whom?*
> *For the serpent who has taken away the plant.*
> *I descended into the waters to find the plant*
> *and what I found was a sign telling me to*
> *abandon the journey and what it was I sought for."* [45]

Thus, when Gilgamesh at last returns to his city, he comes empty-handed. This quiet ending has seemed anticlimactic to many of the poem's readers. But it is actually integral to the story's theme—quite similar in form and function to how J. R. R. Tolkien closes the "Lord of the Rings" trilogy, with Sam Gamgee's quiet return to the Shire:

> *He drew a deep breath. "Well, I'm back, he said."*
> *The End*[46]

When Gilgamesh returns to his own city, a calm descends upon him. The city seems to restore him to a sense of meaning and purpose. In the poem's closing lines, he tells his boatman, Urshànabi, to regard the city:

> *"Study the brickwork, study the fortification;*
> *climb the great ancient staircase to the terrace;*
> *study how it is made; from the terrace see*
> *the planted and fallow fields, the ponds and orchards.*
> *One league is the inner city, another league*
> *is orchards; still another the fields beyond;*
> *over there is the precinct of the temple.*
> *Three leagues and the temple precinct of Ishtar*
> *measure Uruk, the city of Gilgamesh."* [47]

These are the words that close the poem, uttered by Gilgamesh to his boatman, Urshànabi. But it may be recalled that we have heard these very lines before—in the poem's opening lines:

> *Study the brickwork, study the fortification;*
> *climb the great ancient staircase to the terrace;*
> *study how it is made; from the terrace see*
> *the planted and fallow fields, the ponds and orchards.*
> *This is Uruk, the city of Gilgamesh. . . .*[48]

The poem's structure is a great circle. Its first lines "repeat" Gilgamesh's closing lines. They distill what he will learn (and teach) about himself, life, and leadership. And what is that? That leadership is, ultimately, not about heroics, or conquest, or mastery, but about the city.

Ironically, and against all expectation, the quest succeeds. Gilgamesh does find life beyond his own life—where he started, in the city of Uruk. It is through this city that he built, made strong, and sustains that he will be remembered. But yet Uruk is a city like Utnapishtim's lost Shuruppak that eventually, beyond the poem's boundaries, is lost. But when George Smith and other explorers follow their own quest and recover Gilgamesh, they also recover a memory of his city. Poetry, like all art, may allow leaders—and more importantly the communities they serve—to live forever. But, of course, that depends on the contingencies of history: what is remembered, what is lost, what is recovered. It also depends on us, readers and listeners. By reading and exploring the stories of leadership, we play our own active role. We breathe life into long-forgotten or scarcely remembered—but perhaps not quite dead—men and women.

NOTES

1. *Gilgamesh: A New Rendering in English Verse.* Translated by David Ferry (New York: Farrar, Straus, and Giroux, 1992), 3. Most quotations from the poem are from this inspired translation (exceptions are noted).

2. John Maier, ed., *Gilgamesh: A Reader* (Wauconda, IL: Bolchazy-Carducci Publishers, 1997).

3. E. A. Wallis Budge, *The Rise and Progress of Assyriology* (London: Martin Hopkinson, 1925), 152–153; quoted in David Damrosch, *The Buried Book: The Loss and Rediscovery of the Great Epic of Gilgamesh* (New York: Henry Holt, 2006), 11–12.

4. For instance, the *New York Times* reported Smith's discovery as "The Deluge: Discovery and Promulgation of the Chaldean History of the Flood" (December 20, 1872). Available at http://query.nytimes.com/mem/archive-free/pdf?res=9902E2DB163 BEF34BC4851DFB4678389669FDE. This early account reports Smith's original, mistaken reconstruction of Gilgamesh's name as "Izdubar." The Babylonian tablets from Nineveh that Smith translated are now known as the "standard version" of the epic. They represent a late and highly polished version of the story, which in various forms stretches back to the third millennium BCE. The tablets are 12 in number, though the great majority of scholars see only the first 11 tablets as integral to the epic, and see the twelfth is a later accretion. (See A. R. George, "Tablet XII: What, When, and Why," in *The Babylonian Gilgamesh Epic: Introduction, Critical Edition and Cuneiform Texts*, ed. A. R. George, 2 vols. (Oxford and New York: Oxford University Press, 2003), Vol. 1, 47–54.

5. John Maier, "Most Commentators Consider the Flood Story in *Gilgamesh* a Digression," in *Gilgamesh: A Reader*, ed. Maier, 25.

6. Rivkah Schärf-Kluger, *The Archetypal Significance of Gilgamesh: A Modern Ancient Hero* (Einsiedeln, Switzerland: Daimon, 1991).

7. G. S. Kirk, *Myth: Its Meaning and Functions in Ancient and Other Cultures* (Cambridge, England: Cambridge University Press, 1970), 144–145; quoted in Jeffrey H. Tigay, *The Evolution of the Gilgamesh Epic* (Philadelphia: University of Pennsylvania Press, 1982), 7.

8. Notable gender-sensitive readings include Rivkah Harris, "Images of Women in the *Gilgamesh* Epic," chap. 7 of *Gender and Aging in Mesopotamia: The Gilgamesh Epic and Other Ancient Literature* (Norman: University of Oklahoma Press, 2003), 119–128; and Tikva Frymer-Kensy, *In the Wake of the Goddesses: Women, Culture, and the Biblical Transformation of Pagan Myth* (Old Tappan, NJ: Free Press, 1991).

9. See, for instance, Benjamin Foster, "Gilgamesh: Sex, Love, and the Ascent of Knowledge," in *Love and Death in the Ancient Near East: Essays in Honor of Marvin H. Pope*, ed. John H. Marks and Robert M. Good (New Haven: Four Quarters, 1987); reprinted in John Maier, ed., *Gilgamesh: A Reader* (Wauconda, IL: Bolchazy-Carducci, 1997), 63–78.

10. Uruk: Richard McCormick Adams, *Heartland of Cities* (Chicago: University of Chicago Press, 1981), 71; J. N. Postgate, *Early Mesopotamia: Society and Economy at the Dawn of History* (London: Routledge, 1992), 112. Nineveh: Tertius Chandler, *Four Thousand Years of Urban Growth: An Historical Census* (Lewiston, NY: St. David's University Press, 1987). David Damrosch tells the whole remarkable story in *The Buried Book*.

11. *Gilgamesh*, trans. Ferry, 3.

12. *Gilgamesh*, trans. Ferry, 3.

13. *Gilgamesh*, trans. Ferry, 3–4.

14. *Gilgamesh*, trans. Ferry, 4.

15. *Gilgamesh*, trans. Ferry, 4.

16. Tigay, *The Evolution of the Gilgamesh Myth*, 180.

17. *Gilgamesh*, trans. Ferry, 4–5.

18. *Gilgamesh*, trans. Ferry, 5.

19. *Gilgamesh*, trans. Ferry, 5.

20. *Gilgamesh*, trans. Ferry, 12.

21. *Gilgamesh*, trans. Ferry, 14–15.

22. *Gilgamesh*, trans. Ferry, 15.

23. *The Epic of Gilgamesh: The Babylonian Epic Poem and Other Texts in Akkadian and Sumerian*, trans. Andrew George (London: Penguin Books, 1999), 17–18. Roman text in square brackets indicates editorial textual restorations with high certainty; italic text in square brackets indicates restorations that are conjectural or not certain.

24. *The Epic of Gilgamesh: The Babylonian Epic Poem and Other Texts in Akkadian and Sumerian*, trans. George, 18. One phrase—"my heart was made to ache"—is taken from George's full critical edition, *The Babylonian Gilgamesh Epic: Introduction, Critical Edition and Cuneiform Texts*, Vol. 1, 565.

25. George, *The Babylonian Gilgamesh Epic*, Vol. 1, 571.

26. *Gilgamesh*, trans. Ferry, 16.

27. *Gilgamesh*, trans. Ferry, 19–20.

28. *Gilgamesh*, trans. Ferry, 20.

29. *Gilgamesh*, trans. Ferry, 26. Compare George, *The Babylonian Gilgamesh Epic*, Vol. 1, 605–607: "[on] one, one alone [. . .] / [Two] garments, however, [. . . ,] / [though]

it is a glacis slope [...] two [...] / Two triplets [...] / a three-ply rope [*is not easily broken.*]

30. *Gilgamesh,* trans. Ferry, 30.

31. *The Epic of Gilgamesh: The Babylonian Epic Poem and Other Texts in Akkadian and Sumerian,* trans. George, 54.

32. *Gilgamesh,* trans. Ferry, 37–38.

33. George, *The Babylonian Gilgamesh Epic,* Vol. 1, 643.

34. *Gilgamesh,* trans. Ferry, 43.

35. *Gilgamesh,* trans. Ferry, 43.

36. Damrosch, *The Buried Book,* 60.

37. *Gilgamesh,* trans. Ferry, 48.

38. George, *The Babylonian Gilgamesh Epic,* Vol. 1, 679.

39. George, *The Babylonian Gilgamesh Epic,* Vol. 1, 681.

40. *Gilgamesh,* trans. Ferry, 61.

41. George, *The Babylonian Gilgamesh Epic,* Vol. 1, 691.

42. *Gilgamesh,* trans. Ferry, 62–63.

43. *Gilgamesh,* trans. Ferry, 64. Unfortunately the translator's next two lines, among his most lovely and powerful—"The simple man and the ruler resemble each other. / The face of one will darken like that of the other"—are a poetic invention, not supported by any text, though they are certainly within the spirit of the passage.

44. *Gilgamesh,* trans. Ferry, 79.

45. *Gilgamesh,* trans. Ferry, 81.

46. J. R. R. Tolkien, *The Return of the King* (New York: Ballantine Books, 1965), 385.

47. *Gilgamesh,* trans. Ferry, 81–82.

48. *Gilgamesh,* trans. Ferry, 3.

REFERENCES

Translations

The Epic of Gilgamesh. Translated by Danny P. Jackson. Wauconda, IL: Bolchazy-Carducci Publishers, 1997.

The Epic of Gilgamesh. Translated by N. K. Sandars. London: Penguin Books, 2006.

Gilgamesh: A New Rendering in English Verse. Translated by David Ferry. New York: Farrar, Straus, and Giroux, 1992.

The Epic of Gilgamesh: An Old Babylonian Version. Translated by Morris Jastrow and Albert T. Clay. San Diego: The Book Tree, 2003 [Yale University Press, 1920].

The Epic of Gilgamesh: A Norton Critical Edition. Translated by Benjamin R. Foster. New York: W. W. Norton, 2001.

The Epic of Gilgamesh: The Babylonian Epic Poem and Other Texts in Akkadian and Sumerian. Translated by Andrew George. London: Penguin Books, 1999.

Myths from Mesopotamia: Creation, the Flood, Gilgamesh, and Others. Translated by Stephanie Dalley. New York: Oxford University Press, 2000.

Secondary texts

Abusch, Tzvi. "The Development and Meaning of the Epic of Gilgamesh: An Interpretive Essay." *Journal of the American Oriental Society* 121, no. 4 (October–December, 2001): 614–622.

Adams, Richard McCormick. *Heartland of Cities.* Chicago: University of Chicago Press, 1981.

Beye, Charles Rowan Beye. *Ancient Epic Poetry: Homer, Apollonius, Virgil.* Ithaca, NY, and London: Cornell University Press, 1993.

Bloom, Allan. *Love and Friendship.* New York: Simon & Schuster, 1993.

Chandler, Tertius. *Four Thousand Years of Urban Growth: An Historical Census.* Lewiston, NY: St. David's University Press, 1987.

Damrosch, David. *The Buried Book: The Loss and Rediscovery of the Great Epic of Gilgamesh.* New York: Henry Holt, 2006.

Frymer-Kensy, Tikva. *In the Wake of the Goddesses: Women, Culture, and the Biblical Transformation of Pagan Myth.* Old Tappan, NJ: Free Press, 1991.

George, Andrew. *The Babylonian Gilgamesh Epic: Introduction, Critical Edition and Cuneiform Texts.* 2 vols. Oxford and New York: Oxford University Press, 2003.

George, Andrew. "Introduction." *The Epic of Gilgamesh: The Babylonian Epic Poem and Other Texts in Akkadian and Sumerian.* Translated by Andrew George. London: Penguin Books, 1999.

Gonzalo Rubio, J. "Gilgamesh or the Anguish over Death." *Journal of Near Eastern Studies* 57, no. 2 (April 1998): 148–50.

Harris, Rivka. "Images of Women in the *Gilgamesh* Epic." Chap. 7 of *Gender and Aging in Mesopotamia: The Gilgamesh Epic and Other Ancient Literature,* 119–128. Norman: University of Oklahoma Press, 2003.

Held, George F. "Parallels Between the Gilgamesh Epic and Plato's Symposium." *Journal of Near Eastern Studies* 42, no. 2 (April 1983): 133–141.

Maier, John, ed. *Gilgamesh: A Reader.* Wauconda, IL: Bolchazy-Carducci Publishers, 1997.

Postgate, J. N. *Early Mesopotamia: Society and Economy at the Dawn of History.* London: Routledge, 1992.

Schärf-Kluger, Rivkah. *The Archetypal Significance of Gilgamesh: A Modern Ancient Hero.* Einsiedeln, Switzerland: Daimon, 1991.

Tigay, Jeffrey H. *The Evolution of the Gilgamesh Epic.* Philadelphia: University of Pennsylvania Press, 1982.

Tolkien, J. R. R. *The Return of the King.* New York: Ballantine Books, 1965.

Vulpe, Nicola. "Irony and the Unity of the Gilgamesh Epic." *Journal of Near Eastern Studies* 53, no. 4 (October 1994): 275–283.

Wolff, Hope Nash. "Gilgamesh, Enkidu, and the Heroic Life." *Journal of the American Oriental Society* 89, no. 2 (April–June 1969): 392–398.

PART II

WHAT REAL LEADERS TELL US ABOUT LEADERSHIP

4

Personal Memoirs of U. S. Grant, and Alternative Accounts of Lee's Surrender at Appomattox

GEORGE R. GOETHALS

On the afternoon of April 9, 1865, President Abraham Lincoln waited anxiously for word from the battlefront. It was Palm Sunday, and there was no news of General Ulysses S. Grant's continuing skirmishes with Robert E. Lee's forces near Appomattox, Virginia. If Grant could finally capture Lee's army, the four-year Civil War would be very nearly over. But Lee had escaped destruction before, and the outcome was by no means certain. Just as the day was coming to an end, fretful officials at the war department received the following telegram:

> *Headquarters Appomattox C. H., Va.,*
> *April 9th, 1865, 4:30* P.M.

Honorable E. M. Stanton
Secretary of War,
Washington

General Lee surrendered the Army of Northern Virginia this afternoon on terms proposed by myself. The accompanying additional correspondence will show the terms fully.

> U. S. Grant,
> Lieut.-General

Needless to say, Lincoln was greatly relieved. Celebrations in the nation's capital began immediately.

Historians and biographers writing about Grant and the end of the Civil War have discussed two features of this telegram. One is its understatement: "the day's outcome produced a curious flatness in Grant. He sent the most expressionless of victory messages"; "there was a curious restraint in Grant's tepid victory message passed on to Washington"; "No brag, no bluster, no stirring words . . . just a simple statement succinctly summarizing the day's events." [1] The second is that Grant needed to be reminded to send it at all: "Porter asked Grant if he did not think the news of the surrender was worth divulging to the War Department. Grant confessed, without embarrassment, that he had forgotten all about it"; "He had not gone far before someone asked if he did not consider the news of Lee's surrender worth passing on to the War Department."; "It was left to someone else to remark that perhaps it would be a good idea to notify the authorities at Washington what had happened." [2] Grant himself, in Volume II of *Personal Memoirs of U. S. Grant*, simply wrote, "After Lee's departure I telegraphed to Washington as follows: . . ." [3]

Not only have different authors characterized the writing of the telegram and the message itself in different ways, they have also varied greatly in what they have inferred about Grant's frame of mind on this occasion, exactly how he behaved when reminded to wire, and what his thoughts and actions reveal about his personal qualities. And, of course, other writers have not characterized or even quoted the telegram, or mentioned that Grant needed to be reminded to send it.

These different treatments of a small matter that took place on an immensely important day in U.S. history illustrate how our understanding of that history, and the principal actors in its unfolding, are influenced by the interpretation that different writers put on such matters. It is somewhat troubling that as we try to understand leaders and leadership we are confronted with the problem that our knowledge of central historical events is highly subject to the differing perspectives of various scholars. What can we know? How can we know it?

This chapter considers these questions by examining the implications of a particular variation on the general problem of differing historical perspectives. That is, how do we weigh autobiographical accounts of events by the actors themselves? Is there something distinctive about these accounts, or are they best thought of as just one more rendering of history, to be compared on an equal footing with treatments by other writers? We will approach these questions by considering one of the most famous autobiographies in American history, the aforementioned *Personal Memoirs of U. S. Grant*. Its treatment of Lee's surrender at Appomattox is fascinating in its own right, but it also stands in interesting comparison to those of other biographers, of Lee as well as Grant, and of various Civil War historians.

In considering these accounts the overall aim of the chapter is to address two sets of questions. First, what can we learn about what Grant thought, felt, and did on that historic day, and what can we learn more generally about Grant as a leader and about leadership itself? Second, in our efforts to learn these things, what challenges are posed by the existence of so many different accounts of what took place at Appomattox? We will proceed as follows. First, Grant's *Memoirs* will be described briefly. Second, we will compare several aspects of his account of meeting Lee at Appomattox with other accounts. Third, we will do our best to address the questions above about Grant and about the problems of learning about Grant. Finally, we will discuss the implications of our efforts.

PERSONAL MEMOIRS OF U. S. GRANT

Ulysses S. Grant was born in 1822, graduated from West Point in 1843, and fought in the Mexican War in 1846 and 1847. After serving in the peacetime army until 1854, he rejoined his wife and four children and tried unsuccessfully to make a living in several independent business ventures. In 1860 he became a clerk in his father's store in Galena, Illinois, where he was supervised by his two younger brothers. The next year the Civil War broke out and Grant rejoined the army as a colonel. Three years later he was head of all Union military forces, and in another four years he was elected president of the United States, serving from 1869 to 1877. By the summer of 1884 Grant faced financial ruin and impending death from throat cancer. He was persuaded to write his memoirs to provide financial security for his family. Samuel Clemens (Mark Twain) arranged to publish the memoirs (and, in the same year, *Adventures of Huckleberry Finn*) with his own publishing firm. Grant wrote the two-volume, 275,000 word memoirs in less than a year, while enduring extreme pain during the final months of his illness. He died on July 23, 1885, a few days after finishing the final editing.

Since their publication *Personal Memoirs* have been regarded as a masterpiece of autobiographical military history. (They also secured his family's financial future, earning nearly $500,000 in royalties.) For example, twentieth-century biographer William McFeely notes that Grant's "force informed the work of other bold writers including Gertrude Stein and Sherwood Anderson." McFeely also quotes from one of Gore Vidal's "brilliantly iconoclastic essays": "it simply is not possible to read Grant's memoirs without realizing that the author is a man of first-rate intelligence."[4] The writing is direct, clear, fast-moving narrative. It is modest but not humble. The author shows great respect for his opponents, especially Lee. The day after the surrender at Appomattox,

I thought I would like to see General Lee again; so next morning I rode out beyond our lines toward his headquarters. . . . Lee soon mounted his horse, seeing who it was, and met me. We had there between the lines, sitting on horseback, a very pleasant conversation of over half an hour. . . . I then suggested to General Lee that there was not a man in the Confederacy whose influence with the soldiery and the whole people was as great as his, and that if he would now advise the surrender of all the armies I had no doubt that his advice would be followed with alacrity. But Lee said, he could not do that without consulting the President [Confederate president, Jefferson Davis] first. I knew there was no use to urge him to do anything against his ideas of what was right.[5]

The Surrender at Appomattox

Following victories in Kentucky, Tennessee, and Mississippi during the first three years of the war, most notably at Vicksburg in 1863, Grant became head of all Union armies. He came east, and starting in May 1864 engaged Robert E. Lee in a series of battles that ended in the siege of Petersburg, Virginia, the next month. The siege lasted until the spring of 1865 when, on April 2, Lee abandoned Petersburg and the Confederate government abandoned the nearby capital at Richmond. Lee's army tried to escape to join forces with those of General Joseph Johnston. Grant's and Lee's armies raced west, battling along the way. On April 7 Grant started an exchange of messages with Lee suggesting that Lee surrender so as to avoid further bloodshed. After a final failed attempt to break away from surrounding Union forces at dawn on April 9, Lee agreed to meet Grant later that day to discuss terms of surrender. The meeting took place at the home of Wilmer McLean in the small town of Appomattox Court House.

For this chapter we have primarily considered treatments of the meeting at Appomattox by the following authors in volumes published in the years noted: Douglas Southall Freeman, 1935, in his classic four-volume biography, *R. E. Lee*; MacKinlay Kantor, 1950, in a book for juveniles, *Lee and Grant at Appomattox*; Bruce Catton, 1969, in his second volume on Grant's Civil War leadership, *Grant Takes Command*; Shelby Foote, 1974, in the third of his monumental three-volume *The Civil War: A Narrative*; William McFeely, 1981, in his Pulitzer Prize winning *Grant: A Biography*; Brooks Simpson, 2000, in *Ulysses S. Grant: Triumph Over Adversity, 1822–1865*, the first of two expected volumes; Jean Edward Smith, 2001, in *Grant*, today widely considered the best single volume biography of Grant; and Charles Bowery, 2005, in his military and management-oriented book, *Lee & Grant: Profiles in Leadership from the Battlefields of Virginia*.[6] These treatments are compared with Grant's own account in his memoirs.

Relevant to such comparisons is a widely discussed paper in social psychology by Edward E. Jones and Richard E. Nisbett, "The actor and the observer: divergent perceptions of causality."[7] Jones and Nisbett argue that actors tend to attribute their behavior to external causes—objects, people, and events in the environment. They see their behavior as appropriate responses to what surrounds them. Observers of another person's behavior tend to attribute that behavior to internal causes, that is, personal qualities of the actor. The divergent perspectives are illustrated, for example, when an individual laughing during a movie attributes his or her laughter to the quality of the film while an observer of the person's laughter attributes it to the individual's good sense of humor. Jones and Nisbett argue while particular attributions are influenced by many factors, there is a pervasive tendency for actors and observers to lean toward external versus internal explanations, respectively. They specifically contend that biographers generally attribute their subjects' behavior to personal qualities, while autobiographers attribute their behavior to situations or external contingencies. As we consider the treatments of Grant at Appomattox, we will keep this attributional divergence in mind. However, we must note that all recent treatments of Appomattox are influenced to some extent by Grant's *Personal Memoirs*. Thus in this case biographers sometimes adopt the external perspective of the autobiographer.

There are a number of specific incidents at Appomattox about which different authors have written. We will consider four: Grant's migraine headache; Grant getting lost when Lee tried finally to arrange the surrender meeting; Grant's mud-spattered appearance; and the dynamics of the meeting itself, especially Grant acceding to Lee's request to permit cavalry and artillery soldiers to keep their horses.

The Headache

Grant suffered a severe migraine on the night before and the day of the surrender meeting. He describes it in some detail.

> On the 8th I had followed the Army of the Potomac in the rear of Lee. I was suffering very severely with a sick headache, and stopped at a farmhouse on the road some distance in rear of the main body of the army. I spent the night in bathing my feet in hot water and mustard and putting mustard plasters on my wrist and the back part of my neck, hoping to be cured by morning.

A few sentences later he writes of the next day: "I proceeded at an early hour in the morning, still suffering with the headache, to get to the head of the column." Shortly thereafter, when he received a message from Lee finally agreeing to meet to discuss surrender, he writes: "When the officer reached me I was still suffering from the headache; but the instant I saw the contents of the note I was cured."[8]

Grant does not make any explicit attributions about the cause of his headache but implicitly attributes relief to Lee's decision to surrender. Even more implicit is the attribution that his headache was caused by uncertainty and tension about what Lee would do. Some other writers treat the matter as did Grant. Bruce Catton: "his headache left him altogether the moment he read Lee's last letter." [9] Charles Bowery: "When he received Lee's dispatch asking for a meeting to discuss the surrender of the Army of Northern Virginia, the headache magically disappeared." [10] Brooks Simpson is more explicit about the tension and uncertainty linked to the headache: "If the promise of finishing the job in the morning pleased Grant, the notion that Lee would not surrender until compelled to do so suggested that finishing the job might be bloody work. Grant's head continued to ache." [11] Jean Edward Smith goes further. He suggests that more than the hoped for but still uncertain surrender was at work. In addition, Grant was characteristically troubled by such symptoms at such times: "Grant, who was sometimes beset by psychosomatic ailments leading up to major events, was suffering from a severe migraine." [12] Thus Smith places the headache into a more complete picture of Grant's psychological makeup.

Grant Gets Lost

Another aspect of the surrender day is treated in a more varied way by different writers. The meeting was actually delayed for several critical hours because Grant could not be found. Lee contributed greatly to the confusion. On the 8th Grant wrote to Lee, outlining the terms of surrender: "there is but one condition I would insist upon, namely: that the men and officers surrendered shall be disqualified for taking up arms ... until properly exchanged." [13] In response Lee wrote Grant proposing to meet the next morning, not to discuss surrendering his army, but rather an overall political settlement to the war. But then at dawn on that next morning, as noted above, Lee ordered a final attack on Union forces in an effort to escape. At about the same hour as Lee's attack, Grant responded to Lee's message with one saying that he could not discuss political terms—only the surrender of Lee's army. Several hours later Lee finally realized the hopelessness of his position and, in response to Grant's most recent note, wrote the headache-relieving message:

> I received your note of this morning on the picket-line whither I had come to meet you and ascertain definitely what terms were embraced in your proposal of yesterday with reference to the surrender of this army. I now request an interview in accordance with the offer contained in your letter of yesterday for that purpose.[14]

Unfortunately for Lee, Grant had taken Lee's previous message proposing to discuss a political settlement as a sign that Lee meant to keep fighting (which Lee did), and that he must do the same. Thus he pushed forward to get to the front. But then he had to take a detour. In *Personal Memoirs* he explained: "to go direct I would have to pass through Lee's army . . . I had therefore to move south in order to get upon a road coming up from another direction." [15] Thus Grant was for a time out of communication with some of his staff. Almost no one knew where he was. Grant's explanation for taking the detour makes an attribution to obvious external contingencies: he could not ride through Lee's army. But not all writers accept so simple an explanation.

For starters, we note that some writers do not mention that Grant was hard to find. MacKinlay Kantor does note the fact, without explaining it: "The trouble with the whole thing was that General Grant was hard to find. He was on a different road from the one where some of his subordinates thought him to be." [16] Shelby Foote mentions the problem and essentially repeats Grant's attribution: Grant "had to make a wide detour to avoid running into Confederate" forces.[17] However, Foote does mention a further consideration. Grant was annoyed that Lee's penultimate message suggested that he meant to fight on, and Grant did not think it important to wait around for further word. He needed to move forward, as best, and as fast, as he could.

The wild card in discussing these excruciating hours is William McFeely.

> One would expect that with hopes so high for an affirmative message from Lee, he would have alerted officers to his whereabouts at every imaginable point. Instead, finding one road blocked, he went off with Rawlins, Porter, and Babcock to look for another, without leaving word of his destination. Perhaps there was a curious want of confidence at a moment when none but Grant could imagine such a thing; perhaps he dreaded still another rebuff by Lee . . . he . . . put himself out of touch with his own generals—and with Lee.[18]

McFeely also notes that Grant had made himself hard to find on other occasions, though he does not attribute those events to lack of confidence. But the implication is that there is something about Grant that causes him to separate himself from others at critical moments.

McFeely's treatment is important in a number of respects. Published in 1981, it was the first major biography of Grant in several decades, and it stood alone as a major study for almost 20 years. Because it stood alone for so long, and because it won the Pulitzer Prize, McFeely's biography was the received wisdom until only recently. Furthermore, McFeely's overall perspective is more negative than most all of the subsequent treatments of Grant. Although he treats Grant's overall behavior at Appomattox quite favorably ("From the moment Lee's note arrived, Grant was in perfect command of himself, and from then on every move of the day was a quiet triumph played out with consummate skill"),[19] his global impression of Grant is best revealed in his Introduction: He wrote that Grant is

> a curious choice for the subject of a biography if the writer is not an admirer of warfare and is not inordinately fascinated by political corruption. . . . No amount of revision is going to change the way men died at Cold Harbor, the fact that men in the Whiskey Ring stole money, and the broken hopes of black Americans in Clinton, Mississippi, in 1875. . . . I am convinced that Grant had no organic, artistic, or intellectual specialness. He did have limited but by no means inconsequential talents to apply to whatever truly engaged his attention. The only problem was that until he was nearly forty, no job he liked had come his way—and so he became general and president because he could find nothing better to do.[20]

As we turn below to the matter of Grant's appearance at the surrender meeting, we will see again that McFeely treats the Appomattox surrender differently from most other writers. And again, he ascribes Grant's behavior to somewhat negative personal qualities.

Grant's Appearance

It has become part of the Appomattox folklore that Lee looked resplendent and that Grant looked, basically, like a slob. One of his aides wrote "Grant, covered in mud in an old faded uniform, looked like a fly on a shoulder of beef." [21] Lee "wore a bright new uniform, with a sash and a jeweled sword, looking every part the patrician he was." [22] In his memoirs Grant mentions the matter twice.

> When I had left camp that morning I had not expected so soon the result that was then taking place, and consequently was in rough garb. I . . . wore a soldier's blouse for a coat, with the shoulder straps of my rank to indicate to the army who I was." Two paragraphs later he writes: "In my rough traveling suit, the uniform of a private with the straps of a lieutenant-general, I must have contrasted very strangely with a man so handsomely dressed, six feet high and of faultless form. But this was not a matter that I thought of until afterwards.[23]

Most authors make the same attribution that Grant does. His baggage train had been delayed two nights before and he was moving fast to keep up with Lee. For example, Smith writes: "He had left all of his baggage behind on that night ride to Sheridan and was still wearing the mud-splattered uniform in which he started out." [24] However, McFeely suggests that the matter is more complicated, and that Grant's appearance is intentional, not accidental, and, like getting lost, is attributable to Grant's want of confidence, rather than the exigencies of travel during combat. Furthermore, he characterizes Grant's claim about not expecting to meet Lee so soon as a "disingenuous apology." [25] In making this case McFeely cites several passages in *Personal Memoirs* where Grant mentions having left his uniform and baggage behind on other occasions. The key to his argument is a quote where Grant mentions being teased by a young boy for wearing his West Point uniform shortly after he graduated from the military academy: "The conceit was knocked out of me . . . by circumstances . . . which gave me a distaste for military uniform that I never recovered from." [26] McFeely argues that Grant

> could have rearranged the Appomattox meeting if it were not going to be conducted exactly as he wanted it to be. He had wanted to be away from headquarters when called to talk to Lee; he had wanted to ride straight in from the field. His attire had been chosen as long ago as the day the little boy mocked the fancy-dress uniform of the West Point graduate; the worn clothing gave him the same sense of confidence that the elegant uniform gave Lee.[27]

McFeely is not the only writer who makes an internal attribution. Charles Bowery does as well, but he only suggests that Grant's dress was in keeping with his character:

> The patrician Lee looked every inch the general in his immaculate dress uniform and sword, but Grant looked, if anything, like a common soldier. . . . Instead of a sword, Grant carried field glasses. He was, as always, all business. The way the two men dressed reflected perfectly their contrasting styles.[28]

The Meeting

When Grant met Lee in the small parlor of Wilmer McLean's home in Appomattox, there were nearly a dozen aides present. Most were Grant's. Lee's sole attendant was Colonel Charles Marshall, grandnephew of Chief Justice John Marshall. Nearly all of those present wrote accounts of the meeting. There was little disagreement about what was said. And subsequent writings all agree as to the sensitivity, generosity, and wisdom of Grant's actions. In contrast, there is more variation in reports about what each man was thinking and feeling. And there are diverging attributions about why Grant acted as he did. While there is widespread consensus that this was Grant's finest hour, there is some disagreement about whether his actions that day reflected a deep and genuine magnanimity or whether he simply rose to the occasion at that moment. Somewhat overlooked in the many treatments of the meeting are Lee's actions and demeanor, and how both men effectively negotiated the details of the surrender.

After the final exchanges of notes established that Grant and Lee would meet, Charles Marshall selected the McLean house as the venue. Lee arrived at around 1:00 PM accompanied by both Marshall and Grant's aide, Orville

Babcock. The three waited silently for about a half hour until Grant rode up, and entered the room with several staff members. Grant wrote:

> We greeted each other, and after shaking hands took our seats.... What General Lee's feelings were I do not know. As he was a man of much dignity, with an impassable face, it was impossible to say whether he felt inwardly glad that the end had finally come, or felt sad over the result, and was too manly to show it. Whatever his feelings, they were entirely concealed from my observation; but my own feelings, which had been quite jubilant on the receipt of his letter, were sad and depressed. I felt like anything rather than rejoicing at the downfall of a foe who had fought so long and valiantly, and had suffered so much for a cause, though that cause was, I believe, one [of] the worst for which a people ever fought, and one for which there was the least excuse.[29]

For a time Grant and Lee discussed old times, particularly meeting each other briefly during the Mexican War: "Our conversation grew so pleasant that I almost forgot the object of our meeting." Lee refocused the discussion and asked Grant for the terms he would propose for the surrender of his army. Grant replied that they were the same as stated in his written messages: "I said that I meant merely that his army should lay down their arms, not to take them up again during the continuance of the war." After falling off again into "matters foreign to the subject which had brought us together," Lee suggested "that the terms ... ought to be written out. I called to General Parker ... for writing materials, and commenced writing."[30]

Grant remarked "When I put my pen to paper I did not know the first word that I should make use of in writing the terms. I only knew what was in my mind, and I wished to express it clearly, so that there would be no mistaking it."[31]

There are two remarkable aspects of the terms that have been discussed differently by various writers. After Grant put in writing the stipulation that the men of Lee's army should lay down their arms and related equipment, he then concluded:

> This will not embrace the side-arms of the officers, nor their private horses or baggage. This done, each officer and man will be allowed to return to their homes, not to be disturbed by United States authority so long as they observe their paroles and the laws in force where they may reside.
>
> Very respectfully,
U. S. Grant
Lt.-Gen.[32]

With these words Grant allowed the officers to keep equipment that would ordinarily have been surrendered. More extraordinary, especially given his refusal the day before to discuss any political issue, Grant essentially issued amnesty to all the men in Lee's army, including most importantly, Lee himself. There certainly were many members of the federal Congress who thought that Lee, President Jefferson Davis, and other Confederate leaders should be tried for treason and hanged. What accounts for Grant's actions?

Before addressing these issues, one other fascinating and consequential aspect of the meeting must be described. Since it involves a great deal of non-verbal behavior, it is somewhat difficult to convey. Indeed it has been described in slightly but importantly different ways by different writers. In describing it here, we will use documented words from their exchange, but add our own sense of the emotions that accompanied them, based on the various accounts in the works we have been discussing. We will also treat their significance for ending the Civil War. Finally, we will take the liberty of trying to capture the sense of the moment as a scene from a play, with stage directions, starting where Grant finishes writing the words above.

- - - - - - - -

Grant rises from the small table at which he wrote the surrender terms, crosses the room, and places the order book in Lee's hands.

Grant *(gently)*: Will you read this, General Lee, and see if it covers the matter fully?

Lee places the book on the table before him, takes out his glasses, and polishes them carefully, one lens at a time. He crosses his legs, puts on the glasses, and reads slowly without expression. Finally,

Lee *(somewhat more warmly than heretofore)*: This will have a very happy effect on my army.

Grant: Unless you have some suggestions to make in regard to the form in which I have stated the terms, I will have a copy made in ink and sign it.

Lee *(hesitating)*: There is one thing I would like to mention. The cavalrymen and artillerists own their own horses in our army. I would like to understand whether these men will be able to retain their horses.

Grant *(flatly, gazing squarely at Lee)*: You will find that the terms as written do not allow this.

Lee *(slowly rereading the terms, regretfully)*: No, I see the terms do not allow it. That is clear.

Grant *(pausing, musing aloud)*: Well, the subject is quite new to me. Of course I did not know that any private soldiers owned their animals, but I think this will be the last battle of the war—I sincerely hope so—and I take it that most of the men in the ranks are small farmers, and it is doubtful whether they will be able to put in a crop to carry themselves and their families through the next winter without the aid of the horses they are now riding. I will arrange it this

way. I will not change the terms as now written, but I will instruct the officers
I shall appoint to receive the paroles to let all the men who claim to own a
horse or mule take the animals home with them to work their farms.

Lee *(relieved and appreciative):*   This will have the best possible effect upon
the men. It will be very gratifying, and will do much toward conciliating
our people.

- - - - - - - -

Thus Lee, who had very little bargaining leverage to begin with, succeeded in
making a good deal better.

   Like the differences in appearance between Grant and Lee, their exchange
about horses has become part of American folklore. In 1962 President John
F. Kennedy made a witty reference to it. Kennedy had responded furiously
and forcefully when the head of the United States Steel Corporation, Roger
Blough, announced a large increase in steel prices. Kennedy felt this action
violated a carefully negotiated labor contract his administration helped hammer out with the steel workers union. Under great pressure, Blough
rescinded the increase. Kennedy wanted to maintain cordial relations with
Blough and invited him for a meeting at the White House. When an aide
asked how the meeting had gone, Kennedy remarked that he had let him
keep his horses for the spring plowing.

   As noted above, these exchanges have been both described and explained
very differently by the authors considered in this chapter. There is consensus
that Grant was sensitive and wise in being so generous. By acting as he did,
he ensured that Lee moved toward reconciliation himself. Both commanders'
examples of good will were followed quickly by most men in their respective
armies and by many people outside those forces. But the reasons that Grant
behaved so magnanimously have been treated very differently. These treatments reflect different authors' mind-sets about Grant and Lee, as well, it
seems, as their "worldviews," or core beliefs, implicit or explicit, about causality and human nature.[33]

   Grant himself merely describes the exchange with Lee. After writing "Lee
remarked again that this would have a happy effect," he simply continues.
"He [Lee] then sat down and wrote out the following letter:. . ."[34] Douglas
Southall Freeman picks up at the moment after Lee says, "No, I see the terms
do not allow it; that is clear":

> Grant read his opponent's wish, and, with the fine consideration that prevailed
> throughout the conversation—one of the noblest of his qualities, and one of the
> surest evidences of his greatness—he did not humiliate Lee by forcing him to
> make a direct plea for a modification of terms that were generous.[35]

   Writing in 1935 from Richmond, Virginia, Freeman is, of course, extremely
generous in all that he writes about his subject in his four-volume *R. E. Lee*.

More generally Freeman takes a benign view of the people he writes about, with notable exceptions such as Lee's subordinate general James Longstreet. Thus it is in keeping with Freeman's overall view of the world that Grant had greatness. It took a great man to defeat Lee, and then to treat him so generously. Charles Bowery, writing 70 years later, shares Freeman's sunny perspective on both Lee and Grant: "The exchange that then occurred reminded everyone present of the greatness of these two men. . . . Grant's magnanimity and Lee's concern for his men touched all of those present." [36] Both authors attribute Grant's behavior to fundamental, and highly admirable, personal dispositions.

Jean Edward Smith and Bruce Catton have a more complex explanation. Grant's behavior reflected not only his own personal qualities but also those of Abraham Lincoln. When Grant wrote that he "did not know the first word that I should make use of in writing the terms. I only knew what was in my mind," it seems clear that very much on his mind was the recent meeting he had with Lincoln at Grant's headquarters at City Point, just east of Petersburg. Lincoln conveyed his general thought that the terms of reunion should be as generous as possible to arrive at a stable, just peace at the earliest possible moment. His approach was "Let 'em up easy." These authors argue that Grant was following Lincoln's approach in departing from the "Unconditional Surrender" Grant of 1862 at Fort Donelson, the Grant that Lee feared might imprison him. Smith summarizes the "Lincoln plus Grant" attribution as follows: "Writing rapidly, he brought the war in Virginia to a close with less than 200 well-chosen words, reflecting the charity that Lincoln desired and his own innate generosity." [37]

Catton makes a similar assessment.

> Grant's powers today were limited: he was allowed to do no more than fix the terms on which Lee's army was to be surrendered. Yet in the final sentence of his letter [where Grant wrote that the men would be allowed to return home, "not to be disturbed by U.S. authority"] he reached far beyond this limitation, taking everything that Lincoln felt and everything that he himself felt about the necessity to make a peace that would include no reprisals.[38]

Shelby Foote's treatment is similar to the Smith/Catton Grant/Lincoln account but with a twist, adding a reason why Grant may have permitted soldiers to take their horses home: "Then Grant relented. Perhaps recalling his own years of hardscrabble farming near St. Louis before the war—or Lincoln's remark at City Point—. . . he relieved Lee of the humiliation of having to plead for the modification of terms already generous." [39]

There is a third explanation of Grant's generosity that focuses on an external cause, Lee's sword. This goes as follows: seeing Lee's sword, Grant suppressed a wish to take it, as Lee most likely expected he would. Having suppressed that personal wish, Grant expanded a momentary generous impulse to include under it other officers. MacKinlay Cantor: "momentarily the general stopped writing. His glance was resting, not on the proud hurt face of his defeated enemy, but on the beautiful sword at Lee's side." [40] Brooks Simpson expands this description:

> he outlined in simple language the process by which the officers and men ... would stack their arms and record their paroles. That done, he paused and pondered what to write next. For a moment he looked at Lee, his eyes coming to rest on that beautiful sword. There was no reason, he decided, to humiliate Lee by asking the Confederate general to hand over that ceremonial side arm as a trophy of war. Nor was there any need to deprive officers of their side arms, horses, or baggage.[41]

Both imply that Grant was spurred to generosity by seeing Lee's sword.

It is possible that the sword account was prompted by the way Grant discussed it in his memoirs.

> The much talked of surrendering of Lee's sword and my handing it back, this and much more that has been said about it, is the purest romance. The word sword or side arms was not mentioned by either of us until I wrote it in the terms. There was no premeditation, and it did not occur to me until the moment I wrote it down.[42]

Thus Grant mentions the sword but then says it had nothing to do with his generous terms. Perhaps in denying that the sword had any impact, Grant stirred the suspicion that it did.

Sometimes what authors do not say is as interesting as what they do. William McFeely discussed in some detail an essentially psychological explanation—Grant's lack of confidence—for two rather minor pieces of the Appomattox story, Grant's getting lost and Grant's appearance. However, after saying that Grant attained "perfect command of himself" after reading Lee's final note, McFeely is quite spare in his account of Grant's writing the terms of surrender and the subsequent exchange about letting the cavalrymen and artillerists keep their horses. When Grant is behaving "with consummate skill," little is made of it. But McFeely explores in more detail the awkward elements in Grant's behavior at Appomattox.

The Surrender

I have asserted that the final exchange between Lee and Grant concerning horses and side arms was consequential and set a model for both armies, as well as others in both the Union and the Confederacy. Lee himself remarked that Grant's generosity would "do much toward conciliating our people." The tone that was set on that occasion played out three days later during a formal surrender that Grant had insisted upon. The Union officer in charge of the ceremony was future Medal of Honor winner, future president of Bowdoin College, and future governor of Maine, Joshua Lawrence Chamberlain. His Confederate counterpart was General John B. Gordon, future governor of Georgia, the man to whom Lee had assigned the final breakout attempt at dawn on April 9. As the proceedings began, Chamberlain was inspired by the sight of the Confederate columns moving toward him to surrender their arms. He suddenly gave the order for the Union soldiers on either side of the long lines moving past them to "carry arms," a sign of respect. Chamberlain wrote,

> At the sound of the machine-like snap of arms, General Gordon started ... then wheeled his horse, facing me, touching him gently with the spur so that the animal slightly reared, and, as he wheeled, horse and rider made one motion, the horse's head swung down with a graceful bow, and General Gordon dropped his sword-point to his toe in salutation.

The sign of respect was returned. Chamberlain continued: "On our part not a sound of trumpet more, nor roll of drum; not a cheer, nor word, nor whisper or vain-glorying, nor motion of man ... but an awed stillness rather, and breath-holding, as if it were the passing of the dead." [43] (Chamberlain's eloquence, of course, inspired the title for Bruce Catton's 1954 Pulitzer Prize winning *A Stillness at Appomattox*.) Thus the magnanimity of Grant's comportment radiated through the ranks of both armies and beyond.

SUMMARY AND CONCLUSIONS

We have considered how Ulysses S. Grant wrote about the surrender at Appomattox in his own memoirs, and how a number of other writers have characterized and explained the same events. The other writers include three Grant biographers, McFeely, Simpson, and Smith; two civil war historians, Catton and Foote; a Lee biographer, Freeman; the author of a book for juveniles, Kantor; and a management specialist from the military, Bowery. The authors remark upon different details of the surrender day, describe them somewhat differently, and make in some cases quite divergent attributions for Grant's behavior. They quite clearly vary in their overall opinion of Grant, though they all believe that his actions in the crucial moments of his meeting with Lee were both generous and wise. The differences in their global understanding of Grant color their descriptions and attributions. Further, though this is our own much more subjective reading, their assumptions about human nature and causality in general also flavor their writing.

The points on which there is most divergence concern Grant's disappearance, his dress, and his magnanimity. Regarding Grant's being lost for several hours, those who even mention it generally go along with Grant's own explanation, that he was simply reacting to the external circumstances. He could not ride through Lee's forces. Foote adds that he did not think waiting on Lee was in order since Lee had indicated an unwillingness to surrender. McFeely proposes a unique explanation: Grant absented himself on similar momentous occasions so as to regain confidence.

Regarding Grant's dress and appearance at McLean's house, most writers endorse Grant's own explanation that in the race of the two armies, his baggage had been lost. Once again McFeely differs. He explicitly dismisses Grant's explanation as "disingenuous" and again links Grant's behavior to a childhood humiliation and a compensatory attempt to gain confidence. Bowery also notes the impact of the childhood humiliation.

The events at the actual meeting between Grant and Lee on the day of the surrender are the most fully treated. All accounts characterize Grant's actions as both magnanimous and wise. Grant himself makes no attempts to explain them. He simply narrates Lee's behavior and his own. Others have put forth a range of explanations. The simplest (Freeman and Bowery) is that Grant's personal generosity and greatness were at work. The more complicated version (Catton and Smith) is that Grant's own magnanimity combined with Lincoln's wishes, themselves due at least in part to Lincoln's own magnanimity, paved the way for Grant's generous behavior. Other explanations include the notion that Grant's difficult early career contributed to his actions (Foote) and that Grant's suppressed wish for Lee's sword led him to be generous (Kantor and Simpson). McFeely, who speculated about the earlier elements in the story, does not at all characterize or explain Grant's behavior in the meeting. He does resume characterizing Grant's behavior, as noted at the beginning of this chapter, in describing the "flatness" in "the most expressionless of victory messages."

What does all of this mean? First, it is notable that there is support for the Jones and Nisbett theory of actor/observer divergences in attribution. Implicitly or explicitly Grant consistently explains his behavior as the natural and reasonable thing to have done in the particular situation. Some of the writers cited here endorse Grant's explanations, and others make attributions to various personal characteristics. Assuming that the descriptive and attributional divergences we see in this case are part and parcel of many historical accounts of people and events, we must be guarded about any sense of knowledge and understanding we have of leaders, and therefore leadership. But readers, like writers, form their own views, probably whether they want to or not. We know from the psychological literature that our conclusions about people are informed by what the culture teaches us, and those conclusions take hold automatically, without our awareness. We can at least be aware of the fact that there is quite literally a "received wisdom" that inhabits

our perceptions and evaluations, and that it is probably a good idea to con-
sciously consider and think critically about what we have perhaps uncon-
sciously come to believe.

Despite whatever efforts we might make to be open- and fair-minded, it is
extremely difficult, perhaps impossible, not to make our own attributions, to
draw our own onclusions. As noted above, it is an automatic process. But
we can at least do so with our eyes wide open—as much as possible—both
to the biases transmitted from others and to the ones developed on our own.

With these caveats we hope it is appropriate to relate our own construction
of Grant's behavior at Appomattox, the quality of his *Memoirs,* and his overall
leadership. Certainly Grant's behavior at Appomattox was generous. There
is no divergence among authors on this point. There are differences in
explaining the causes of his generosity, but not the generosity itself. Our
concern is that Grant's generosity is a behavior that psychologist Fritz Heider
would say "engulfs the field." [44] It is so powerfully salient that neither other
aspects of Grant's behavior nor nonobvious causes of his generosity get
much attention.

It seems to us that Grant's generosity "engulfs" or overshadows a more
basic quality of Grant's personality—his intelligence. Like Lincoln, Grant's
goal was first to crush the rebellion, but then construct a peace that would
get the South back on its feet and back to work as quickly as possible. This
demanded extremely fine-tuned measures of firmness and flexibility. At the
crucial moment when Lee asked whether artillerists and cavalrymen could
keep their horses, Grant's immediate response was no. He quickly reversed
field, not because he felt sorry for Lee or saw a ceremonial sword or because
of strong impulses toward generosity. Rather, he was smart enough to realize
that it was the best way to achieve the goal of a stable peace. Certainly Lee
wanted such a peace as much as Grant, but both those above (Jefferson Davis)
and below him (many Confederate officers) were pushing hard for a continu-
ation of the war, most likely through endless guerilla fighting. Grant's wise
concession made it easy for Lee: "I will arrange it this way ..." Lee was
induced to feel gratitude and relief, which forged in him a commitment
"toward conciliating our people." Importantly, that commitment soon led
Lee to accept the presidency of Washington College in Lexington, Virginia
(now Washington and Lee University), providing for the South a vivid example of peaceful, constructive reengagement in normal life.

We also hope that the quotes from *Personal Memoirs of U. S. Grant* have
given the reader a sense of their direct, forceful modesty, and thus that of
Grant himself. Grant was not generally regarded as much of a speaker or con-
versationalist. He is regarded as a clear, fluid writer. When he was commanding general, one of his subordinates, George Meade, commented, "There is
one striking thing about Grant's orders: no matter how hurriedly he may

write them on the field, no one ever had the slightest doubt as to their meaning, or ever had to read them over a second time to understand them." [45] This
same clarity appears in Grant's statement of the surrender terms to Lee: "each
officer and man will be allowed to return to their homes, not to be disturbed
by United States authority." Likewise, Grant's presidential rhetoric is notable
for its directness and clarity.

What can be said about Grant's overall leadership, and what of that overall
picture can be drawn from the preceding discussion? Of course, Grant led in
two quite different domains, as commanding general and as U.S. President.
In a 2006 volume in a "Great Generals Series," which includes books on
Eisenhower, Patton, Stonewall Jackson, and MacArthur, series editor General
Wesley Clark writes, "Grant was the general whose strategic brilliance, tacti-
cal acumen, and courage won the Civil War for the Union"; and "Above all,
Grant had the unique combination of almost instinctive common sense in battle and strategic vision . . . to . . . which every program of military leadership
development ultimately aims. . . ." [46] This appraisal has emerged as the consensus view of military historians since J. F. C. Fuller's 1929 *The Generalship
of Ulysses S. Grant* first made such an assessment.[47]

No such consensus exists about Grant's presidential leadership. In recent
"greatness" ratings Grant has risen from one of the two or three worst presidents to some position above the bottom ten. One recent article (seriously)
suggested he should be regarded as our greatest president.[48] Grant accomplished much of what he wanted in foreign and economic affairs but suffered
serious defeats in efforts at reform, protecting Native Americans, and, most
importantly, Reconstruction. But what is most remembered about his two
administrations are various scandals. None involved him personally, but several involved people close to him.

Can the qualities that produced *Personal Memoirs* and Lee's surrender at
Appomattox also be seen in Grant's overall military and political leadership?
I think they can. Wesley Clark points to Grant's strategic vision and brilliance.
Grant was highly intelligent and generally had well-grounded good
judgment. Grant also had a coolness under pressure (in combat and in politics) that was remarkable, and that enabled him to use his intelligence and
good judgment under the most trying and dangerous circumstances. Clark
notes his "common sense in battle." One of his officers, amazed that Grant
seemed to be unperturbed by shells exploding all around him, said "Ulysses
don't scare worth a damn." [49] Grant also had a raw force and drive. It was by
no means flamboyant, but his energy and capacity to do things forcefully and
quickly are notable.

Writing in 1962, the critic and commentator Edmund Wilson argued that
qualities of cool confidence and great energy marked *Personal Memoirs*.

> This capacity for inspiring confidence, this impression Grant gave of reserves of force comes through in the *Personal Memoirs* without pose or premeditation. Grant faltered a little in the later chapters ... when his suffering blurs the text; but in general the writing of the *Memoirs* is perfect in concision and clearness, in its propriety and purity of language. Every word that Grant writes has its purpose, yet everything is understated. These literary qualities, so unobtrusive, are evidence of a natural fineness of character, mind and taste; and the *Memoirs* also convey the dynamic force and definiteness of his personality ... the narrative seems to move with the increasing momentum that the soldier must have felt in the field.[50]

In addition to intelligence, common sense, and inspiring drive, in *Personal Memoirs* and in his meeting with Lee, Grant manifested an unusual trust in other people. If it were not for that, Lee and Grant might never have concluded the Appomattox surrender. They both had subordinates who mistrusted the other and opposed their meeting. However, Lee was reassured that Grant would be lenient by his "old war horse," General James "Pete" Longstreet, who had been a groomsman in Grant's wedding. Grant had no one to reassure him. On the contrary, on the morning of the surrender, Generals Meade and Sheridan strongly urged Grant to finish the destruction of Lee's army rather than negotiate a surrender. Bruce Catton writes "If any general ever had the killer instinct it was Phil Sheridan."[51] But Catton continued, "Grant wanted a victory that could be turned into a lasting peace, and Sheridan did not have the recipe for it."[52] In the event, the wisdom of Grant's decision to meet Lee would be tested by whether or not Lee used the cease-fire to try to escape. The memoirs state:

> I was conducted to where Sheridan was located with his troops drawn up in line of battle facing the Confederate army near by. They were very much excited, and expressed their view that this was all a ruse to enable the Confederates to get away.... and they would whip the rebels in five minutes if I would only let them go in. But I had no doubt about the good faith of Lee, and pretty soon was conducted to where he was. I found him at the house of Mr. McLean with Colonel Marshall ... awaiting my arrival.[53]

Suffice it to say that Grant's faith in others served him well on April 9, 1865. It did not serve him well at several junctures prior to the Civil War, on many instances during his presidency, and, most poignantly perhaps, when he trusted others with his finances just prior to commencing *Personal Memoirs*.

In addition to Grant's highly trusting disposition, there is another more elusive and dissonant quality, related perhaps to his faith in others, that contributed to some of the disappointments of his life prior to the Civil War, his presidency, and his business endeavors toward the end of his life. As recent biographer Josiah Bunting notes, there is an occasional "torpor" that overtook Grant at times.[54] He could be surprisingly passive. This quality stands in great contrast to the determination, drive, and force he manifested consistently during the war, inconsistently as president, and once again in finishing *Personal Memoirs* days before his death.

In sum, there is a consistency to the direct, grounded, intelligent, and generous prose in *Personal Memoirs*. Those qualities also governed Grant's actions at Appomattox. Others have painted and explained those actions in different ways. Like the actors described in Jones and Nisbett's theory of actor/observer divergences in attribution, Grant simply saw them as the right thing to do under the circumstances.

NOTES

The author gratefully acknowledges the research assistance and insight of independent study student Cara J. Scmidt.

1. William S. McFeely, *Grant: A Biography* (New York: W. W. Norton, 1981), 220; Jay Winik, *April 1865: The Month That Saved America* (New York: Harper Collins, 2001), 191; Brooks D. Simpson, *Ulysses S. Grant: Triumph Over Adversity, 1822–1865* (Boston: Houghton Mifflin, 2000), 436.

2. Bruce Catton, *Grant Takes Command* (Boston: Little, Brown, 1968), 468; Shelby Foote, *The Civil War: A Narrative*, Volume 3 (New York: Random House, 1974), 950; Simpson, *Ulysses S. Grant*, 436.

3. Ulysses S. Grant, *Personal Memoirs of U.S. Grant.* (Cambridge, MA: Second DeCapo Press edition, 2001), 559. (Original publication, New York: Charles W. Webster, 1885, 1886, two volumes.)

4. William S. McFeely, "Introduction to the First DeCapo Edition," *Memoirs* (Cambridge, MA: DeCapo Press, 1982), xix.

5. Grant, *Personal Memoirs*, 559.

6. Douglas Southall Freeman, *R. E. Lee: A Biography*, Vol. 4 (New York: Scribners, 1935); MacKinlay Kantor, *Grant and Lee at Appomattox* (New York: Random House, 1950); Catton, *Grant Takes Command*; Foote, *The Civil War*; McFeely, *Grant*; Simpson, *Ulysses S. Grant*; Jean Edward Smith, *Grant* (New York: Simon & Schuster, 2001); Charles Bowery, *Lee & Grant: Profiles in Leadership from the Battlefields of Virginia* (New York: AMACOM, 2005).

7. Edward E. Jones and Richard E. Nisbett, "The Actor and the Observer: Divergent Perceptions of Causality," in *Attribution: Perceiving the Causes of Behavior*, ed. E. E. Jones, D. E. Kanouse, H. H. Kelley, R. E. Nisbett, S. Valins, and B. Weiner (Morristown, NJ: General Learning Press, 1972).

8. Grant, *Personal Memoirs*, 552–554.

9. Catton, *Grant Takes Command*, 462.

10. Bowery, *Lee & Grant*, 212.

11. Simpson, *Ulysses S. Grant*, 431.

12. Smith, *Grant*, 401.

13. Grant, *Personal Memoirs*, 551.

14. Ibid., 554.

15. Ibid., 553.

16. Kantor, *Lee and Grant at Appomattox*, 83.

17. Foote, *The Civil War*, 938.

18. McFeely, *Grant*, 218.

19. Ibid., 218.

20. Ibid., xi.

21. Catton, *Grant Takes Command*, 464.

22. Ibid., 464.

23. Grant, *Personal Memoirs*, 555–556.

24. Smith, *Grant*, 398.

25. McFeely, *Grant*, 219.

26. Grant, *Personal Memoirs*, 17.

27. McFeely, *Grant*, 219.

28. Bowery, *Lee & Grant*, 213.

29. Grant, *Personal Memoirs*, 555–556.

30. Ibid., 556.

31. Ibid., 557.

32. Ibid., 557.

33. James David Barber, *The Presidential Character: Predicting Performance in the White House* (Englewood Cliffs, NJ: Prentice-Hall, 1992).

34. Grant, *Personal Memoirs*, 558.

35. Freeman, *R. E. Lee*, 139.

36. Bowery, *Lee & Grant*, 213.

37. Smith, *Grant*, 405.

38. Catton, *Grant Takes Command*, 465.

39. Foote, *The Civil War*, 948.

40. Kantor, *Lee and Grant at Appomattox*, 123.

41. Simpson, *Ulysses S. Grant*, 434.

42. Grant, *Personal Memoirs*, 558.

43. Winik, *April 1865*, 197.

44. Fritz Heider, *The Psychology of Interpersonal Relations* (New York: Wiley, 1958).

45. Mark Perry, *Grant and Twain: The Story of a Friendship that Changed America* (New York: Random House, 2004), 234.

46. Wesley K. Clark, "Forward" to John Mosier, *Grant* (New York: Palgrave Macmillan, 2006), xi.

47. J. F. C. Fuller, *The Generalship of Ulysses S. Grant* (London: J. Murray, 1929).

48. Nathan Newman, "Ulysses Grant: Our Greatest President." Available at http://tpmcafe.talkingpointsmemo.com/2006/07/04/ulysses_grant_our_greatest_pre/

49. John Keegan, *The Mask of Command* (New York: Viking, 1987).

50. Perry, *Grant and Twain*, 234–235.

51. Catton, *Grant Takes Command*, 462.

52. Ibid., 463.

53. Grant, *Personal Memoirs*, 554.

54. Josiah Bunting III, *Ulysses S. Grant* (New York: Henry Holt, 2004), 153.

5

Ressentiment as a Political Passion

RUTH CAPRILES

Fair is foul, and foul is fair.

—*Macbeth: (I.1)*

There are moments, historical experiences, when events seem driven by irrational forces or hidden wills that upset all values, emotions, and daily life, when the "Beast" [1] comes out and seems to be winning the round of our own destiny. Such has been the experience in Venezuela, with the rise of Hugo Chávez to power by democratic vote in 1998.[2] The impression we have of a befallen phenomenon is due to our historical experience. Venezuelans have lived in a setting like the Garden of Eden from the beginning of historical time. It was, and still is, a land of abundance and multiple riches; a wonderful climate and beautiful, wild, nature; and an untamed but reliable provider. People of mixed races and colors were, or were always recorded as, "of good disposition," even through times of tyranny and fratricidal wars during the nineteenth and first half of the twentieth centuries.

In 1958, the people ousted the last dictator of the twentieth century and embarked in the experiment of an open society and democratic government —a project that resulted in 40 years of relative political stability and social and economic growth. Venezuela was among the "Democracies on the way to Development" and one of the very few countries in Latin America that did not suffer from the military intervention in politics during those years. Such sustained and positive growth in the 1970s led Venezuela into debt to finance gigantic modernization projects that were far from its capacities to handle, skyrocketing its international obligations in part because the international banking and financial conditions had changed suddenly.

Economic and social conditions changed in the 1980s; some experts spoke of scarce resources and the need to make changes in ways of spending. Since then, the "adjustment packages" and the pressure from the International Monetary Fund were imposed while all indicators of progress and modernity fell. The old tropical diseases became renewed endemics; education rates decreased and poverty grew geometrically, multiplied by indiscriminate immigration. Meanwhile the new international "epidemics," inflation, debt, unemployment, and growth of a third sector economy, battered the country.

The economic adjustment brought rejection from the people, and the ruling elites were unable to be firm and sustain neoliberal measures within populist regimes. Although they backed off from the adjustments, the political parties in government lost their constituency. Corruption and incapacity of the ruling elites were blamed for the failure of the country's development. By 1990, public opinion signaled the desire for a change in the political system, maybe as an easy answer to the real change needed in the economic dimension. A social uprising on February 27, 1989, and two coups in 1992 (February and November) show malaise enough to have warned the establishment.

That is how a lieutenant from the army came to be noticed through a failed coup d'état in 1992. His name is Hugo Chávez. He emerged as a self-styled leader of the poor, a messiah to heal all evils of inequality and injustice. For many, he meant a change, a slap in the face of politicians. For the opposition, he meant a menace to democracy and an open society. In eight years of government, with the intent to stay in power for life, and despite strong opposition, he has now managed to curb all resistance.

After Chávez's first inflammatory speeches as a candidate in 1998, and later as elected president, Venezuelans experienced a sudden change in their "social mood." It seemed as if one day the easygoing disposition of Venezuelan citizens disappeared and was replaced by *ressentiment*. It spread from Chávez's words and deeds to his admirers and detractors. By such a contagious process, Chávez took Venezuela from the promising path of decentralization and empowerment of the people back to the worst state-controlled economy, polity, and society ever experienced in this country. How could this happen? How could Chávez induce Venezuelans to voluntarily give up their freedom and democracy? And perhaps more importantly: What can we learn from the attraction/repulsion bond Chávez has with his followers and opposition?

One answer may come from the way Chávez cultivated and manipulated ressentiment in his followers. In this chapter I will use literature and philosophy to explore the phenomenon of ressentiment; then I will briefly apply the model derived from that exploration to the case of Hugo Chávez to show how a leader uses it to gain and retain power.

RESSENTIMENT IN PHILOSOPHY AND LITERATURE

An outright definition of "ressentiment" will ease our plunge into the cluster of meanings attached to that emotion and word. It will explain why this chapter uses the French spelling of the word. Both Friedrich Nietzsche and Max Scheler use the French word "ressentiment" to refer to a kind of brooding emotion. Scheler says that Nietzsche has made it a term of art with no equivalent in German language:[3]

> In the natural meaning of the French word I detect two elements. First, ressentiment is the repeated experiencing and reliving of a particular emotional response reaction against someone else. The continual reliving of the emotion sinks it more deeply into the center of the personality, but concomitantly removes it from the person's zone of action and expression. It is not a mere intellectual recollection of the emotion and of the events to which it responded—it is a re-experiencing of the emotion itself, a renewal of the original feeling. Secondly, the word implies that the quality of this emotion is negative, i.e. that it contains a movement of hostility.

Friedrich Nietzsche

Ressentiment enters Nietzsche's moral theory, in *The Genealogy of Morals*, as a corollary of his postulates on "Good and Evil; Good and Bad."[4] He defines "good" and "bad" as words appropriated by the superior "race" to designate itself; he equates good to the noble ("the powerful," "the masters," "the commanders") and conversely equates "bad" to the common man, the plebeian, the weak, the poor.[5] Nietzsche does not imply that the masters are good and the plebeians are bad; what he says is that the distinction good or evil is made by conquerors or rulers and emerges from their feelings of superiority. Rulers create values and enforce them as a "triumphal affirmation of themselves."[6] They transform thus the political concept of mastery into a spiritual concept of moral value. Morality, then, is born out of a power relationship. Ressentiment subverts that order, devaluates the aristocratic values and "*itself becomes creative and engenders values.*"[7]

But the new values are different from the aristocratic values because they are not affirmative nor active but negative and passive or reactive:

> While all noble morality grows out of a triumphant self-affirmation, slave morality from the start says "No" to what is "outside," "other," "a non-self." And this "No" is its creative act. This transformation of the glance which confers value— this necessary projection towards what is outer instead of back onto itself—that is inherent in ressentiment. In order to arise, slave morality always requires first an opposing world, a world outside itself. Psychologically speaking, it needs external stimuli in order to act at all. Its action is basically reaction.[8]

The catalyzing agent of that inversion is the hatred and impotency of the weak:

> As is well known, priests are the most evil of enemies—but why? Because they are the most impotent. From their powerlessness, their hate grows into something immense and terrifying, to the most spiritual and most poisonous manifestations.[9]

From that hatred emerges the "slave revolt" in morality, and ressentiment comes out as a forceful agent in history. It is not the weak, though, who end up dominating over the strong, active people throughout written history. The resented are not the plebeian, the poor, common people who accept their destiny. Ressentiment emerges from the split in the higher "caste" and the inversion of aristocratic values accomplished by those who abandon (or maybe are not fit for) war.

As to the origin of ressentiment, Nietzsche points to the accounts of psychologists.[10]

> *In my view, only here can we find the true physiological cause of resentment, revenge,* and things related to them, in a longing for some anaesthetic against pain through one's *emotions.*[11]

In sum, for Nietzsche, ressentiment results from superiority and domination.

Max Scheler

Scheler builds upon Nietzsche's theory of ressentiment even though he disagrees with Nietzsche's application of it to history. Scheler aims to "penetrate more deeply into the *unit of experience* designated by the term."[12] He describes the phenomenon as a progression of feeling:

> Ressentiment is a self-poisoning of the mind which has quite definite causes and consequences. It is a lasting mental attitude, caused by the systematic repression of certain emotions and affects which, as such, are normal components of human nature. Their repression leads to the constant tendency to indulge in certain kinds of value delusions and corresponding value judgments. The emotions and affects primarily concerned are revenge, hatred, malice, envy, the impulse to detract, and spite. Thirst for revenge is the most important source of ressentiment.[13]

We have then an operational definition. Ressentiment is a disease of the mind and a mental attitude. There is also some kind of progression into the emotion or different levels of those reactive emotions.

> It is always preceded by an attack or an injury. Yet it must be clearly distinguished from the impulse for reprisals or self-defense. . . .

> There is a progression of feeling which starts with revenge and runs via rancour, envy, an impulse to detract all the way to spite, coming close to ressentiment.[14]

Scheler takes an interesting turn from Nietzsche's approach. For him ressentiment is a dynamic term with a sociological dimension:

> the manner in which ressentiment originates in individuals or groups, and the intensity it reaches, is due primarily to hereditary factors and secondarily to social structure. Let us note, however, that the social structure itself is determined by the hereditary character and the value experience of the ruling human type. Since ressentiment can never emerge without the mediation of a particular form of impotence, it is always one of the phenomena of "declining life." But in addition to these general preconditions, there are some types of ressentiment which are grounded in certain typically recurrent "situations" and whose emergence is therefore largely independent of individual temperament. It would be foolish to assert that every individual in these "situations" is necessarily gripped by ressentiment. I do say, however, that by virtue of their formal character itself—and quite apart from the character of the individual concerned—these "situations" are charged with the danger of ressentiment.[15]

Scheler even posits a law:

> There follows the important sociological law that this psychological dynamite will spread with the *discrepancy* between the political, constitutional, or traditional status of a group and its *factual* power.[16]

The collective phenomenon unfolds in several phases: First there is the repression of the original impulse to get back at the person who has injured or oppressed an individual or group; then the emotion is detached from any particular reason or any particular individual and it turns into a negative attitude towards certain traits and qualities no matter in whom they are found (i.e., class hatred) resulting in an inversion or falsification of collective values; then it is directed against any other person's and group's very essence and being.[17]

> When the repression is complete, the result is a general negativism—a sudden, violent, seemingly unsystematic and unfounded rejection of things, situations, or natural objects whose loose connections with the original cause of the hatred can only be discovered by a complicated analysis.[18]

"The slave revolt" and the installation of the "false" set of values in place of the "true" values mark the victory of ressentiment. The new "true" values—poverty, suffering, illness, and death—replace power, health, beauty, freedom, and independence.

Manuel García Pelayo

This Spanish Venezuelan political scientist addresses the issue of ressentiment from a political perspective. He draws a distinction between ressentiment as a psychological trait ("a constant revival of a humiliation") and ressentiment as a historical agent. The historical agent permeates ideas and institutions with an inversion of values that destroys old values and social arrangements, institutions, and groups of actors. This is a useful distinction because both Scheler and Nietzsche place ressentiment in the individual (be it physical or psychological), yet both apply the concept to collective behaviors and processes.

García Pelayo focuses on the political content of ressentiment, which is contingent on the political position of the resented and in the cultural process of incubation. Ressentiment then is about power, violence, domination, and leadership. That is probably what Nietzsche meant when he spoke of the "slave revolt" being a whole group's reaction of the weak to the domination by the supermen. For García Pelayo, the first precondition for ressentiment to emerge is impotence to satisfy revenge or envy. The second is the pretension of equality by a class of people who are in a position of inferiority.

Gregorio Marañón

Marañón takes a psychological approach to ressentiment that seems to corroborate García Pelayo's emphasis on the importance of the individual who is in a position of influence. He defines resentment as "a passion; a passion of the animus which may lead to sin and, sometimes, to madness or crime." [19] He also separates the "cause" of resentment from the original aggression or offense given: "It does not depend on the quality of the aggression but on the individual who receives it." Marañón wants to understand the resented person by understanding the kinds of people who are prone to resentment.

> The resented is always someone without generosity. Without doubt, the contrary passion to ressentiment is generosity, which we must not confuse with the capacity to forgive.[20]

Forgiveness is a virtue and can be granted by a moral imperative, but generosity is a passion born from understanding—as only one who loves can know.[21] The resented person is ill-fitted to love and, thereby, a person of mediocre moral quality. It is not simple evil.

> The bad man is only a criminal . . . The resented is not necessarily a bad person; he can even be good if life is favorable. It is only in face of injustice and adversity when he becomes resented. [22]

Marañón points to the same characteristics of resentment and the resented person we have found in all authors: the long incubation time of resentment between the offense and the revenge, or the "poor in spirit," who accepts adversity, and the intelligent person, who believes he deserves more than what he gets and becomes resented.[23]

William Shakespeare

Shakespeare is the master writer on human strong passions. Several of his characters express ressentiment. Shylock is the classic figure of group ressentiment. He is impotent but powerful, conniving, and revengeful for an offense committed at the beginning of time and reenacted over and over through centuries. The individual reenactment of an ancient grudge is best expressed in one of Shylock's parliaments. Notice the impossibility to forgive that may be the reason for the "incurable disease."

> *I hate him for he is a Christian,*
> *But more for that in low simplicity*
> *He lends out money gratis and brings down*
> *The rate of usance here with us in Venice.*
> *If I can catch him once upon the hip,*
> *I will feed fat the ancient grudge I bear him.*
> *He hates our sacred nation, and he rails*
> *...Cursed be my tribe,*
> *If I forgive him!*[24]

The conjunction of the individual, the sociological, and the political contents in ressentiment is wonderfully revealed in that first meeting of Antonio and Shylock:

> *Shylock:*
> *Signior Antonio, many a time and oft*
> *In the Rialto you have rated me*
> *About my moneys and my usances:*
> *Still have I borne it with a patient shrug,*
> *For sufferance is the badge of all our tribe.*
> *You call me misbeliever, cut-throat dog,*
> *And spit upon my Jewish gaberdine,*
> *And all for use of that which is mine own.*
> *Well then, it now appears you need my help:*
> *...*
> *What should I say to you? Should I not say*
> *'Hath a dog money? is it possible*
> *A cur can lend three thousand ducats?'...* [25]

The grudge is between different values of different cultures. Antonio squanders and "lends out money gratis"; he spits and despises Shylock who finds a blessing in thrift and usury. "Sufferance is the badge" of a whole tribe over time, breeding ressentiment in their hearts.

The power relation is thus revealed. Antonio belongs to the dominant culture; he is a prosperous honorable merchant, fair, loved, and moved by love.
Shylock remonstrates alone in the shadow of tribal disgrace; he is depicted
as mean and ugly, chased and hated; but he has some leverage over the other:
he has the money the "good men" need.

Shakespeare also depicts ressentiment in the Moor, Aaron, in *Titus Androni-
cus*. He pronounces that cry full of agony of reaction to racism:

> *'Zounds, ye whore! is black so base a hue?*[26]

The character Aaron helps us appreciate the difference between revenge and
ressentiment when one compares his motives to Tamora's, Queen of the
Goths. Although both are captives of the Romans, Tamora is driven by
revenge towards Titus and the Romans for the execution of her son. She
pleaded as a mother and as a valid enemy of Rome, yet she did not obtain
mercy or justice (in accordance to the custom to spare royal blood except in
battle) so she is full of hate and seeks revenge.

Aaron's motives are different. He was himself captive or servant to the
Queen, although he has risen to be her lover and master.

> *Away with slavish weeds and servile thoughts!*
> *I will be bright, and shine in pearl and gold,*
> *To wait upon this new-made empress.*
> *To wait, said I? To wanton with this queen. . .*[27]

Aaron is in reality the main character of the play; he is the leader in the
action and the plot unravels by his agency. Titus and Tamora end up being
his victims. He expresses well the cluster of feelings that contribute to the
emotion we have called ressentiment:

> *Madam, though Venus govern your desires,*
> *Saturn is dominator over mine:*
> *What signifies my deadly-standing eye,*
> *My silence and my cloudy melancholy,*
> *My fleece of woolly hair that now uncurls*
> *Even as an adder when she doth unroll*
> *To do some fatal execution?*
> *No, madam, these are no venereal signs:*
> *Vengeance is in my heart, death in my hand,*
> *Blood and revenge are hammering in my head.*

Here we see the process of value inversion by "the art of slander":

> *Some devil whisper curses in mine ear,*
> *And prompt me, that my tongue may utter forth*
> *The venomous malice of my swelling heart!*[28]

And the superb, dramatic effect of a passion that can never be satisfied, nor quenched:

> *Ten thousand worse than ever yet I did*
> *Would I perform, if I might have my will;*
> *If one good deed in all my life I did,*
> *I do repent it from my very soul.*[29]

Ayn Rand

This author is worth reviewing because her novel *Atlas Shrugged* is a treatise on ressentiment. According to Rand, the novel was meant to develop her philosophy of "Objectivism." Her philosophical penchant affects the literary quality of the novel. It flattens the personalities of the characters who keep on repeating the same postulates that do not really amount to a complete philosophical system. Nevertheless, it catches the reader in such a way that even today Rand awakens admiration among the young and is a model for the entrepreneurial spirit.

The plot of the novel is set in a future United States, whose economy and society is collapsing as a result of the political domination of the resented and their installation of a set of values that submit the rich and enterprising innovators to the common good and the welfare of the poor and the weak. It is the battle between individualism and collectivism with an optimistic final victory of the individual mind and his "motive power" that moves society: the power of the human mind and will to conquer and create.

In response to the inversion and imposition of a set of values that are contrary to the logic of reason and to the excellence of human action and creativity, a group of heroes, *prima movers*, decide to go on strike. They cease to contribute to the ideas and values of collectivism and social welfare sustained and dictated by the resented.

In Rand, as in Nietzsche, human beings are of two kinds:

1. The heroes are warriors, entrepreneurs, innovators, creators, who have feelings such as envy, jealousy, anger, sadness, but of a pure kind different from base emotions such as pity, revenge, ressentiment, and they strive forward into the infinite process of excellence and happiness. Heroes are wise in an existential sense, and they reach happiness by the continuous practice of excellence or action based on moral principles.

2. The looters are moved by envy, spite, ressentiment. They are incapable of sustaining themselves or society without the action of the heroes and are too lazy to do the job the best way possible. They argue collectivism out of mediocrity and lack of the motivation, reason, and the spiritual conviction of creative men who move the world. The looters have inverted values and continuously proclaim the priority of the "common good" over the individual greed.

Atlas Shrugged is supposed to stage the battle of reason versus passion, which is the battle of individualism versus collectivism, or good versus evil. But notice the catch in this particular eternal battle. In Rand's battle, passion is in one side only: evil's part. The heroes in Rand do not have passions; they have feelings, so pure and genuine that they are both enjoyed and controlled by their superior rationality. As Nietzsche's "priests caste," Rand's villains are mediocre, impotent, and revengeful; their purpose is to get power and, to achieve it, they invert values, transmute a political concept into a spiritual concept, and convert revenge in a spiritual act. Such transmutation is expressed by the humble, but sharp, wife of Taggart to one of the looters:

> All of you welfare preachers—it's not unearned money that you are after. You want handouts, but of a different kind . . . it is the spirit that you want to loot . . . the unearned in spirit.[30]

Rand's characters need not explain among equals their motives or behavior. It is unnecessary because each one is equally intelligent and shares the same principles, logic, and thoughts. Heroes do not need to convince the looters of their false code of morals. Heroes know humanitarian love, love of mankind, public welfare, altruism, collectivism, pity, compassion, and generosity are part of an inverted code of morals and do not even try to convince others; they just act and show them what excellence is.

Like Scheler, Rand relates ressentiment to a vacuum, a feeling of nothingness. Nevertheless, Scheler would not agree with Rand's moral code. Whereas for Nietzsche and Rand, value lies in action, in the merit acquired by one's own effort, and both blame the resented for holding values in themselves: love of humanity, brother compassion, people's welfare.

Honoré de Balzac

Balzac's *Human Comedy* is a *tableau* showing the smallness and meanness of human beings; their different reactions to inequality and injustice in eighteenth century bourgeois French society. There are no heroes in that *tableau;* even winners are losers and all actors are victims one way or another. This is not naïve optimistic fiction, as Rand's. This novel offers a bleak albeit humorous look at society. It is ironic that in defense of individualism, Rand draws two types of shallow, uniform characters, whereas Balzac's characters present a rich tapestry of psychological distinctions.

The resented are less powerful in Balzac than in Rand, maybe because for him evil or perversity is a characteristic of society, not a quality of individuals. He does not even use the word in the "French sense," as understood by Nietzsche and Scheler. It is ironic that Balzac uses the English meaning of the word—the verb "to resent"—and does not refer to the kind of emotion we have been discussing. Balzac uses "resentment" to describe a simple feeling or reaction to an immediate stimulus, such as someone saying: "I resent your words" or "I resent your indifference." Notwithstanding such lack of explicit conceptualization of the emotion in relation to the word, ressentiment is behind many of his characters. One of the most striking examples is Lisbeth Fischer or "la cousine Bette" from the novel of the same name.

"La cousine Bette" is another type of the resented person that has sort of a passive ressentiment, the kind that derives more from envy than from revenge. It is not the looter-resented person but the parasite-resented person: the one who does not do evil with her inverted values but simply sits back to enjoy the roundabouts of life and history that allow you to see the corpse of thy enemy pass by your window. Bette is the audience in the eternal battle of vice and virtue, a malicious aid to evil's round.

> She gave up all idea of rivalry and comparison with her cousin after feeling her great superiority; but envy still lurked in her heart, like a plague-germ that may hatch and devastate a city if the fatal bale of wool is opened in which it is concealed.[31]
>
> In 1837, after living for twenty-seven years, half maintained by the Hulots and her Uncle Fischer, Cousin Betty, resigned to being nobody, allowed herself to be treated so. She herself refused to appear at any grand dinners, preferring the family party, where she held her own and was spared all slights to her pride.[32]

In his initial description of his main character, Balzac outlines the basic traits we have seen in ressentiment: a situation of inferiority or grievance. Bette is ugly and poor. She relies on the benevolence of her beautiful and good cousin and the benevolence of Baron Hulot. She slanders the people who have the values she blames for her inferiority or offense. This leads to a diminishing of desired and unattainable value, the negation of value itself, and insatiable revenge.

> Lisbeth Fischer, though the daughter of the eldest of the three brothers, was five years younger than Madame Hulot; she was far from being as handsome as her cousin, and had been desperately jealous of Adeline. Jealousy was the fundamental passion of this character, marked by eccentricities. . .[33]
>
> Gifted with a cunning which had become unfathomable, as it always does in those whose celibacy is genuine, with the originality and sharpness with which

she clothed her ideas, in any other position she would have been formidable. Full of spite, she was capable of bringing discord into the most united family.[34]

Her eccentricities were her expression of the inversion of values. She stressed her lack of beauty by mocking herself and by wearing dresses especially redesigned to be outmoded and make her look like an old maid. She lived off charity and rejected the support offered by Baron Hulot to open her own embroidery atelier and his attempts to find her a husband. As in the tale of the fox and the grapes, interpreted by Scheler and Pelayo, her initial step in the process of ressentiment was to invert her values and behave as if beauty, independent wealth, marriage, and social prestige were not important to her, as if her lack of all those qualities made her happiness.

V. S. Naipaul

Ressentiment and colonialism are the main characters in the Indian-Trinidadian novelist V. S. Naipaul's writing. Most of his books are mirrors on the detritus of colonialism. They seem to say to the conquerors, "Hey, here is what you brought about." But they also serve as a mirror to the weak, to serfs, slaves, and people of the South—"Hey, here is the face of your ressentiment."

Naipaul's bleakest book, *Guerrillas* (1980), offers insight into ressentiment. In the novel, all characters are mean, resented, lost in either denial or a hopeless quest for vengeance of a primeval injustice and harm. They live in a "place at the end of the world, a place that had exhausted its possibilities." [35] Among them, Jimmy epitomizes South American defeated left. He is the Muslim, dark Chinese, Trinitarian, leader of a "Thrushcross Grange, People's Commune, for the land and the Revolution," a project supported by politicians and financed by corporations because he is considered "The only man that stands between them and the revolution." A bogus project: "Everybody is pretending that something exists that doesn't exist." [36]

The fictional truth is that Jimmy is not really a leader, the grange is not "communal," productive of crops for the people, or revolutionary. It is not even a refuge for guerrillas, which are extinct by that time and were only a diffuse menace. Thrushcross Grange is barely a space in the jungle where a few derelicts stay in a kind of non-being and no-story, but end up killing for no reason at all. Nothing happens in the novel. It epitomizes the triviality of evil, the banality of power and leadership with no echo, no mirror. Naipaul writes: "He's like the others. He's looking for someone to lead." [37]

Naipaul offers a different perspective on ressentiment. In Nietzsche and Rand, emotion is the key motivation in the long battle for power, an important battle between two opposite strategies of cultural survival:

individualism, creation, and love versus collectivism, destruction, and rancor. In Nieztsche, Rand, and Scheler, history shows us epochs when ressentiment has dominated the world, times when the supercreative man prevailed. Naipaul's view is much darker. In Naipaul's world ressentiment is human nature and cultural reality. There is no hope for construction or bettering. There is no battle. "There is nothing for me there." Naipaul teaches us that there is no gratification in ressentiment.

RESSENTIMENT AND THE PROCESS OF POLITICAL PASSION

Through the literature reviewed, one can discern a "shadow" of meanings of ressentiment, a cluster concept, shared by all authors.

All authors, starting with Nietzsche, found ressentiment a major political force driving societies. From the previous schema we can see its collective character: It causes a collective inversion of values; is caused or motivated by social situations of impotence, inequality or inferiority; is conditioned by relational qualities as a lack of social opportunities or "class" consciousness; and has important social effects.

But what kind of "force" are we talking about? At the individual psychological level, we can posit ressentiment as a motive of behavior; but those categories are not good to explain collective behaviors and processes. Scheler's words are pointed towards this question: "Quite independently of the characters and experiences of individuals, a potent charge of ressentiment is here accumulated by the *very structure of society*." [38]

Ressentiment is not only an individual motive but also a social condition that places a high probability that an individual will be resented or will resent. He talks of "lasting situations which are felt to be injurious but beyond one's control." [39] There is accumulation of grievances and long lasting unfair situations, but he does not understand those as causes but as preconditions.

How do individual emotions aggregate and explode suddenly into a "slave revolt"? It is not an easy question. The answer may lie in leadership and political passion. Passion is the moment when emotions, not reason, take over the control of behavior, be it individual or collective. Passion answers to the question "when?" not to "what?" Regarding collective behavior, we can say that a passion controls collective, groups or mob, behavior when it does not follow the usual, rational proceedings in that society or when it does not pursue the social goals chosen by public choice or posited social goals.

Let us start by discerning several ways ressentiment becomes a political passion.

a. *A power relation:* Having impotence and disadvantage at its origin, its activation implies getting power. Scheler depicts ressentiment as a power

1.1	R is
	Repression of emotion
1.2	R implies, causes, provokes, is the source of
	An inversion of values
1.3	R is provoked by, caused by, motivated by
	Impotence in face of aggression
	Incapacity
	Inequality
	Inferiority
1.4	R is conditioned by
	Unattainability of positive values
	Inacceptance of ranks among pairs
	Pretensions of equality
	Weakness of the dominant consciousness
	Decrease of dominant's right to lead
1.5	R has signs or effects
	No gratification of revenge or envy
	Incurable disease
	Important social effects
	Domination by blackmail or looting
1.6	R is a phenomenology
	Aggression
	Repression
	Incubation
	Redirection to diffuse or collective universe
	Revolt
	Substitution of previous value code
	Investing value code with the new ruler's power

process from an aggression through revolt until the substitution of value codes. And as Marañón and García Pelayo noticed, when the resented are in positions of power, they will have tremendous effect in historical events.

b. *A total process:* As it is directed to a diffuse other, it becomes a reaction against the whole of society in a battle for ultimate material and spiritual power.

c. *An inversion or inversions of values:* What comes out of the "black box" of the ressentiment process is in sum an inversion of values and/or a recurrent battle among values: A double inversion should recover original values or create new ones that will be inverted again *ad infinitum.*

d. *A historical "disease":* Its incurability and pervading character, emphasized by Nietzsche and accepted by all authors, allows it to become an extended social characteristic, passed over through generations. "Cursed be my tribe, if I forgive him," exclaims Shylock. The way people react to an aggression or an inferior position in life is certainly an individual and psychological question, but both the aggression and the inferior position are social conditions. Ressentiment lurks behind many socialist parties and the rancor that some public functionaries and terrorists have against entrepreneurs and capitalists. Osama Bin Laden's terrorism and Chávez's revolution are all but the same expression of the "concept of political superiority" of ressentiment.

e. *A leadership relationship:* Ressentiment needs voices to express the inverted values and attract followers into "the slave revolt." Ressentiment that seems to start as a shared social emotion becomes a collective passion through the leader-follower relationship. Leadership is a double mirror relationship. Leaders become so when there are followers to empower them and to reflect their ideas, goals, passions, and wishes. The regard of followers allows people to be leaders and to see themselves as such. Equally, leaders empower followers and give them the assurance they need to overcome impotency and initiate revolt.

Ressentiment becomes a social passion when that double reflection takes place between leader and followers. Nietzsche's priests, Scheler's humanitarians, and Rand's looters are people who have emerged from impotence, people who have become potent or feel and believe they can do it. The real resented characters are always losers: Cousine Bette, Jimmy, Aaron, even Rand's looters when they are defeated. According to Rand, looters are not potent but suck the strength of doers. The resented may win, but if they cannot surmount their ressentiment they will be defeated again and die like cousine Bette, surrounded by the love of the "superior" group.

Max Weber's type of charismatic leader[40] applies to this kind of leadership that relies on emotions, not institutions. If it wants to last, it must convert itself into a rational institutional authority. Institutionalization may depend on conditions of several kinds but rational leadership is paramount. In the time span of the polity, it may have to do with the capacity of leaders to distribute with a certain amount of equity and social justice or with their blindness and deafness regarding the demands of followers. The qualities of the leaders, their sincerity and expertise in the leading, their language and their actions, are important factors. But it will also depend on the followers who can choose to go out of the realm of ressentiment. So, to overcome ressentiment we need good leaders, it is true, but we also need good followers to choose the right leader and empower him or her.

f. *A revolution of expectations:* Another social condition for ressentiment to emerge has to do with inequality, social permeability, and the "revolution of expectations." We have seen that to become resented there has to be some comparison (be it in beauty, richness, power, force, honor, or fame), but the uneven situation must be felt as unjust, unnatural, unjustified, or undesired. It is the pretending to be as lucky as the other, the desire itself to be other than oneself, that allows such emotion to emerge. So, for ressentiment to become a social or political drive there has to be some situation where there is social difference in a society and people not only want to be other but could be so. The slave revolt is an upturn of the accepted status and roles in society.

Marañón says the opposite of ressentiment is generosity. I would rather think the opposite of ressentiment is contentment in one's own place in society. Inequality then is a "cause" of ressentiment inasmuch as it depends on the expectations. To be second and happy requires the acceptance of the proper place and the other's excellence. If you are unhappy with inequality, you expect more of yourself than you can get or are willing to strive for.

APPLICATION OF THE MODEL

The application of the model does not assume that ressentiment is a characteristic for the whole of Venezuelan society. This study distinguishes particular individuals or groups that suffer from ressentiment. We also need to distinguish between "being," "acting," "using," etc. It is one thing to be resented, another to resent, and another to use ressentiment's symbols or behaviors as tools to conquer or dominate.

In December 1994, a few months after being pardoned and released from prison by the interim president, Rafael Caldera, Chávez went to Cuba and laid out his plans to start a revolution in Venezuela. One line of strategy was expressed thus in his speech at the University of Havana: "This year (referring to 1995, electoral year) we aspire, with the Bolivarian Movement, the Bolivarian National Front, to polarize Venezuela."[41] Since then, in increasingly inflammatory speeches, he has deepened the polar division of Venezuelan citizens between "poor-rich," "black-white," "exploited-exploiters." By August 2007, a polling agency explained the recovery of 10 percent of his lost popularity between May 2007 and July 2007 this way: "He keeps on fueling the polarized social schema to interpret all conflicts and confrontations in terms of 'poor-rich,' 'black-white,' 'exploited-exploiters.'"

Before Chávez, this was not so. Venezuelans were of "good disposition," socially and politically intermingling in a "good note"[42] all colors of skin, creeds, customs, and behaviors. Inclusion set the social atmosphere in

Venezuela 1966–2000. After Chávez, that changed. Anger, hate, and envy arose, as if dormant emotions had arisen from a long-forgotten time; an old grudge against someone redirected towards society. Venezuela has been divided in two: evil and good people. Bad people are the "oligarchs" or "lackeys of imperialism." The president raised an old flag of the egalitarian, extreme federalists who in 1860 cried: "Death to all white and oligarchs!" These terms have a wide range of meanings in presidential speech, but mainly refer to those who oppose the new creed, mostly people who believe in a pluralistic society, in competition and merit, and in a free market. These are considered wrong values; for pursuing them some are menaced daily and subject to intimidation by an all-powerful state.

Reducing the revolutionary quest to a "poor-rich" issue suggests that the dominant repressed emotion leading the Venezuelan process is envy. There is anger, yes, and desire for revenge from the extreme left leaders for their old political disadvantage, but the message for the people is this: "You should have what others have" not to prosper but to stay poor. Chávez made this explicit. While he has never promised to make all Venezuelans rich, he has specifically told them that they have to be equally poor, Cuba being an example of what is called "The Sea of Happiness."

An example will suffice to prove the point. In a recent invasion of a sugar cane farm by a group organized under the front of a "cooperative of the people," an invader asked the wife of the owner:

> How many years have you been here?
>   50 years, she answered, working this land with our own hands.
>   Well, you know what? Now it is our turn.

The invaders were not workers of the farm, which could make them desire revenge from an unjust patron. Like Rand's looters, it is a diffuse claim for equality without having to work for it. The invaders destroyed the crops and, when told by the displaced owner to take advantage of that crop, which meant not only money but 1,200,000 kilograms of sugar for Venezuelan consumers, they answered: "No, we are going to make *conucos*[43] for the people." Two months later, while invaders had been condoned and even encouraged by the authorities, the army stormed into the farm to rescue a person held in kidnapping by the "cooperativists."

The inversion of values has been systematic. The rise of poverty to the level of virtue is a typical example. Chávez said that theft and murder are justified when people are hungry, so now delinquents rob and assault in the name of the revolution. Freedom, a cherished value to Venezuelans, is now rendered meekly to the will of the president along with democratic values such as plurality of political parties and autonomy of institutions. Suffice another anecdote:

> On entering a subway [car], a middle-aged woman chided me by asking:
> Do you have a police record?
> No, I answered, amazed
> "Ja . . . , she replied, then you will never be a Minister nor get a job in this administration. To get a job these days you need to be a thief or a murderer."

She kept on asking everyone around her the same question, adding in every instance:

> "Every thing my parents taught me to be wrong, now is good; and what was good is bad. Corruption, stealing, killing is what the government teaches." She was not crazy nor hysterical. She was decently dressed and spoke so coherently that, during the 30 minutes ride, people around her ended coinciding with her and expressing similar ideas.

Venezuela was ripe for ressentiment when Chávez became president. It was largely fueled by poverty but also by the inferior position of the extreme left after the first democratic governments defeated the guerrillas in the 1960s.[44] The left was excluded from the party system in 1960. After 1967 they began to be included,[45] and by 1969 an armistice, "pacification policy," invited all guerrillas left in hiding to join the political system. They entered electoral processes, won seats in Congress, enjoyed pivotal power, got appointments to the executive, and were even financed by majority parties during 30 years of democracy.

They were part of the establishment but apparently suffered from the poor "cousin Bette" syndrome. Only after Chávez came into power did people realize that the extreme left had subverted the army. One guerrilla leader named Douglas Bravo never surrendered and was free to do as he pleased. He had stayed in hiding and, unencumbered by police and immigration, came back one day and dedicated himself to recruiting officers in the army to his cause. One of those officers was Hugo Chávez with whom Bravo collaborated in the 1992 coup. Like Bravo, Chávez was also pardoned by President Caldera.

By 1992, there were at least three subversive groups working towards a coup d'état. Two of them were within the military, and one of them included civilians from the legal left parties, eminent politicians, the former president, and intellectuals. So we can say that in Venezuela, the revolt of the resented was not brought about by the "slaves" or the dominated classes but by a weaker fraction of the ruling class: the leaders of the extreme left. They were later joined by the extreme right who were repulsed by the surging of a new phenomenon in politics called "civil society."

The conditions for ressentiment to arise, as stated by the model, were also present in Venezuela since 1990. Modernization and the extension of democracy produced a revolution of expectations in third world countries. For rich

oil-producing countries such as Venezuela, high expectations started in the
1960s and 1970s but were cut short in the 1980s and fell dramatically in the
1990s. The UN document, "The Millennium Development Goals: A Latin
American and Caribbean Perspective,"[46] expresses the question succinctly:

> The pivotal theme of this report is the question of inequality. Despite the major
> strides made in relation to a number of social issues, the Latin American and
> Caribbean region still has the dubious distinction of being the most inequitable
> region in the world.[47]
>
> The optimism that prevailed at the start of the 1990s gave way to disillusion-
> ment with the outcomes of the reforms undertaken during that period.[48]

Venezuelans, who were accustomed to easy wealth and open society,
were unhappy with the economic restrictions and the corruption of leaders.
A situation of diminished expectations, due to global economic conditions
and also by the inefficiency and corruption of the leaders, was the broth from
which ressentiment awakened. The parties' "right to lead" plummeted in
10 years, and their diminished capacity to satisfy voters led to obtuse
decisions. For example, a Christian-democratic party chose a former "Miss
Venezuela" to run against Chávez because of her popularity. Chávez easily
won the election. It is worth noting, also, that a considerable number of
professionals,[49] who had some space to try to influence public opinion,
shared and spread discontent, revealing the "weakness of the dominant consciousness," a condition typical of ressentiment. For many of them this weakness felt like shame. Some were ashamed of their dominant position and
having things that others do not have such as higher education, a family,
and a job.

Chávez's revolution invoked slogans and heroes from the Independence
Wars (1810–1829), the Federal War (1858–1863), and the guerrilla war (1960–
1970). His heroes are first, the father of the land, Simón Bolívar, to symbolize
liberation from a foreign power. The second is Ezequiel Zamora, an unmerci-
ful rebel, extreme federalist at around 1846–1860. And third is "Maisanta" or
Pedro Pérez Delgado, an extreme, and somewhat obscure, rebel of the early
twentieth century who happens to be an ancestor of Chávez.

The use of symbols, heroic ancestors, and death vows is quite common in
history. What is special here is the importance that Chávez gives to old warriors and battles to symbolize the continuity of his war, as he likes to call it.
It is a war that Bolívar started that has had at least three eruptions in 150 years,
in 1858, 1960, 1992, and that Chávez is going to win.[50] He persistently
declares an eternal war, a war diffused in time and space against the devil
himself. Sometimes the devil is George W. Bush, at others the devil is the Venezuelans, or Spaniards,[51] or whoever can be made an enemy of the revolution.
Such insistence on an eternal and diffuse war suggests the incurable disease

of ressentiment, a claim lost in history that cannot be fulfilled and vengeance cannot be satiated.

As to other effects considered by our model, one must consider Venezuela's extraordinary government income, which is based on the constant rise of oil prices and is solely controlled by Chávez. There are innumerable cases of big corruption (of the military, the ministers, the deputies, the judges, and the magistrates) and small corruption within public offices and the innumerable parallel agencies (the so-called social "missions," cooperatives, etc.). While crime escalates and the government seizes private property in the name of equality, government officials display an astounding show of illicit wealth.

The immense oil wealth fund bribery is the main medium of domination. The whole society is caught in a bribe system. It is not only the civil servants who earn enormous salaries and get 10 months of "aguinaldo" (Christmas allowances), or the "poor" who are paid in cash only by subscribing to the social programs (missions), it is also banks and private business, and even the opposition, who manage to keep a comfortable standard of living by taking advantage of the exchange control system or, worse, money laundering for businesses and government officials. It is obvious that the huge oil income and the general looting of Venezuelan resources sustain Chávez's government. Chávez has Venezuelans caught between two passions: Ressentiment and greed.

The case of Chávez's leadership in Venezuela illustrates the progression of ressentiment. It began with the crushing of the guerrilla in the 1960s, the persistent economic inequality, the repression of the emotion during the years of democracy, incubation within the armed forces, the redirection towards a collective and diffuse universe, the revolt, and the inversion and substitution of values. Finally, there emerged a new value code and leadership that gained legitimacy first by democratic means, later by manipulation of electoral results, and finally by ruling by presidential decree.

LEADERSHIP BY RESSENTIMENT

The process of ressentiment in Venezuela is the result of a leader who has put in place a so-far-unstoppable political machine. Every opposition leader has been destroyed, and Venezuela seems caught in an inertia that is independent of the characters and experiences of individuals. Individually, 75 percent of the population is inclined towards freedom and democracy (based on real, expected statistics, results of the Revocatory Referendum against Chávez in 2004). Yet, as a whole, Venezuelans are driven by political passion—an emotion that involves most citizens, including Chávez followers and the opposition. One measure of bad leaders may be their capacity to stir a considerable amount of emotion in their followers and enemies at the same time—the more enemies, the worse the leader.

There are a percentage of indifferent people in Venezuela[52] (a category polls call "the Ni-Nis") who are not ravished by political passion, although some in this group may simply be tired and defeated. Nevertheless, we must allow for indifferent people who are not consumed by this political passion. Yet they cannot escape its collective effects even if they emigrate, which thousands are doing as a direct result of this regime.

Chávez has used ressentiment to accomplish an inversion on ethics. He is implementing an extensive campaign to indoctrinate and universalize the new values, "to make the revolutionary new Venezuelan," to create the utopian cooperative society mediated by the all-powerful state. Will the new values, invested by such power, substitute old values? Will those values sustain themselves in time? It may depend on the creativity of the new leaders. At some point, the negative values have to become positive or become institutional, as Weber explained regarding charismatic authority.

As a leader, Chávez has extraordinary skills. He has emotional intelligence and appeal, the capacity to make decisions, a compelling vision, fixed goals, and an ideological (communist) agenda. He avidly seeks power and has decided to take it and keep it as long as he lives. We cannot say which of these qualities constitute his charisma, but what we can say is that his leadership is charismatic according to Weber's typology.[53] It is based on his personal power. He does not obey rules, nor do bureaucracy or institutions sustain him. Some of his followers even attribute supernatural powers to him.[54] We can also say, according to the standard definition of leadership, that his charisma is the reflection of the collective emotion we have identified as ressentiment.

Chávez's message would not have found an echo in a society where private enterprise and individual effort are ranked as important values. The message of the resented leader catches or lights up when it is reflected, or finds an echo, in some population with the same emotion and similar set of values. The emotional bond with his followers, and also with his enemies, proceeds from that ressentiment that many Venezuelans have against the political elite, against the United States, and against their destiny in general. The responsibility lies as much on Chávez as on the rest of the Venezuelans, his followers and his detractors.

AFTERWORD

Finding the conditions that may arouse ressentiment into a violent battle will not stop the eternal battle or the momentous eruptions of hate and ressentiment accumulated through history, but it might give us some insight on the type of leadership behavior that sparks destructive reprisal. It helps us understand the legacy of leaders who fail to tackle the problems of those who are or feel that they are marginalized in society. Such leaders fail to assess what is too much—too much poverty, too much inequality, too much waste, and too much abuse of power and injustice. Moreover, in today's world we see how ressentiment plays itself out in the growing number of terrorists who often live under bad leaders, and/or feel slighted, left out, and ready to turn upside down the most basic moral values of human societies.

As with any emotion, collective ressentiment can subside, go into latent mode, or be superseded by some positive drive of good leadership. This is possible only if we overcome the human blindness to the limits of a people's ethical sense of fair distribution of material goods and respect for others' spiritual goals. It is important to realize that the problem of ressentiment is not Venezuela's or the Muslim world's or that of any one group. It is potentially a global problem, which not only comes as a backlash of history (so it cannot be helped) but also as a result of ongoing inequality and injustice at home and in the world.[55] There is a joint responsibility between those who resent and the resented. In this sense we should heed Naipaul and see not only our resented face but also the mirrored image of the industrial world. Only then we can find the answer to the Toflers' questions:

> When should we forget old rancours? When do sons get free from the sins of their parents? When is the right moment to stop worrying about the past and put us to think about the future?[56]

NOTES

1. In the Biblical Books of Revelation and Daniel, "the Beast" is a monster with seven heads and ten horns that arises from "the Abyss" or the sea and brings destruction. One of the heads of such a beast has been understood as the Antichrist, which is linked, usually, to the number 666. In some contexts the term refers to the physical universe (Kabbalah) or universal love (Adventists). In political thought it has mostly been understood, starting from Hobbes's Leviathan, as absolute, destructive power.

2. Although Chávez actually got into power by democratic elections, his first try was through a coup that failed on February 4, 1992.

3. Max Scheler, *Ressentiment* (Milwaukee, WI: Marquette University Press, 2003), 21. In Spanish, though, the word "resentimiento" usually has the same connotation as the French word. The meaning of the English word "resentment" comes from the French. It describes aggrieved feelings of insult, injury, or ill treatment towards something or someone that people tend to hold on to over time.

4. Federico Nietzsche, *Obras Completas, Mas Alla del Bien y del Mal* (Buenos Aires: Ediciones Aguilar, 1951), I:2.

5. Ibid., I:1–10.

6. Ibid., I:283.

7. Ibid., I:10.

8. Ibid.

9. Ibid., I:7.

10. The refutation of English psychologists' theories on the origins of morals seems to be one main purpose of the *Genealogy of Morals*. In the prologue, Nietzsche recognizes as a motive to publish his ideas on the origin of morals the reading of Dr. Paul Rée's book *The Origin of the Moral Feelings* and the impulse to deny it "statement by statement, conclusion by conclusion."

11. Ibid., III:15.

12. Scheler, *Ressentiment,* 24.

13. Ibid., 25.

14. Ibid.

15. Ibid., 36.

16. Ibid., 28.

17. Ibid., 43–47.

18. Ibid., 43.

19. Gregorio Marañón, *Tiberio, Historia de un Resentimiento* (Madrid: Espasa-Calpe, S.A., 1959), 25.

20. Ibid., 26.

21. Ibid., 26–27.

22. Ibid., 27-28.

23. Ibid., 23.

24. William Shakespeare, *The Tudor Edition of the Complete Works* (London and Glasgow: Collins, 1951), I:3, 36–47.

25. Ibid., 1:3, 101–124.

26. Ibid., 4:2, 71–72.

27. Ibid., 2:1, 13–19.

28. Ibid., 2:3.

29. Ibid., 5:3.

30. Ayn Rand, *Atlas Shrugged* (New York: A Signet Book, 1996), 814.

31. Honoré de Balzac, *La Cousine Bette* (Paris: Le livre de Poche Librairie Générale Francaise, 1972), 41.

32. Ibid., 42.

33. Ibid., 43.

34. Ibid., 42.

35. V. S. Naipaul, *Guerrillas* (London, Great Britain: Penguin Book, 1980), 50.

36. Ibid., 30.

37. Ibid.

38. Ibid., 28.

39. Ibid.

40. Max Weber, *Economy and Society,* trans. and ed. Guenther Roth and Claus Wittich (New York: Bedminster Press, 1968), 193–203.

41. Quoted by Fidel Castro in http://www.granma.cubaweb.cu/secciones/visitas/venezuela/art12.html

42. Humboldt had characterized Venezuelans, back in the nineteenth century, as of "good disposition." Before Chávez we used to say that Venezuelans are "buena nota," meaning, I believe, people who do not confront but include.

43. Small patches of ground.

44. Presidents Rómulo Betancourt (1959–1963) and Raúl Leoni (1964–1968) unleashed a determined war on guerrilla until their extinction. By the end of Leoni's administration the main leaders were dead or ready to surrender.

45. In 1968, the VIII Plenary of the Communist Party decided to abandon armed fight and concur to elections at the end of that year. The president elected, Rafael Caldera issued the policy of "pacification" and legalized all leftist parties.

46. UN. 2005: *The Millenium Development Goals: A Latin American and Caribbean Perspective*. Available at www.eclac.cl/publicaciones/xml/0/21540/lcg2331.pdf

47. Ibid., 19.

48. Ibid., 29.

49. I contributed to that collective feeling of rejection of the political party system by producing a dictionary of corruption in Venezuela from 1959 to 1993 in several volumes.

50. In his usual long speech on Friday, September 14, 2007, broadcast on government controlled media, he finally said he is the reincarnation of Bolívar. He had previously said he was the reincarnation of Maisanta and Zamora, and that he was inspired by Bolívar, but had not dared to get that far.

51. Some followers of Chávez tore down and vandalized the statue of Cristóbal Colón in Caracas as a symbol of colonialism.

52. Recent polls show that up to 48 percent of the sample's population define themselves as "Ni-Ni, even if many in that category express they are against the reform of the Constitution sought by Chávez."

53. Gladys Villarroel and Nelson Ledesma, "Carisma y Politica," *Politeia* 39, no. 30 (2007).

54. Weber, *Economy and Society*, 193–204.

55. http://ontology.buffalo.edu/smith//courses01/rrtw/Postrel.htm; http://www.racematters.org/muslimrootsofresentment.htm; Stephen Smith and Sandy Tolan, *Muslim Roots of Resentment*; http://americanradioworks.publicradio.org/features/resentment/

56. Alvin Toffler and Heidi Toffler. "La reparación y la historia," *La Nación*, September 27, 2004. Available at http://www.lanacion.com.ar/opinion/nota.asp?nota_id=639818

PART III

HOW PHILOSOPHY SHEDS LIGHT ON LEADERSHIP

6

Understanding Leadership: Is It Time for a Linguistic Turn?

ANTONIO MARTURANO

Leadership studies is an established area in the field of organization studies, but its roots date back to the earlier philosophical Greek thought. Plato is seen as one of the forerunners of leadership studies.[1] Leadership was a philosophical topic for Aristotle, St. Thomas Aquinas, Niccoló Machiavelli, Thomas Hobbes, David Hume, and Immanuel Kant, just to mention a few philosophers. They all talked about the important qualities that a great "man" should possess, and they sought to understand the ideal nature of the leader-followers relation. As a philosophical endeavor, the study of leadership was entrapped in the political debate of the times. Indeed, all the authors mentioned above focused on very fundamental problems such as democracy, rights, and ways to shape a just government.

Despite its roots, leadership scholars today rarely pay attention to contemporary philosophy. Contemporary philosophy, especially its analytical side, provides a new set of tools and concepts, especially in philosophy of language and philosophy of logic, which were unavailable before. Leadership studies have not attempted to use formal analytical methods from philosophical logic, philosophy of language and semiotics, and modern epistemology to analyze leadership.

This failure of leadership scholars to reflect on the epistemological foundations of leadership studies lies behind the disagreement that they have about the definition of leadership. Leadership studies are largely based on work in psychology. Using arguments from the history of modern philosophy and philosophy of logic, I will argue that psychology does not provide a strong or, for that matter, a weak epistemological basis for leadership studies. As a consequence, I advocate for a linguistic turn in leadership studies because in the end, what is it that leaders do if they do not use, change, manipulate, and create new meanings? I will analyze leadership as a linguistic phenomenon using tools from the philosophy of language, semiotics, analytic and postanalytic philosophy, and logic. My focus will be on the linguistic phenomenon that is at the basis of leadership creation and its recognition by the followers. Finally, I will propose a new language-based way to look at the leadership that is based on the works of the Italian semiotician Umberto Eco.

EPISTEMOLOGY AND LEADERSHIP STUDIES

According to several authors, the state of leadership studies appears to be quite fragmented, and more and more scholars are unsatisfied with the predominance of social science perspective in this field.[2] Indeed, according to philosopher Joanne B. Ciulla, "Most of the leadership literature comes from business schools and researchers with backgrounds in organizational behavior and social and industrial psychology."[3] Psychology is the dominant paradigm in leadership studies and de facto provides a foundation for leadership studies.

I would suggest that such fragmentation in leadership studies is a result of the failure of scholars to discuss its foundations. In this respect, as a branch of human inquiry, leadership studies are in the same place that philosophy was at the dawn of the twentieth century. Philosophers at that time were concerned about the future of philosophy, because it appeared that psychology might be able to provide all of the answers to questions about human knowledge. In particular, there was a heated debate about the validity of logical truths. Some authors, notably the English philosopher John Stuart Mill, held the view that logical and mathematical truths were truths about psychology. So, for example, numbers might be equated with a person's mental images, and truths of mathematics might be equated with laws of human thought. On the contrary, some other authors, notably the German philosopher Gottlob Frege, believed that logic prescribed laws about how people *should* think (*normative level*) and was not the science of how people *do* think (*descriptive level*).[4] Logical truths would remain true even if no one believed them nor used them in their reasoning. If humans were genetically designed to think using the rules of logic, would that not make their thinking logically valid? According to Frege, what is true or false, valid or invalid, does not depend on one's psychology or beliefs. To think otherwise is to confuse something's being true with something's being-taken-to-be-true. Numbers cannot be equated with mental images nor can the truths of mathematics be equated with psychological truths. Mathematical and logical truths are objective, not subjective and, more importantly, psychology cannot provide a foundation for mathematics, logic, or even human knowledge.

In a similar way, one of the often-repeated refrains of some leadership scholars is that leadership is "in the mind and the heart" of followers and leaders rather than an intersubjective (albeit historical) process. I suspect that this view comes from research that focuses on the motivations behind leadership rather than research on the basic mechanisms of leadership. Here I argue that if we just look at psychological processes as the foundation of leadership, it is not possible to come to an agreement on the nature of leadership. That is why we need another way to explain it, which, like other contingency theories, takes into account psychological factors as well as environmental and historical factors.

We use language (which should be understood as a system of signs and rules to manipulate them) to communicate more than knowledge and emotions. It is the most important tool that a leader uses to interact with her followers.[5] Language provides an intersubjective tool that is more helpful than psychology to understand the machinery of leadership. In the following section I will begin a linguistic analysis of leadership. That is the basic mechanism people use to recognize someone as a leader and therefore establish a leadership process.

REFERENTIAL OPACITY AND LEADERSHIP

A number of leadership scholars have discussed the problems with the definition of leadership. For example, Joseph Rost has argued that leadership scholars need to agree on a common definition of leadership, whereas philosopher Joanne B. Ciulla argues that disagreements about definitions are not about the denotation of the term, but rather its connotation.[6] Philosophers of language offer insights into the logic of how we use the term to designate a wide range of people in a variety of contexts and circumstances as leaders.

Different names or words may be used to refer to the same thing and can be freely substituted for each other. Hence, in a true statement of identity, one of its two terms may be substituted for the other and the result will be true. This is called the rule of substitutivity or the principle of identity of indiscernibles or Leibniz's Law.[7] The philosopher Gottfried Wilhelm Leibniz argued that for A and B to be identical they had to share all of the same properties. If A and B have *different* properties, then they cannot be the same thing. If we find some property that B has but A does not, then we can conclude that A and B are not the same thing.

For example, the sentences

(1) Silvio Berlusconi is the owner of Mediaset
(2) Silvio Berlusconi is a known supporter of Milan FC (football club)

are true. We can substitute in the sentence (2) "Silvio Berlusconi" with "the owner of Mediaset" and we will still have a true sentence. This is called "referential transparency." [8] On the contrary, when the subject of the sentence (Berlusconi) follows a mental state verb or what is called a *propositional attitude*[9] such as "it is thought that," "it is believed that," or "it is known that," we cannot tell if it is true that the owner of Mediaset is the same person as the supporter of Milan FC. This is called *referential opacity* or *opaque context* because it is not clear that both sentences are true and refer to the same person.

Now, let us consider the following sound argument:

(A) The Italian prime minister is the owner of Mediaset
(B) The owner of Mediaset is a successful leader
(C) The Italian prime minister is a successful leader

The fact that the third sentence (C) follows from (A) and (B) is due to a certain property of the identity relation, that is Leibniz's Law, or the law of substitution of identicals. This law asserts that if two things are identical, meaning if they share each and all their properties, we are allowed to freely substitute them in a sentence. In statement (A) we can substitute (at least in 2006) the expression "The Italian prime minister" with "The owner of Mediaset." Therefore the property of "being a successful leader" belonging to "The owner of Mediaset" can also be attributed to "The Italian prime minister" according to Leibniz's Law.

Sentences (B) and (C) are implicit attributions of propositional attitude. Their utterance implies the belief (in followers and others) that the owner of Mediaset is a successful leader. Thus a propositional attitude is implied in sentences (B) and (C). To make it a genuine attribution of propositional attitude, we should restate the sentence thus:

(B*) Tony believes that the owner of Mediaset is a successful leader

Let us take this up in the following argument, wherein we make exactly the same claim as the first premise and use the same structure of reasoning but, now that we recognize the implicit propositional attitude, the result turns out to be the opposite.[10] Since it is possible for the premises to both be true and the conclusion false, the argument is fallacious or is invalid:

(D) The Italian prime minister is the owner of Mediaset
(E) Tony believes that the Italian prime minister is a successful leader
(F) Tony believes that the owner of Mediaset is a successful leader

In order to make the above argument valid we have to add another premise, which follows:

(G) Tony believes that (D) The Italian prime minister is the owner of Mediaset

The structure of this reasoning is the same, because a property belonging to "the Italian prime minister" is the property of being-believed-to-be-a-successful-leader-by-Tony. According to Leibniz's Law, such a property should also belong to the owner of Mediaset. But (without G) Tony would not understand such an identity, namely the owner of Mediaset is the same person as the Italian prime minister (that is Mr. Berlusconi). This is exactly what is called *referential opacity*. This example shows that something intrinsic to logic must have changed when we went from sentences stating X is Y to propositional attitude Tony believes that X is Y. When we recognize (B) as a propositional attitude, which we do in (E), we are obliged to recognize (F) and (G) as attributions of belief too. When we add epistemic operators such as "belief" to standard logic, we get puzzling cases that seem to violate Leibniz's Law. Consider the following sentences:

(H) Tony believes that the Italian prime minister is a successful leader
(I) Tony believes that the owner of Mediaset is not a successful leader

They could both be true. Let us imagine that Tony is not able to understand that "the Italian prime minister" and "owner of Mediaset" are referring to the same person, yet both sentences could still be true. There is nothing unsound in recognizing these two sentences as true, that is believing (E)—that Mr. Berlusconi the politician is a successful leader—is not incompatible with believing (F)—believing Mr. Berlusconi is an unsuccessful business leader, or vice versa. But even if Tony knows that Mr. Berlusconi is actually both the Italian prime minister and the owner of Mediaset, he may still make these utterances without committing a logical contradiction because he is using "successful leader" in two different *senses* attached to two different beliefs about "being a leader" in business and in politics. In the first case "Italian prime minister" has a different *sense* than "owner of Mediaset," even if we employ "successful leader" in the same sense. In the second case, "successful leader" is employed with two different senses.

Propositional attitudes are relational. The truth of a belief statement is based on what one believes, and not on whether someone or something has a certain property. In other words, the truth of the statement "Tony believes that Mr. Berlusconi is charismatic" is based on whether Tony actually does believe that Mr. Berlusconi is charismatic and not on whether Mr. Berlusconi actually has the property of charisma. This is true even though natural language sometimes masks this fundamental difference.

The concept of leadership, which we assume to be dependent upon a contingent framework, is now clarified. We use the word "leader" to refer to a set of beliefs and values in a speaker or a set of speakers. For example, Hitler was indisputably a leader because of his position and because he came to embody the values, norms, and beliefs of a majority of the German community in Germany at his time. Embodying values (and eventually manipulating them) in a particular community is *conditio sine qua non* for a leader to gain supremacy and power. According to the French postmodern critical scholar Michel Foucault, "power is in the system ... it is embedded in social relations and institutions."[11] Indeed, characteristics of "leaderness" are different in each community because different values, norms, and beliefs are embedded in social relations and institutions from which power is nourished.[12]

In leadership studies, scholars may assess Hitler's leadership by, for example, evaluating his effectiveness and/or morality. This is a metanarrative, free from the set of the values, norms, and beliefs (in a sense similar to Weber's notion of *Wertfrei* or value-free), which actually made Hitler seem "leaderful" to the German people when he was alive.

LANGUAGE AND CULTURE

Furthermore, a linguistic approach can explain the limits of some leadership scholarship on culture. For example, in the article "Culture Specific and Cross-Culturally Generalizable Implicit Leadership Theories: Are Attributes of Charismatic/Transformational Leadership Universally Endorsed?" Deanne Den Hartog et al. claim that "specific aspects of charismatic/transformational leadership are strongly and universally endorsed across the cultures."[13] The authors claim that such attributes are "universally seen as contributing to outstanding leadership."[14] They refer to a set of abstract traits but do not tell us anything about the meanings that these traits have in different cultures and language practices. A more abstract definition can always be found starting with the different cultural aspects of a concept. For example, the concept of *quiet leadership* can be understood in different ways. Lao Tzu expresses the Chinese sense of quiet leadership in the following sentence:

> As for the best leaders, the people do not notice their existence. The next best, the people honor and praise. The next, the people fear; and the next, the people hate ... When the best leader's work is done the people say, "We did it ourselves!"[15]

In Western culture, a quiet leader can be best described as *eminence grise* or a person who exercises power or influence in certain areas without holding an official position. The term *eminence grise* originally referred to François Leclerc du Tremblay, the right-hand man of the infamous Cardinal Richelieu, who was King Louis XIII's chief minister. These are two different instances of quiet leadership that cannot be collapsed within a general label of quiet leadership, without getting lost in the real, living meaning that it has in particular societies.

Indeed, a very abstract definition of quiet leadership will still be able to unify different cultural meanings of the word by means of a semantic ascension, which would mean talking *about* language and general concepts instead of talking of *how* words are actually used. This sort of definition cannot take into account that real, living meaning of the different cultural aspects. For example, the fact that a leader needs to be recognized as such by his or her followers would be understood as an element of leadership shared by every culture. But it fails to address the particular differences that each culture uses to individuate a leader or to provide a meaning for her leadership. Den Hartog et al., in other words, confuse a metalinguistic abstraction where we talk *about* the term "quiet leadership" with the relative way in which each culture addresses quiet leadership over time. Den Hartog and her colleagues claim that there are universal traits that explain leadership at the level of a meta-language; however, the way that a culture recognizes and identifies a leader can only be explained at the level of an object language in relation to a set of beliefs, norms, and values. Den Hartog and colleagues simply confuse these two different levels.

It is important to note that "traits" (interpreted as propositional attitudes) attributed to leaders have, so to speak, a *psychologically independent* status. They have *meaning* (sense plus reference) only in the linguistic practice of a particular community and therefore are not rooted in someone's actual psychology. Moreover, trait theory is often viewed as an alternative to style theory (authoritarian, facilitative, etc.), but in this analysis I have shown that they are not really alternatives in that neither deals with the relational nature of leadership. Like traits, styles are defined by the beliefs of community members.

In other words, styles like "authoritarian" are not pure perceptions. Rather it is, according to the philosopher Charles Sanders Peirce, a *percept,* that is a perceptual (social) construction.[16] When someone is talking about "authoritarianism," it does not entail that she has, so to speak, seen it. Surely, she has an image of authoritarianism, but her asserting that something has the attribute of being "authoritarian" is a judgment that is a propositional attitude. In an analogous way, according to Umberto Eco, the very fact that soldiers on different occasions perform a regular action every time the order "at ease!" is uttered implies that such a behavior is embedded in a concept and it turns into an abstraction, or a law, or a regularity.[17] In analogy with the soldiers' behavior, someone's behavior comes to have embedded in it the quality of being authoritarian. In other words, the sentence "the Leader X has an authoritarian style" denotes a prescription to followers about how they should perform symbolically to obtain a perceptive contact with the object of the word, namely the leader.[18] A symbol's meaning is all the classes of actions aimed at causing some perceived effects.

By producing a series of immediate feedbacks, a sign establishes a habit, which is a tendency to behave likewise in future similar circumstances. According to Peirce, we turn the correspondence between a sign and its representation into a law. Understanding a sign implies learning what is needed in order to produce a concrete state of affairs (such as what soldiers do when they hear the order "at ease!").[19]

Thus, in this sense, styles and trait theories are not alternatives—they are both forms of attribution of propositional attitudes. We have shown how a very important part of leadership language works. It arises from the beliefs and values of people in all communities, and the beliefs and values are expressed as propositional attitudes.

LEADERSHIP, LINGUISTIC PRACTICES, AND PSYCHOLOGISM IN SOCIAL SCIENCES

The concept of leadership in our perspective appears to be an instance of referential opacity because linguistic practices we use to talk about leadership are imbued with propositional attitudes. We have seen that it is not possible to have a well-grounded concept of "leader" in the abstract. The concept of leader depends on a relationship between the players (namely, followers and leaders).[20] These relationships can be viewed as ascriptions of propositional attitudes, in particular as sentences about beliefs. Followers ascribe or believe that leaders have certain attributes or capacities.[21] The mutual acknowledgment of such qualities is created through particular language practices. Leaders do not really have characteristics such as charisma; people only believe that they do. Such traits are ascriptions of propositional attitudes. We do not know whether or not such mental objects (that is propositional attitudes) have any foundation outside our minds. In other words, the words we use to describe a particular leader are just names that refer to groups or classes of individual things.[22] In this way we can bypass psychological assumptions about the nature of those traits. Traits are representations that have meaning only in a particular social context, and only as attributions within propositional attitudes.

The full understanding of a trait's meaning is linked to social conventions (namely, values and beliefs) used in that believer's community. As the Austrian philosopher Ludwig Wittgenstein pointed out in his critique of private language, semantic characteristics of a language, such as definitions, are *public* characteristics.[23] This is different from a private language in which one makes up names for his or her sensations and other subjective experiences. The individual who speaks a private language determines the meaning of the term (i.e., a particular trait).[24] Such a language is accessible only to that person and no one else. Because the primary characteristic of a language is to be understandable to anyone in order to communicate something, her language is inaccessible or it is meaningless because it is not linked to any social construction. Using an often-repeated philosophical slogan, the meaning of a word comes from its use, not the meaning in an individual's mind. The meaning of words in any language has to be public to be understood.

Let us now turn our attention to the so-called situational analysis of leadership.[25,26] According to philosopher of science and social scientist Karl Popper, social sciences rely on building models to explain certain kinds of events (such as "Why is unemployment in the construction industry a seasonal trend?").[27] These events are built on the empirical conditions of the event (i.e., the weather, unemployment statistics, or the nature of the construction industry). If we want the models to be representations of how the elements in the models interact, we also need universal laws (analogous to Newton's laws of motion in natural sciences). How are leadership models usually applied to the real world? They usually use general "laws" from individual and group psychology. This is what Popper calls *psychologism.*[28] Situational theories replace concrete psychological experiences with abstract situations that are supposed to trigger certain kinds of behavior in people. Popper argues that the only triggering principle in human behavior is *the principle of rationality.* The principle of rationality states that a person's actions are always "adequate" or "appropriate," that is, "in accordance with the situation."[29] This principle is not subject to any kind of scientific control. In other words, Popper thinks that psychology does not think that people are smart enough to avoid behaving in ways that are more or less predictable to those who are aware of all the relevant parameters of the situation. Such a claim, equivalent in content to Popper's rationality principle, may be described as an "empirical conjecture."[30]

AN ALTERNATIVE LENS ON LEADERSHIP

I will sketch now an alternative way to study leadership based on language. We will start with an analogy between a leader and a "work of art."[31] There is no agreement on the definition of a leader; but everybody seems to agree with what we can call Drucker's *minimal definition of leadership:* "a leader is someone who has followers." [32] This is an interesting statement albeit an ambiguous one. Drucker's statement can be understood in two ways: "a leader is someone who has *actual* followers" or "a leader is someone who *potentially* has followers." If the first hypothesis holds, someone is a leader when de facto he or she has followers. Retroactive leadership cannot count as true leadership. Vincent Van Gogh, the Flemish painter, cannot be called a leader because during his life he did not have followers. He had followers only after he died. In my opinion, this idea is too restrictive and might allow room only for a sociological exploration of leadership.

Let us turn our interest to the second way in which I tried to understand Drucker's statement. In this case, we can certainly list Van Gogh as a leader because he had "potential" followers who become actual followers after his death. But, before analyzing this conjecture, I will first need to refer to the idea of "work of art" and how Eco analyzed this idea in semiotics. I will compare leadership to aesthetics and, in particular, to the contemporary study in textual theories. Textual theories are interesting methodologies for analyzing texts. A "text" is any message preserved in a form whose existence is independent of both sender and receiver, like a book or a painting. Leadership studies shares with textual theories the impossibility of describing the subject matter of their discipline. "What is a work of art?" is analogous to the question "What is a leader?" What makes P. Manzoni's "Artist's Shit"[33] and Leo Tolstoy's *War and Peace* "works of art"? What makes Nelson Mandela and Pol Pot leaders? It is difficult to find a reasonable answer, unless we rely on our previous analysis of opaque contexts. We call something "leadership" or a "work of art" based on the values, norms, beliefs, and needs of followers or readers.

In this very sense we can understand that both disciplines share the idea that a work of art and leadership *presupposes* the existence of readers and followers.[34] A work of art and leadership also presuppose a "potential" reader or follower (or, as Eco[35] calls it, a "model reader"—by analogy we will call it a "model follower"). Leadership, indeed, is also a chain of expressive devices that need to be actualized by some receivers called followers, but leadership (according to our analogy) is, so to speak, an "incomplete text." By analogy with Eco's reconstruction of a text,[36] we can say that any expression in the text called "leadership" remains just mere words without significance until it is related to (according to a particular code) its conventional contents. Such conventional content can be found in an ideal encyclopedia —or set of all the meanings associated with the same concept—which includes anything publicly known in a particular community (i.e., "man" is a male, a human; but it also will have bodily, psychological, social, and literary characteristics).[37] Dictionaries are those repertoires including all the properties—or definitions—of terms in a particular language. In other words, a follower is able to give meaning to attribution of propositional attitudes such as "charisma" or "authoritarian" to leaders by relating those terms to a preexisting (public) understanding encoded in a dictionary. According to Eco, a model follower is able to "unfold" a dictionary every time she comes across traits and styles (that we reduced to attributions of propositional attitudes). For example, when she comes across charisma and authoritarianism, she must relate them to a preexisting series of rules that allow her to understand the function of those traits and styles in a particular leadership context.

In this very sense, Eco argues, a dictionary sets up the rules we use for the meanings of words in a language (how to use "authoritarian" in an appropriate way), and the encyclopedia will show us all the known occurrences of "authoritarian" in a culture (in history, in politics, in movies, in theatrical plays, and even in jokes). A follower will understand the characteristics of a leader when she finds them based on a dictionary and an encyclopedia. In fact, in order for a follower to decode the system of meanings a leader is embodying, she needs not only a linguistic competence but also a capacity to manage anything about her culture that enables her to trigger a series of presuppositions, repressing idiosyncrasies, etc.[38]

This explains why in our previous analysis about propositional attitudes, the same follower can understand someone as a leader in one place but not in another, or two persons can disagree about a person's leadership and how leadership's characteristics are situation and culture dependent. The leadership process is a sort of "textual cooperation" between a leader and followers. Such cooperation should be based on a leader's "structure," that is, her traits *plus* behaviors that we have previously reduced to meanings. These meanings must be decoded by followers (starting with their dictionary and encyclopedia), and then used (through propositional attitudes) to recognize her as a leader.

CONCLUSION

I will not take this attempt to analyze leadership further, as it is a work in progress. According to my reconstruction, leadership is a product in which its effectiveness should be part of its own very generative mechanism or leadership generates itself. Producing leadership means actualizing strategies that include the followers' strategies. Leadership strategy—according to our analogy with a work of art—is not leader-centric. On the contrary, it is follower-centric. The main activity of the leader is to make followers flourish—so to speak. In a sense, leaders have to give followers the latitude to add meaning to their leadership (we can see here the role of ethics in this model). This captures some of Burns' theory of *transforming leadership*.[39]

Leaders and followers help to create competencies in each other. What a leader expects in a model follower (that is, as we saw at the beginning, a potential follower) is someone who will be a partner in constructively shaping the meaning of leadership.

NOTES

1. Plato, *The Republic*. Available at http://classics.mit.edu/Plato/republic.html (see especially chap. XVIII and following).

2. See, for example, J. B. Ciulla, who claims that "Leadership, unlike physics, is about human behavior, which does not lend itself to deductions from a theoretical system," quoted in J. T. Wren, "A Quest for a Grand Theory of Leadership," in *The Quest for a General Theory of Leadership,* ed. G. R. Goethals and L. J. Sorensen (Northampton, MA: Edward Elgar, 2006), 1.

3. See J. B. Ciulla, "What We Learned Along the Way: A Commentary," in *The Quest for a General Theory of Leadership,* ed. Goethals and Sorensen, 221.

4. It is worth noting that most leadership theories express the same ambiguity as representation of logic theories within a psychological framework. In other words, most leadership theories are ambiguously normative and descriptive or they do not explicitly say whether they are theories about how leadership *is* or about how leadership *should be.*

5. B. Russell, *Human Knowledge: Its Scope and Limits* (London: George Allen and Unwin, 1948), chap. 1.

6. See J. Rost, *Leadership in the Twenty-First Century* (New York: Praeger, 1991); and J. B. Ciulla, "Leadership Ethics: Mapping the Territory," *The Business Ethics Quarterly* 5, no. 1 (1995): 5–28.

7. Leibniz's Law says that if A and B are one and the same thing, then they have to share all the same properties. If A and B have *different* properties, then they cannot be one and the same thing. If we find some property that B has but A does not, then we can conclude that A and B are not the same thing.

8. W. V. A. Quine, *Word and Object* (Cambridge, MA: MIT Press, 1960), 142n.

9. Most propositional attitude attributions use a propositional attitude verb that is followed by a *that* clause, a clause that includes a full sentence expressing a proposition. Attributions of cognitive relations to propositions can also take other kinds of clauses though: *Beckham wanted to play* or *Hillary wished Bill to succeed,* for example. These still attribute propositional attitudes, cognitive relations to an identifiable proposition (*Beckham will play, Bill will succeed*), though the proposition is not so directly expressed. The weakened form of the sentence, although apparently more active, disguises the presence of a propositional attitude, as in *Hillary wished that Bill would succeed.*

10. In logic, this is called a *hypothetical syllogism,* that is, a valid argument of the following form:

> If P then Q.
> If Q then R.
> Therefore, if P then R.

In other words, this kind of argument states that if one implies another and that other implies a third, then the first implies the third.

11. Quoted in Wren, "A Quest for a Grand Theory of Leadership," 17.

12. R. C. Tucker, "The Theory of Charismatic Leadership," in *Philosophers and Kings: Studies in Leadership*, ed. D. A. Bastow (New York: Braziller, 1970), 69–94.

13. D. N. Den Hartog, S. A. House, S. A. Hanges, S. A. Ruiz-Quintanilla, and P. W. Dorfman, "Culture Specific and Cross-Culturally Generalizable Implicit Leadership Theories: Are Attributes of Charismatic/Transformational Leadership Universally Endorsed?" *Leadership Quarterly* 10, no. 2 (1999): 219–256.

14. Ibid.

15. Lao Tzu, *Tao Te Ching*, quoted in D. McIlroy, *The Pragmatic Leader. A Guide to Mastering Key Management Concepts* (Lincoln, NE: iUniverse, 2004), 71.

16. C. S. Peirce, *Collected Papers* (Cambridge, MA: Harvard University Press, 1931), §2.141.

17. U. Eco, *Lector in Fabula: La Cooperazione Interpretativa nei Testi Narrativi* (Milano: Bompiani, 1979), 42.

18. Peirce, *Collected Papers*, §2.330,

19. Ibid., §5.491

20. We will see below that leadership even presupposes the existence of followers.

21. Ascriptions of propositional attitudes should be not confused with attributions in the sense of attribution theory. Ascribing a person a particular trait means that someone believes that someone else has a particular property. Attribution theory, on the contrary, is a theory about how people explain things. When we offer explanations about why things happened, we can give one of two types. One, we can make an external attribution. Two, we can make internal attribution. An external attribution (get ready for this) assigns causality to an outside agent or force. Or as kids would say, "The devil made me do it." An external attribution claims that some outside thing motivated the event. By contrast, an internal attribution assigns causality to factors within the person. Or as the sinner would say, "I am guilty, grant me forgiveness." An internal attribution claims that the person was directly responsible for the event.

22. I am proposing here a nominalistic or a nominalistic-conceptualistic idea of leadership. Nominalism is the philosophic position that abstract or general terms, "universals," are not real entities either in the world or in the mind, but names that refer to groups or classes of individual things. These terms are canonically used to designate the theories that have been proposed as solutions of one of the most important questions in philosophy, often referred to as the problem of universals, which, while it was a favorite subject for discussion in ancient times, and especially in the Middle Ages, is still prominent in modern and contemporary philosophy.

23. L. Wittgenstein, *Philosophische Untersuchungen* (Oxford: Blackwell, 1953).

24. "The words of this language are to refer to what can be known only to the speaker; to his immediate, private, sensations. So another cannot understand the language." Ibid., §243.

25. F. E. Fiedler, *A Theory of Leadership Effectiveness* (New York: McGraw-Hill, 1967).

26. P. Hersey and K. H. Blanchard, *Management of Organization Behavior: Utilizing Human Resources*, 4th ed. (Englewood Cliffs, NJ: Prentice-Hall, 1977).

27. K. R. Popper, "Models, Instruments and Truth. The Status of the Rationality Principle in the Social Sciences," in K. R. Popper, *The Myth of the Framework. In Defence of the Science and Rationality*, ed. M. A. Notturno (New York: Routledge, 1994), chap. VIII.

28. Popper was strongly critical of psychologism; see his criticism in his *Logic of Scientific Discovery* (§2 and §25). In particular, Popper believed that no scientific theory can be justified using experience (epistemological antipsychologism). K. R. Popper, *Logic of Scientific Discovery* (London: Hutchinson, 1959).

29. Popper, "Models, Instruments and Truth," 169.

30. M. Lagueux claims that "It is the epistemological cost of such a move that Popper attempted to reduce in his paper by discussing its implications and by rejecting well known aprioristic and instrumentalist ways out of the problem." M. Lagueux, "Popper and the Rationality Principle." Available at http://www.univie.ac.at/karlpopper2002/abstracts/ContributedPapers/Lagueux.pdf (accessed July 5, 2007), h. 22, 30.

31. I would recommend to see it just as an "as if," that is, a structural analogy (i.e., a model) between a "work of art" and leadership. Ordinary uses of the notion of model today tend to collapse the distinction between a model and the theory about which it is a model. There is, indeed, a one-to-one correlation between the propositions of a theory and those of a model. Propositions, which are logical consequences of propositions of the theory, have correlates in the model, which are logical consequences of the correlates in the model of these latter propositions in the theory and vice versa. But the theory and the model have different epistemological structures (they are not *isomorphic*): in the model, the logically prior premises determine the meaning of the terms occurring in the representation of the calculus of the conclusions. In the theory the logically posterior consequences determine the meaning of the theoretical occurring in the representation in the calculus of the premises. American philosopher of science Richard B. Braithwaite suggests that confusing a theory with a model for it is one of the most important dangers in the use of models. R. B. Braithwaite, *Scientific Explanations* (Cambridge: Cambridge University Press, 1955), 93.

32. P. Drucker, "Managing Oneself," *Harvard Business Review* 77, no. 2 (1999): 65–74.

33. The 90 cans of "Merda d'artista" ("Artist's Shit, content 30 gr., freshly preserved, produced and tinned in May 1961") were first exhibited in the Galleria Pescetto (Albisola Marina) on August 12, 1961. Manzoni calculated the value of the 90 cans—all numbered, each with a net weight of 30 grams—in accordance with the daily exchange rates for gold. Manzoni's cans of "Artist's Shit" have some forerunners in the twentieth-century art, like Marcel Duchamp's urinal ("Fontaine," 1917) or the Surrealists' coprolalic wits. Salvador Dalì, Georges Bataille, and, first of all, Alfred Jarry's "Ubu Roi" (1896) had given artistic and literal dignity to the word "merde." The link between anality and art, as the equation of excrements with gold, is a leitmotiv of the psychoanalytic movement (and Carl G. Jung could have been a point of reference for Manzoni). Manzoni's main innovation to this topic is a reflection on the role of the artist's body in contemporary art. (See http://www.pieromanzoni.org/EN/works_shit.htm)

34. Eco, *Lector in Fabula*, 50ff.

35. Ibid.

36. Ibid., 50

37. U. Eco, *Kant e l'Ornitorinco* (Milan: Bompiani, 1997), 195.

38. Eco, *Lector in fabula*, 53.

39. J. MacGregor Burns, *Transforming Leadership* (New York: Grove Press, 2003); see 2–3 and chap. 10.

7

Why "Being There" Is Essential to Leadership

JOANNE B. CIULLA

The first and greatest imperative of command is to be present in person.
—John Keegan[1]

One of the first things Americans hear on the TV or radio news each day is where the president will be and what he will be doing. In England, you can tell when the queen is staying in her castle if her flag is flying over it. People like to know where their leaders are, and that information is readily available to the public. In an era of video conferencing and satellite feeds, leaders can be seen and heard anywhere at anytime in the virtual world. Nonetheless, the presence of a leader on TV is sometimes not good enough. There are times when it is crucial for leaders to physically be in the right place, at the right time, doing the right sort of thing. This is especially the case when there is a disaster or crisis. Leaders who fail to understand the importance of "being there" in a crisis usually face public condemnation. When something bad happens, people want to know where their leaders are and what they are doing. This is about more than symbolic gestures or a sense of timing. Leaders have a moral obligation *to be there* for us because it is their job and it is part of what the job of leaders means to followers. This chapter examines how place and time are embedded in what it means to be a leader and the moral expectations of leadership.[2]

ON METHOD

The idea that leaders need to be at the right place at the right time is not particularly profound. It is almost a cliché. While from a common sense point of view, the statement "leaders who are not in the right place at the right time risk condemnation" seems true, a leadership scholar from the social sciences would ask, "What evidence do we have that this is indeed true?" A social psychologist might create an experiment that tests how people react when a leader is or is not present in various scenarios, whereas a political scientist might collect data from polls and news articles on public reactions to leaders who did not show up at important events. Social scientists can tell us whether the statement is true and under what conditions it is true, but they do not tend to focus on questions such as "What does this expectation mean?" "Where did it come from in human history?" In leadership studies, the social sciences have gone a long way to describe and explain leadership, but they only scratch the surface of understanding; to dig deeper, we must turn to the humanities.[3]

The goal of this chapter is to explore why followers expect leaders to be at a certain place at a certain time. My goal is to understand what this means in relation to how we think about leadership. To do this I will draw from history, the classics, literature, and philosophy. One might call my approach hermeneutic. Hermeneutics is the art of interpreting texts and language. Theologian Friedrich Schleiermacher and historian Wilhelm Dilthey characterize "hermeneutics" as a theory of knowledge for scholars who study "culture, rituals, images, examples of the useful arts—in short, for such products as are the result of man's deliberate ingenuity rather than of nature's blind working."[4] The idea of leaders and leadership clearly falls into this category. As the philosopher Hans-Georg Gadamer notes, the hermeneutic approach allows one to discover the meaning of a part in the context of the whole.[5] In what is called "the hermeneutic circle," a scholar goes back and forth between interpretations of meaning that are explicit and implicit in the phenomenon under investigation.

In this chapter we will begin by looking at the container for "being there"—the normative aspects of time and space in general and in a particular piece of literature. We go on to examine a historical vignette about the Roman Emperor of Nero and what it came to mean to us in the present. Then we consider a contemporary case involving the former Russian President Vladimir Putin and use philosopher Martin Heidegger's work on time and care to pull together our analysis of why being there at the right time is morally important for leaders.

SOME GENERAL OBSERVATIONS ON THE HISTORY AND THE MEANING OF TIME

Time marks the space between birth and death in which we live our lives. In the past, events were the measure of time. For example, in Madagascar, one-half hour was measured by the time it took to cook rice. The time it took to fry a locust measured a moment. In Chile, it took one Ave Maria to cook an egg and an earthquake could last two credos.[6] In the early days of Christianity, the Catholic Church gave a moral sense to time because it said that time belonged to God. Sloth was not, as people think today, the sin of not working. It was the sin of not caring. Sloth was considered a sin because God, having given us the gift of time, wanted us to pay attention to what we do in it and to enthusiastically attend to the things that we do in the time we have.[7]

Agrarian societies chart time by natural events, and in many cultures, people still primarily use religious events to mark the passing of time. Today, time measures events rather than events measuring time. We regard clocks and calendars as objective and rational ways to decide when to do things and when to go places. Even the kind of watch that a person wears portrays time differently. Traditional analog clocks allow you to see where you have been, where you are, and where you are going. The digital clock literally and figuratively depicts modernity—you only see time in the present. Clocks and calendars give us two different imperatives for action. The first imperative is based on objective measures of time: "It is June 4th hence, according to my schedule, I must go to New Orleans and be there by noon." The second is based on events that create a feeling of obligation such as, "New Orleans has been hit by a flood and people are suffering. I have an obligation to go there as soon as possible."

Even our objective concept of time is a bit of a fiction. It used to be true that a watch measured every event and synchronized watches worn by different people would agree on the time interval between two events. However, when Albert Einstein noticed that the speed of light appeared the same to every observer, no matter how fast they were moving, scientists abandoned the idea that there was a unique absolute time. Instead, according to relativity theory, observers would have different measures of time as recorded by a clock that they carried. Different observers wearing different watches would not necessarily agree.[8] This is a more personal notion of time, relative to the space that is occupied by the observer who measures it. Time then is more than the numbers used to measure it. While clocks and calendars tell us when events take place, events still define time and place for us. Most people do not remember the date when John F. Kennedy was killed or when the Challenger crashed, but they usually remember where they were and what they were doing. Events tend to mark our memories more than calendars and clocks.

WHERE YOU ARE, WHAT YOU KNOW, AND WHO YOU ARE

We cannot treat space and time as separate containers or environments of human experience because they usually bleed together. Where we are influences our moral outlook on the world. Edwin Abbott illustrates this point in the novel *Flatland*. Abbott creates a fantasy about spatiality to critique the arrogance and narrow-mindedness of colonial and Victorian morality of his day.[9] The book explores the complexities of imagining spatial and moral dimensions. In the story, a character named "A Square" sets out on a journey and discovers the epistemic limitations of living in his two-dimensional world of Flatland. Along the way, he meets up with the Sphere from Space-land, who patiently helps A Square recognize a third dimension. Once A Square begins to see in three dimensions, he wants to continue in the "divine" search of knowledge about more dimensions, but Sphere arrogantly dismisses the possibility of more than three dimensions. Eventually, A Square returns to Flatland. This part of the story is similar to Plato's allegory of the cave. When a person breaks free from looking at shadows on the cave wall, and climbs out of the cave, he too sees reality in three dimensions. Like Plato's cave man,[10] A Square will never be at home again in the two-dimensional reality and morality of Flatland. By being somewhere else, he becomes someone else. He is a square who no longer fits in with the other squares.

Flatland raises an interesting question about physical reality and our moral perceptions of the world. Does watching the two-dimensional pictures of war, floods, and famine on the news have the same moral impact as being there? How does being there enhance a leader's capacity to empathize and meet the moral expectations of his or her followers? For our purposes, how does being there at the right time alter or perhaps make a leader? For example, on 9/11 the physical presence of Rudolph Giuliani at the site of the disaster played an enormous role in the public perception of him as a leader, regardless of the quality of what he did at the time or before it. In other words, in times of crisis, being there in body, heart, and mind may be as important or more important than what a leader actually does at the time.

DID NERO FIDDLE WHILE ROME BURNED?

The significance of *where* you are, when you are there, and what you are doing is contingent on *who* you are. The meaning of a leader occupying a certain place at a certain time is unique. For example, we all know the story of Nero playing his fiddle while Rome burned. There is nothing wrong with Nero playing the fiddle on the roof of his palace; however, there is something that is not only wrong but also immoral about Nero playing the fiddle on his roof at the time in which Rome burns below. It is this point that connects space and time to the implications of Nero's identity as the leader of Rome. If Nero were an ordinary citizen who lived alone, his behavior in that place at that time would be considered odd, but not necessarily immoral. The fact that Nero is a leader makes his location at that time morally significant, because there is a sense in which we expect him to be somewhere else in Rome attending to the disaster. In this case Nero is physically looking down on Rome, but it does not appear that his heart and mind are on the fire.

The story of Nero playing his fiddle has come down to us through the ages. It is repeated in various forms by a number of ancient historians and then it shows up (as do so many things from the past) in William Shakespeare's work as well as in the work of a number of modern writers. Today we sometimes use the phrase as shorthand to describe a leader who is self-centered, inattentive, and irresponsible, and who fails to look after something that is important—"She is like Nero who played the violin while Rome burned." To fully understand the significance of this story for our understanding of leadership, we must first ask, is it true that Nero played the violin while Rome burned? Curiously, for our purposes the truth of the story is not that important. The more interesting question is, Why have people from Nero's own time up until now kept repeating this story?

In AD 64 there was a huge fire in Rome. It lasted six days and wiped out large portions of the city. One of the more reliable accounts of the fire comes from the Roman historian Gaius Cornelius Tacitus (AD 56–120). Tacitus reports that Nero was not in Rome when the fire started. The emperor was at his summer home in Antium and did not return to the city until the fire got close to one of his houses in town. When Nero finally arrived in Rome, Tacitus tells us:

> But as a relief for the evicted and fugitive people, he opened up the Plain of Mars and the Monuments of Agrippa, in fact even his own gardens, and he set up improvised buildings to receive the destitute multitude; and comestibles were sailed up from Ostia and nearby municipalities, and the price of grain was reduced to three sesterces. All of which, though popular, proved unavailing, because a rumor spread that at the very time of the City's blaze he had actually mounted his domestic stage and sung of the extirpation of Troy, assimilating present calamities to olden disasters.[11]

If this really was rumor going around Rome, be it true or false, it is one that speaks volumes about how Nero was perceived as a leader. (Imagine President George W. Bush ordering disaster relief after Hurricane Katrina and then getting up on his home stage and singing a song that compared the disaster to the destruction of Troy!)

Ancient historians were known to present gossip as fact and embellish history to make the story more interesting. Tacitus was no admirer of Nero, but his account seems more measured than other historians (and he was a near contemporary of Nero's). For example, the historian Gaius Suetonius Tranquillus (AD 69–140) claims that Nero set the fire to plunder and destroy ancient monuments and the houses of the rich and powerful in the city.

According to Suetonius, "Pretending to be disgusted by the drab old buildings and narrow, winding streets of Rome, he brazenly set fire to the city." [12] Suetonius then writes:

> Nero watched the conflagration from the tower of Maecenas, enraptured by what he called "the beauty of the flames"; then put on his tragedian's costume and sang "The Sack of Ilium"[13] from beginning to end. He offered to remove corpses and rubble free of charge, but allowed nobody to search among the ruins, even of his own mansion; he wanted to collect as much loot and spoils as possible himself. Then he opened a Fire Relief Fund and insisted on contributions, which bled the provincials white and practically beggared all private citizens.[14]

This is a far more sinister account of the event. One in which Nero does, as the saying goes, "fiddle while Rome burns." Later writers followed Suetonius's story line, only some had Nero singing a different song or playing a different instrument while others, such as Cassius Dio (AD 150–235), had him singing and watching the fire from the roof of his palace.[15]

Despite any exaggeration or poetic license, we know that Nero was an immoral and somewhat bizarre person in his private and public life. He killed his mother and kicked his pregnant wife to death after she complained about him coming home late from the races. Nero perfected the idea of bread and circuses, giving handouts and violent public entertainment to keep the masses happy. Fiddling while Rome burned was nothing compared to the fact that he then blamed the fire on the Christians. After the fire, Nero rounded up the Christians and had them brutally tortured and killed, often as public entertainment. Among those killed were the Saints Peter and Paul. It is all too easy to caricaturize a leader like Nero, but as the classicist Edward Champlin points out, the real Nero may not have been as bad as his monster-like image in history.[16]

CITHARAS AND FIDDLING

Nero was a brutal man and a vain artist. He was a serious musician who liked to compete in music contests and longed for artistic recognition. The story of him fiddling while Rome burned seems to speak to the public perception of him as uncaring, self-centered, and disjointed from the people. One thing we can be certain of is that he did not play the fiddle because it had not yet been invented. According to classicist Mary Gyles, Nero probably played the cithara (a stringed instrument resembling a lyre) because he had coins and statues of himself as a cithara player.[17] So the interesting question is, why do we say that Nero played the fiddle? Here is where we can see how the study of language offers insight into the origin of certain ideas.

According to Gyles, the Latin word "fides" means string, and the Roman writer Marcus Tullius Cicero (106–143 BC) uses fides and the diminutive "fidicula" to refer to a stringed instrument, which in his day would be a lyre or a cithara. She traces the term to the AD 500s and finds that "fidicula" is used in English and Continental Germanic to refer to musical instruments such as the harp, lyre, and rotta. Gyles says that by the fourteenth century the word evolved into the word "fiddle" and applied to the violin when it was invented a century later.

So what does all this have to do with Nero and leadership? The story of Nero playing the fiddle lay somewhat dormant in literature until it re-emerged in the seventeenth century in Shakespeare's *Henry VI* where Henry proclaims:

> Plataginet, I will: and like thee, Nero,
> Play on the lute, beholding the towns burn.[18]

Gyles argues that it is significant that Nero shows up in this play as a musician, but that in *The Taming of the Shrew*, Shakespeare makes it clear that he thinks a lute is the same thing as a fiddle.[19] She then points to a number of authors who follow Shakespeare and repeat the story that Nero fiddled while Rome burned. Because of the Nero story, the verb "fiddled" enters the English language with two very different meanings. Consider the definition from Samuel Johnson's dictionary, written between 1745 and 1755:

1. To fiddle, from the noun.
2. To trifle, to shift the hands often, and to do nothing like a fellow that plays upon a fiddle. Good cooks cannot abide what they justly call fiddling work, where abundance of time is spent and little done.[20]

One rarely associates playing an instrument with "doing nothing," but if we go back to the Nero story we see that both the story and the word for playing the instrument in the story (albeit the wrong instrument) take on a meaning that includes in it moral condemnation of Nero, who was doing something trivial and unhelpful at the wrong time. In modern English it is an even harsher term that can mean to cheat or swindle,[21] to make frivolous movements, and to waste time.[22]

The intent of this (somewhat off the beaten path) account of Nero and fiddling while Rome burns is to show how sayings can be graphic summaries of what people have thought and felt about how leaders should not behave over a long period of time. People expect leaders to attend to the problems of followers. In times of crisis, people condemn leaders who are not there and/or do something at the time of the crisis that the public perceives as pleasant or enjoyable to the leader. When leaders behave this way, the public thinks they are fiddling around. In our next examples, we see that the perception of fiddling around need not involve playing an instrument.

THE PROBLEM WITH NOT BEING THERE

Russian President Vladimir Putin offers a striking instance of a leader who failed to understand the importance of "being there" when he stayed on at his vacation dacha instead of returning to his office in Moscow or going to the port at the Barents Sea after the Russian nuclear submarine *Kursk* sank in August 2000. Consider some of the reactions to Putin's behavior at home and in the world press.[23] "Particularly irksome," declared a Moscow daily, was that "he has not interrupted his vacation . . . if only for an hour, to support the seamen in distress." Igor Chernyak wondered about Putin's ability to empathize.

> How come that in the past five days, Putin, who once spent a night aboard a submarine and knows what being underwater means, has not found time to address the families of the Kursk's seamen? Why does he think he can remain silent these days, with all of Russia keyed up, its heart going out to the people aboard the hapless sub?

In democratic societies, the public is supposed to hold their leaders accountable for where they are in times of crisis. For example, the British paper the *Independent* editorialized (August 18): "No democratic politician can afford to remain on holiday in a crisis." Oslo's *Dagbladet* observed: "every other democratically elected head of state would have gotten as near the site [of the accident] as humanly possible." Michael Backhaus argued in the tabloid *B.Z.* of Berlin (August 18):

> The czars and their Soviet successors simply did not have to take care of public concerns. In their majority, the Russians still want a strong man, a kind of czar, at the lead. But they want someone who takes care of the people and who is with them in times of misery. Putin's heartless silence and the serious shortcomings during the rescue mission could destroy his reputation as the savior of the Russian motherland.

An editorial in the Italian *La Stampa* (August 18) notes:

> According to the Russians, today Putin should be at the Barents Sea . . . following the rescue operations. Yesterday's public surveys, conducted for "Echo of Moscow" radio, heated up its switchboards: Most of the radio listeners wanted Putin to immediately interrupt his vacation, (adding) "Clinton does it all the time."

Putin replied to these criticisms and acknowledged his mistake in an interview with Voice of America:

The only thing which could have been changed in my conduct as head of state, it could be possible to halt my working meetings, to suspend them at the place of my vacation in Sochi, the Black Sea, I could go back to the capital, to Moscow. But, again, it would have been a P-R (public relations) activity since in any city of the country, or all over the world, I'm always linked to the military, I have communication means, I can discuss any problems on the table.[24]

Putin thought that going to his office or to the site of the submarine was simply a matter of public relations. In other words, he cared, but failed to *show* care. The cause of outrage was the public perception that he chose to stay on vacation rather than be where the public thought that he should be. In short, he appeared to be fiddling around when he should have been doing his job as leader. Note that Putin, like Nero, did seem to attend to the problem at hand. The key issue for followers was that they believed that their leaders were not paying attention and were doing something enjoyable while others suffered. Such leaders appear self-interested, callous, and indifferent to the plight of their followers.

Putin's case is particularly revealing when it comes to the difference between caring and showing care. On the one hand, he is a product of his personal background as head of intelligence and growing up in an undemocratic culture. So one might argue that he did not know that leaders were supposed to stop vacationing and go to Moscow or the site of a disaster right away.[25] On the other hand, this does not get at the question of whether Putin really cared about the right things. Some believed that Putin was more concerned with showing that Russia did not need help than caring about the 118 men who were trapped in the submarine. The other rumor going around was that there was something to hide on the submarine.

There are many other cases of leaders who failed to be in the right place at the right time. Coincidentally, a year later, we see another example of this involving a submarine. In February 2001, when Japanese Prime Minister Yoshiro Mori found out that the U.S. submarine *Greeneville* sank a Japanese fishing boat called the *Ehime Maru's*, he actually called and asked his secretary whether it was all right for him to continue his golf game. Apparently she said yes, because he went on to play for two more hours.[26] He was widely condemned by the public and the press. (Mori's political career was already on thin ice at the time.) His response to criticisms of his behavior was more clueless than Putin's. He said: "Why is this an issue of emergency management? It is an accident isn't it? I think I exercised my leadership."[27] In an editorial, Japanese writer Shin'ya Fujiwara criticized Mori's behavior and the failure of the captain of the *Greeneville* to apologize to the Japanese families. Fujiwara aptly sums up the expectations that people have for leaders to be there. He writes, "both men have shown this capacity to go missing when they are needed, leaving us alone again in our grief and frustration."[28]

Being there in a time of crisis is central to leadership in all contexts. As John Keegan notes in the opening quote of this chapter, a leader's presence is central to military leadership for practical as well as moral reasons. Business leaders have also been condemned when they fail to show up in times of crisis. One notable example of this is the failure of Exxon CEO Lawrence G. Rawl to visit the site where the *Exxon Valdez* broke up in Alaska and caused one of the worst oil spills in history.[29] It took him about a week to finally get there, in the meantime making Exxon seem like it did not care or take responsibility for the environmental disaster.

CARE AND BEING THERE

Let us turn now to what "care" means and how it is related to being there. "Care" has two different but interrelated meanings. It can mean anxiety or concern and is often used as a noun as in "She has many cares" or "She has no cares." The verb form of "care" often means solicitous, paying attention *to*, taking responsibility *for*, or even worrying *about* someone or something, as in "I care about or for her." The two different meanings come together in "I must care for her especially when she has so many cares." The word "care" comes from the Latin word "cura," which is also the root of the word "cure."

In *Being and Time* philosopher Martin Heidegger traces the origins of the role of care in life to the fable of Care (Cura) by the Roman writer Gaius Julius Hyginus (64 BC–AD 17).[30] The fable ties the idea of caring to the origins and maintenance of humanity. It goes like this:

> Once when "care" [Cura] was crossing a river, she thoughtfully picked up some mud and began to shape it. While she was thinking about what she had made, Jupiter came by. Care asked him to give it spirit, and this he gladly granted. Care wanted to name the human after herself, but Jupiter insisted that his name should be given to the human instead. While Care and Jupiter were arguing, Earth (Tellus) arose and said that the human being should be named after her, since she had given her own body. Finally, all three disputants accepted Saturn as judge. Saturn decided that Jupiter, who gave spirit to the human, would take back its soul after death; and since Earth had offered her body to the human, she should receive it back after death. But, said Saturn, "Since Care fashioned the first human being, let her have and hold it as long as it lives.[31]

The myth demonstrates how care literally and figuratively makes us what we are and sustains us as human beings.

Heidegger ties the idea of care (Sorge) to what it means to be or to exist. He uses the word "Da-sein," to mean "being there." Heidegger says we not only exist in time, but we exist first and foremost as beings with the capacity to be concerned about our own being or self-identity. We are self-reflective in that we make sense of our ability to make sense of the world. Humans do not exist by themselves. They exist in the midst of a world of other people and things. For Heidegger, care is the uniquely human way of being in this world. It is the experience of care that unifies the self and makes a person into an authentic human being. While Heidegger is looking at the broader philosophic question of "being there," it is instructive to use his observations to think about why care is fundamental to what we are as humans and how we understand our common morality.[32] This last point is most important for the issue at hand concerning leaders. The "being" of a leader has some unique aspects to it. Since leaders cannot exist without followers, they exist in the context of followers. What sets them apart in that context is that their role carries the expectation and obligation to care. Failure to place a value on being there at a particular time is, like the vice of sloth, failure to care.

THE ETHICS OF CARE

One of the oldest and ubiquitous moral principles is the golden rule: "Do unto others as you would have others do unto you" or "do not do unto others as you would not have them do unto you." It assumes a common ability to empathize, and it encompasses expansive notions of space and time. The "others" in the rule are just like you and me no matter where they are or what time it is. The rule implies that people are the same based on their wants and needs. The golden rule gives us guidance on how to treat people, but it still does not quite capture what it means to care. Perhaps that is what makes it such a useful principle. Care requires attention, solicitude, and active involvement. Unlike the golden rule, which is objective and egalitarian, care entails having certain dispositions and feelings, and it is highly subjective and selective.

In the twentieth century, feminist scholars began to formulate an ethic of care.[33] One impetus for this was psychologist Carol Gilligan's surprising discovery that girls progressed up Lawrence Kohlberg's scale of moral development more slowly than boys. Gilligan went on to conduct her own study of moral development of girls and found that women and girls thought about ethical problems in "a different voice" than men.[34] Rather than reasoning from moral principles, females were more concerned with relationships and contexts. One might argue that if a leader thinks about morality in this "female" way, he or she might be more likely to sense why being in the right place at the right time is important for his or her relationship to followers. It is the same disposition that leads mothers and fathers to go to their screaming babies, even when the babies are not hurt or in danger. According to psychologist Erik Erikson, the human inclination to care is rooted in the impulse to "caress" someone who in his helplessness emits signals of despair.[35]

The ethics of care is often contrasted with the ethics of justice. Philosopher Virginia Held describes an ethic of justice as one that focuses on fairness, equality, individual rights, and abstract principles as well as the consistent application of them. An ethic of care is about cultivating caring relations, attentiveness, responsiveness to need, and narrative nuance (which includes time and place). She says, "Whereas justice protects equality and freedom, care fosters social bonds and cooperation." [36]

The basic ideas behind the ethics of care, such as the role of emotions, empathy, and sympathy, have been discussed by many thinkers in the history of philosophy and are not considered feminine or masculine, but merely other ways to think about ethics.[37] For example, Søren Kierkegaard introduced the notion of care as a means of counteracting the excessive objectivity of philosophy in the early twentieth century.[38] The Roman philosopher Seneca (who, by the way, was Nero's tutor) observed that behaving rationally is only part of morality. He said humans were given reason so that they can achieve the good. They were given the capacity to care so that they can perfect the good.[39] The dichotomy between those cold, hard, objective, moral principles based on reason and justice, and moral feelings such as empathy is extremely important when we consider the ethics of leadership. Followers want and expect leaders to have moral principles and moral feelings. Not all leaders have both, but this does not necessarily mean that they are immoral or that they cannot learn or at least compensate for missing moral feelings related to care.

CONCLUSION: HOW DUTY AND PROPRIETY CAN LEAD TO CARE

Looking back on the Putin example, notice that he says that he was monitoring the situation with sophisticated communications at his vacation dacha. There was nothing that he could practically do to help raise the submarine. He appears to have been directing the action from afar. Putin may well have been behaving like a responsible and rational leader, who is in the wrong place at that time. The public controversy over Putin centered on what his absence at the Barents Sea port said about his feelings; however, there is another equally if not more important issue in the case. Putin not only appeared to lack the right feelings that would motivate him to be there, but he lacked the knowledge that he had a duty to be there. Staying at his dasha made him seem slothful—as if he did not care about how or where he did his work—or as if he was not giving the disaster the appropriate kind of attention. Care is about more than concern for others; it is also about concern for what one does in the role that defines what one is.

While we want leaders who have feelings of care for other human beings, there is much to recommend in a leader with a strong sense of duty. First, a leader like Putin does not need to have a tender heart to know when and where he should be in times of crisis. Care is largely about feelings, but it may also be framed in terms of attention to one's duty. Second, the duties of leadership can be taught in ways that moral feeling cannot. Leaders learn from their mistakes when they have a duty to be on the site of a disaster. Putin did. In later disasters, such as the massacre of school children in Beslan by Chechan rebels in 2004, he promptly arrived on the scene. Even if showing up is nothing more than public relations, it still means something to followers. It means the leader is "on the job" and paying attention to their plight. A leader's presence can give followers confidence in the leader, and this confidence can be a source of comfort.

It may be unrealistic to expect all leaders to have finely honed feelings of care, and not all of them do. This is rather like expecting all leaders to have charisma. I would argue that either care for one's duty or the care that comes from feelings is morally sufficient, albeit not as emotionally satisfying to followers. The duty to be with followers in a crisis is also captured by the concept of "propriety" or what is considered proper behavior for a leader. Confucius understood the importance of propriety and ceremony for leaders as a means of showing both respect and humility.[40] Ancient Greek and Chinese writers talked about propriety in terms of the virtue reverence. According to philosopher and classicist Paul Woodruff, the ancients considered reverence the most important virtue for leaders. It was the virtue that made leaders act as if they were a part of a larger whole and kept leaders from acting like gods.[41] As noted earlier, leaders simply cannot exist without followers.

We have been exploring how being there and care are essential elements of the moral obligations of leadership. Being in a certain place at a certain time is the context and existential aspect of leadership. The best leaders care because of how they feel *and* because of their sense of duty, but either motivation may be sufficient for filling their moral obligations and doing their job. A leader's duties are determined by how to do his or her job the right way. As I have argued elsewhere, the ethics of leaders is inextricably tied to and embedded in the skills, knowledge, and competencies of leadership.[42] Leaders can and often do learn their duties and proper behavior on the job. Duty and propriety offer guidance for leaders about where they should be at certain times, regardless of how the leader feels.

Physical presence affects the way that people perceive the world. Visiting the location of a disaster after it has occurred is different from watching it on a flat screen TV. Being at the site of a disaster may cultivate sentiments of care in leaders who do not have them or, at a minimum, help leaders understand why they should be there. When leaders "fiddle while Rome burns," stay on vacation while sailors die, or play golf while families grieve, they fail to understand that these things do not happen to their followers without happening to them. This is why it is so important for presidents to visit wounded soldiers and attend the funerals of those who have fallen in war. Leaders need to experience the feelings of followers up close because they are players in the same tragedy. Since the time of Nero and perhaps before then, people have condemned leaders who fail to understand this point and "fiddle while Rome burns."

NOTES

1. John Keegan, *The Mask of Command* (New York: Viking, 1987), 329.
2. Joanne B. Ciulla, "The State of Leadership Ethics and the Work that Lies Before Us," *Business Ethics: A European Review* 14, no. 4 (2005): 323–335.
3. As C. P. Snow noted in his famous 1959 Rede lecture, there are "two cultures" of scholars, the humanities and the sciences. He said the sciences provide us with descriptions and explanations, but we need the humanities for understanding. C. P. Snow, *The Two Cultures* (Cambridge: Cambridge University Press, 1998), 2.
4. Roy Howard, *Three Faces of Hermeneutics* (Berkeley: University of California Press, 1982), 1.
5. Hans-Georg Gadamer, *Truth and Method,* 2nd ed., trans. Joel Weinsheimer and Donald Marshall (New York: Crossroads Publishing, 1990), 190.
6. E. P. Thompson, "Time Work-Discipline, and Industrial Capitalism," *Past and Present,* no. 38 (1967).
7. Joanne B. Ciulla, *The Working Life: The Promise and Betrayal of Modern Work* (New York: Crown Business Books, 2000).
8. Stephen Hawking, *A Brief History of Time* (New York: Bantam Books, 1988).
9. Edwin A. Abbott, *Flatland: A Romance of Many Dimensions* (New York: Dover Publications, 1992 [1884]).
10. Plato, *Republic,* trans. G. M. A. Grube (Indianapolis, IN: Hackett Publishing, 1992).
11. Tacitus, *The Annals,* trans. A. J. Woodman (Indianapolis IN: Hackett Publishing, 2004), 15.39, 323.
12. Suetonius, *The Twelve Caesars,* trans. Robert Graves and Michael Grant (New York: Penguin Books, 1997), 236.
13. This is a lost epic from Greek literature about the sack of Troy.
14. Ibid., 237.
15. Cassius Dio, *Roman History,* trans. Earnest Gray, Loeb Classical Library Edition, Vol. VIIII (Cambridge MA: Harvard University Press, 1925), sec. 16, 113.
16. Edward Champlin, *Nero* (Cambridge, MA: Belknap Press of Harvard University Press, 2003), 9.
17. Mary F. Gyles, "Nero Fiddled While Rome Burned," *The Classical Journal* 42, no. 4 (1947): 211–217.

18. William Shakespeare, *The Complete Works of William Shakespeare* (New York: Barnes and Noble Books, 1994), Henry VI, Pt. I Act I, Scene 4, 6.

19. Gyles, "Nero Fiddled While Rome Burned," 215.

20. Samuel Johnson, *Dictionary of the English Language,* Vol. I (New York: AMS Press, 1967).

21. It is worth noting here that in the 1530s wandering minstrels had fallen into disrepute and by the seventeenth century were considered idlers and people who spread social unrest. This too contributed to the meaning of the expression "fiddling around," according to Gyles, "Nero Fiddled While Rome Burned," 215.

22. *The Complete Oxford English Dictionary* (Oxford: Clarendon Press, 1991), 585.

23. All press quotes in this section, unless otherwise stated are from Federation of American Scientists. Available at http://www.fas.org/news/russia/2000/russia-000818-sub_comment.htm

24. Voice of America. Available at http://www.fas.org/news/russia/2000/russia-000909.htm

25. Terry L. Price, *Understanding Ethical Failures in Leadership* (New York: Cambridge University Press, 2005).

26. Stephanie Strom, "Sub Incident Erodes Trust in Japan Chief and the U.S.," *The New York Times,* February 18, 2001, N7.

27. Howard W. French, "A Sorry Mess: Taking Measure of Suffering," *The New York Times,* March 4, 2001, WK 16.

28. Shin'ya Fujiwara, "In Japan, Waiting for the Captain to Appear," *The New York Times,* February 14, 2001, A17.

29. Bruce Harrison and Tom Prugh, "Assessing the Damage: Practitioner Perspectives on the Valdez," *Public Relations Journal* 45, no. 10 (1989): 40.

30. Hyginus, *Fabularum Liber* (New York: Garland, 1976 [1535]).

31. In an edited form from Martin Heidegger, *Being and Time,* trans. Joan Stambaugh (Albany, NY: SUNY Press, 1996), 184.

32. See Robert C. Solomon, *From Rationalism to Existentialism* (Lanham, MD: Rowman & Littlefield, 2001).

33. See Nel Noddings, *Caring: A Feminine Approach to Ethics and Moral Education* (Berkeley: University of California Press, 1986); Martha C. Nussbaum, *The Fragility of Goodness* (Cambridge: Cambridge University Press, 1986); and Martha C. Nussbaum, *Sex and Social Justice* (New York: Oxford University Press, 1999).

34. Carol Gilligan, *In a Different Voice: Psychological Theory and Women's Development* (Cambridge, MA: Harvard University Press, 1982).

35. Erik H. Erikson, *The Life Cycle Completed: A Review* (New York: W. W. Norton, 1982).

36. Virginia Held, *The Ethics of Care* (New York: Oxford University Press, 2006), 15.

37. See, for example, Bishop Joseph Butler, *Five Sermons Preached at the Rolls Chapel; and A Dissertation upon the Nature of Virtue* (New York: Bobbs-Merrill, 1950 [1726]); and David Hume, *An Enquiry Concerning the Principles of Morals* (Indianapolis, IN: Hackett, 1983).

38. Søren Kierkegaard, *Johannes Climacus; or, De Omnibus Dubitandum Est; and A Sermon,* trans. Thomas Henry Croxall (Paulo Alto, CA: Stanford University Press, 1958);

Frederick Copleston, *Contemporary Philosophy: Studies of Logical Positivism and Existentialism* (Westminster, MD: Newman, 1966).

39. Seneca, *Seneca ad Lucilium Epistulae. Vol. 3 of Epistulae Morales,* trans. Richard M. Gummere (Cambridge, MA: Harvard University Press, 1953).

40. See Confucius, "Selections from the Analects," ed. and trans. Wing-tsit Chan, *A Source Book in Chinese Philosophy* (Princeton, NJ: Princeton University Press, 1963).

41. Paul Woodruff, *Reverence: Renewing a Forgotten Virtue* (New York: Oxford University Press, 2001).

42. Joanne B. Ciulla, "Leadership Ethics: Mapping the Territory," *The Business Ethics Quarterly* 5, no. 1 (1995): 5–28. Also see Joanne B. Ciulla, "Ethics and Leadership Effectiveness," in *The Nature of Leadership,* ed. J. Antonakis, A. T. Cianciolo, and R. J. Sternberg (Thousand Oaks, CA: Sage Publications, 2004), 302–327.

PART IV

HOW MUSIC AND MUSICIANS LEAD

8

Leadership through Music

KATHLEEN MARIE HIGGINS

"Who has had the most convincing eloquence so far? The drum roll; and as long as the kings command that, they remain the best orators and rabble rousers."[1] Nietzsche reminds us here of an aspect of leadership that is frequently overlooked: the value of music for leading. Leaders use music pervasively. Parades, gatherings of political parties, summit meetings, and so forth, all utilize music to signal the importance of the occasion and its participants, as well as to emphasize the cohesion of groups. Leaders beyond the political realm also employ music. Religious leaders use music to instill reverence and move the faithful. Educators embed teachings in nursery rhymes and other songs.[2] Military leaders rally troops and terrify enemies with music.[3]

My aim here will be to consider why and how music lends itself to serving leaders' purposes, as well as to consider some questions of strategy for leaders to consider. I will focus on the concerns of political leaders. However, my analysis should be relevant to other kinds of leaders, too. Philosophers in both ancient Greece and ancient China theorized that leaders should attend to the role that music plays in their states. In what follows I will focus largely on their grounds for this position, although I will elaborate with examples from current musical experience.

MUSIC AND POWER

Leaders, whether formal or not, occupy positions of authority. One can go forward in a leadership role only by maintaining one's power. But there are various approaches for accomplishing this. One extreme approach is that of the police state, in which noncooperation is met with severe retaliation. The ostensible aim in this case is compliance, not enthusiastic support for one's leadership. But even this method is in practice aimed at affecting the attitudes of the governed. Even draconian leaders are most successful if the threat of punishment suffices to dissuade individuals from undesired actions, and this depends on the threat being internalized.

What this means is that the authoritarian leader has to be concerned with people's emotions, trading on such emotions as self-protectiveness and fear. Indeed, Niccoló Machiavelli's advice to leaders was that they should rule with fear rather than love. But authoritarian leaders are not only interested in the emotions that they want to incite. They need to be vigilant regarding emotions that they inadvertently inspire as well. When their populations feel frustrated, unheard, and/or victimized, such leaders are impelled to do something to keep these potentially confrontational emotions at bay.

Now consider the opposite end of the leadership spectrum, that of the benign leader, whose strategy runs contrary to Machiavelli's recommendation. The benevolent leader is genuinely concerned about the well-being of the population. This leader, too, must be attentive to the emotional climate in the populace, for it reflects societal well-being. In addition, like the authoritarian leader, the benevolent one most probably wants to maintain a position of authority, and this is dependent on the continuing support of at least some of the governed.

Leaders all along the spectrum, in fact, need to attend to their citizens' emotions, and therefore they have good reasons for being concerned with music. Music both reflects and impacts the emotions of participants and listeners. Philosophers have considered several ways that music might relate to emotion. Music may mimic emotions or the behavior they induce. Or music may be an expressive behavior, indicating how some person or persons might feel. Or music may cause listeners to experience certain emotions. All three of these ideas will figure in what follows, for each of them figure in rationales for leaders' strategic employment of music. In practice, however, imitation, arousal, and expression of emotion are usually not separate processes. Emotional expression typically arouses emotion in others, which in turn motivates more emotional expression. Imitating manifestations of emotions can encourage others to adopt similar behaviors. To help focus on various reasons leaders have to work with music, I will begin by discussing traditional accounts of music as imitating emotion, and subsequently consider music as expressive and as arousing emotion. However, the dominant theme will be leaders' use of music to influence people's attitudes and behavior and to provide them with social skills—in other words, for better or for worse, to educate.

MUSICAL AS MORAL INFLUENCE

The notion of music imitating or mimicking emotion might seem a bit bizarre until we consider that emotion (at least as usually understood)

involves multiple aspects.[4] It includes physiological changes (including activation of the sympathetic and parasympathetic nervous systems), sensations,
attitudes, thoughts, behaviors, and dispositions to action (or "action tendencies," as Nico Frijda puts it).[5] If music imitates emotion, presumably it imitates features of emotion that are evident to the normal range of unassisted
human perception. Sensations and behaviors would seem to be the most
obvious bases for musical imitation, though clearly structured thoughts
might be imitable as well.

The idea that music is imitative was a commonplace for ancient Greek philosophers. Plato and Aristotle assume that music imitates emotions. Aristotle,
for example, asserts,

> Rhythm and melody supply imitations of anger and gentleness, and also of
> courage and temperance, and of all the qualities contrary to these, and of the
> other qualities of character, which hardly fall short of the actual affections, as
> we know from our own experience, for in listening to such strains our souls
> undergo a change.[6]

Presumably, Aristotle has in mind the *behavior* associated with certain emotions in this passage. Music "behaves" through rhythms and melodies in a
manner that resembles emotional behavior. Nineteenth-century music theo-
rist Eduard Hanslick, though arguing that music cannot imitate or represent
specific emotions through its own resources, nonetheless explicates this idea
when he proposes that what music actually presents are "tonally moving
forms."[7] It is able to represent "those ideas which relate to audible changes
in strength, motion, and proportion," ideas "of increasing and diminishing,
acceleration and deceleration, clever interweavings, simple progressions
and the like."[8] The reason we see resemblances between music and emotion
is that the dynamic features of music—the gait of its rhythms, for example,
and the patterns of tension and release—resemble the dynamics of feelings
associated with certain emotions. Particular dynamics, according to Hanslick,
are sometimes consistent with a variety of emotions, so simply listening to
musical patterns in the absence of contextual cues will not tell us for certain
that a specific emotion is being represented.

This would not have concerned Plato and Aristotle very much, had they
ever heard an argument like Hanslick's. They did not take "music" to mean
instrumental music alone, in the absence of any other activity. They assumed
that music typically has words conjoined with it, and very often dance. Moreover, music was usually performed in the context of some larger civic event,
such as a theater performance. Music video, in which the music is accompanied by characters acting and dancing, is something of a present-day counterpart of this, though we should keep in mind that our contemporary
possibilities for individual consumption of music (e.g., by the person

watching television in isolation) were unprecedented before the twentieth century. At least, much of the music we listen to resembles that of the ancient Athenians in combining music and verse. But this is typical of song in any time and place.

Plato and Aristotle, and many ancient Chinese thinkers as well, considered music to be an important instrument of moral education. In this they are concerned with consequences of musical activity that are broadly significant for political leaders. Confucius, for example, counsels, "Let a man be first incited by the Songs, then given a firm footing by the study of ritual, and finally perfected by music." [9] Similarly, Aristotle contends,

> Music has a power of forming the character. . . . There seems to be in us a sort of affinity to musical modes and rhythms, which makes some philosophers say that the soul is a tuning, others, that it possesses tuning.[10]

Plato concurs. His character Socrates claims that with respect to education,

> Rhythm and harmony permeate the inner part of the soul more than anything else, affecting it most strongly and bringing it grace, so that if someone is properly educated in music and poetry, it makes him graceful, but if not, then the opposite.[11]

One rationale for the idea that music serves moral education is that the texts conjoined with music might be morally desirable or undesirable, and thus might present good or bad role models for its audience. Treating music as an element of poetry and theater, Plato's Socrates cautions against allowing these arts to display the kinds of conduct (e.g., lewd or disruptive behavior) that leaders would not want citizens to imitate.

However, Plato's Socrates also refers to more narrowly "musical" matters as well. He calls for the restriction of music to only two modes, one suited to military action and one to reverence. This tight linking of features of music with given kinds of activity reflects the fact that music can incite action. By "modes" Socrates means the scales, or sets of particular tone, from which a piece of music could be constructed. The modes differed with respect to the relative distribution of half steps and whole steps between tones. (Half steps are the tonal distance between the sounds of two adjacent keys on the piano; whole steps are the tonal distance between the sounds of two keys on the piano with one key between them.)

Most Westerners are accustomed to two basic modes, major and minor. But our major and minor scales are not the only possible modes. For example, what is called the Dorian mode (though different from what the Greeks would have called Dorian) is the scale that can be formed made by playing all the white piano keys from the D above middle C to the next higher D.[12] The ancient Greeks were aware of a variety of modes, for distinctive modes were associated with individual city-states and their ways of doing things. The "ethos theory" held that the modes themselves had an impact on the character of the people.

Modes linked to societies the Athenians considered barbarian *sounded* barbarian to them. They heard the music makers and their characteristics through the music. Even the use of certain instruments was frowned upon. Both Plato and Aristotle show disdain for the aulos, the double flute. Plato's Socrates complains that it introduces composite harmonies, when he wants modes to be pure and straightforward.[13] Aristotle, too, deems the aulos too exciting to be educationally useful and harmful to the voice.[14] While their explanations do not admit this, the aulos was associated with Dionysian cults; hence, it is likely that their condemnation of the instrument was related to their assessment of the cults themselves. Confucius similarly objects to foreign music on the grounds that it is licentious.[15]

The ethos theory raises the question of how the modes come to have moral influence. Does something inherent to the specific arrangement of notes and intervals in a particular mode affect people spiritually? Some have contended this but are hard put to explicate how this happens. A more obvious explanation is that we learn conventional associations between certain extramusical content and particular music or musical elements. Even the melody of "Happy birthday" makes us think of someone's birth anniversary. The tune of a Christmas carol takes many of us imaginatively to that season of the year. The sound of a pipe organ makes many Westerners think of church, and so on. It is easy to believe that the repeated linking of music written in a particular mode with a given city-state made the connection seem natural after a time, just as most of us in the West feel that it is natural to link minor keys and sad moods, even though this association is historically contingent.[16]

Associations between music's features and particular societies are also common in our era. Even an instrumental version of a national anthem draws listeners' minds to thoughts of the country with which it is associated. The selection of instrumentation can also induce feelings of political membership. For example, the bagpipe connotes Scottish or (more broadly) Celtic identity, while the use of traditional Chinese instruments is evocative of Chinese identity both inside and outside that culture. Stylistic elements of a culture's music also draw listeners' minds to thoughts of that culture. Musical emblems can also be established by recurrently using particular melodies in particular contexts. Such features of music can be useful to leaders who want to inspire patriotic feelings.

Already in ancient Greece, as we have seen, the meanings people associated with music had a marked cultural component. Thus, the meanings one society would associate with particular pieces and elements of music would not necessarily be apparent to foreigners. This is not to deny, however, that some elements and works of music have meanings that are cross-cultural. The human auditory system and the nature of musical perception is species-invariant, and certain features of music that appeal to it are standard across societies. For example, musical rhythm is more salient to human perception than pitch. Musical rhythms tend to be organized in groupings of twos and threes. Given that our own movements and actions are rhythmic, it becomes possible to compare the rhythms of music, whether our own or other peoples', with our own activity. Not surprisingly, then, we hear "imitations" of the behavior of emotional people in the music even in styles with which we are not very familiar. Leaders can suggest authority in the way that they comport themselves physically; but they can also do so through music. Dignified music suggests grandeur. It is a means for a leader to assume the role.

MUSIC AS EMOTIONAL BAROMETER

Part of being a good leader, as Confucius saw it, was to attend to the needs and concerns of subordinates. According to ancient Chinese thinkers one of the chief ways that a ruler could become aware of the concerns of the people was to listen to the music they were making. Their reasoning is premised on the account of music offered in the "Great Preface" of the *Book of Songs (The Shi Jing)*, one of the Five Classics of Confucianism.[17]

> The feelings move inwardly, and are embodied in words. When words are insufficient for them, recourse is had to sighs and exclamations. When sighs and exclamations are insufficient for them, recourse is had to the prolonged utterances of song. When those prolonged utterances of song are insufficient for them, unconsciously the hands begin to move and the feet to dance.[18]

According to this vision, music is a natural outgrowth of our innate need for emotional expression, and it communicates emotion more fully than words.

The implication is that songs reveal what people really care about. The implication is that a ruler can use popular songs as a means for taking the emotional pulse of the population. The practical consequence was, according to Kenneth DeWoskin, that Chinese rulers would often appoint "official bureaus commissioned to collect songs outside of court and introduce them into courtly entertainments."[19] A more recent, related practice was Mao Zedong's enlistment of song collectors to collect and evaluate folk songs and music dramas. The songs of peasants from the countryside were then popularized and used to celebrate agricultural workers and their concerns.[20]

POLITICAL MUSIC

The expression of emotion through music is not only an indication of people's emotions. It can also extend an emotional outlook. Typically, emotional expression is contagious. Listeners usually mirror the emotions expressed in music unless contextual cues or some personal motivation dissuades them.[21] This consideration is important to leaders, for they can expect the proliferation of emotions expressed in popular music. Songs with political content are not just barometers of public sentiment— they are propaganda, often of a most effective kind.

Songs can offer veiled or unveiled political commentary and can explicitly or implicitly call for political action.[22] They often work on emotions, conveying a provocative content through an evocative musical setting. In recent American history, for example, popular music in the 1960s catalyzed the civil rights movement and promoted antiwar sentiment during the Vietnam War. Music is particularly powerful for rallying political support because we tend to identify with music, to imaginatively put ourselves in the emotional place of the protagonist of a song, and to relate to behavior that has affinity with the rhythms we hear. Music with aggressive rhythm to that extent promotes aggressive behavior, for example.

The political influence of music has led some leaders and theorists of leadership to favor censorship. Even Plato's Socrates encourages musical and artistic censorship, although he does suggest that he might be persuaded against it if the music and art in question could be shown to have socially redeeming merit.[23] The idea of censorship raises a number of questions, the most obvious one being whether it can ever be morally warranted. Nineteenth-century philosopher John Stuart Mill argues that the liberty of adult citizens can only legitimately be constrained with respect to actions that would harm another person. If he is right, musical expression could appropriately be curtailed only if it could be shown to harm another person. Such circumstances are not impossible. For example, the public performance of the historical first stanza of "Deutschland über Alles," its national anthem, has been forbidden in Germany since the end of World War II because it is so strongly associated with the Nazi regime that its performance would strike some as a hate crime. One could imagine the performance of a certain provocative work of music in certain contexts being used to promote a riot. However, establishing that a given performance of music causes harm to a given person or persons would probably be difficult to establish in most instances.

Of course, not all political institutions aim to protect people's liberty. Authoritarian regimes have other agendas, and one of the most obvious ways in which they relate to music is to suppress music that they deem subversive. A gruesome example is treatment of Chilean singer-songwriter Víctor Jara by the regime of General Augusto Pinochet. Jara was a supporter of Salvador Allende, who had died in the coup against his administration that was led by Pinochet. Soon after the coup Jara was arrested and tortured, having all of his fingers broken so that he could never again play the guitar. Three days after his arrest, he was shot to death. This case reveals that leaders who take music seriously are not all exemplary.[24]

The prospect of musical censorship raises many questions. What are the criteria for censorship? Who decides when these criteria have been met? Who determines if redeeming social merit outweighs the considerations that argue for censorship? What sanctions should be taken against those who perform banned music?

Music can have propagandistic influence, but this need not be in opposition to a leader's aims. Leaders, too, can use musical propaganda to advertise and promote their agendas. Campaign theme songs fall into this category of propagandistic uses of music. The use of music on public service announcements can attract attention or make the content more attractive.

Sometimes leaders combine musical censorship with more proactive strategies. Mao Zedong's government explicitly promoted the composition of songs praising work and revolutionary ideals with the aim of changing people's thinking. The People's Republic of China also sought to reform Peking opera, which makes use of stock characters and traditional plots. Traditional plots in many cases were eliminated from the repertoire because they were "unsocialist." In particular, Mao Zedong's wife, Jiang Qing, considered such plots objectionable because they reflected the outmoded class structure, fostered Confucianism, and sometimes encouraged superstitions, like belief in ghosts. She directed a crackdown on traditional Peking opera and insisted on their being replaced by "model," revolutionary Peking opera.

Mao and Jiang Qing subscribed to the aesthetic doctrine of socialist realism, which holds that art should portray revolutionary developments, thus contributing to ideological education. They insisted that the plots of the reformed Peking operas should depict communal life, class struggle, and the revolution. The acting should also be easily accessible, and thus devoid of the vocabulary of symbolic gestures that typified the traditional performances.

The resulting model Peking operas were very long and had little dramatic tension, given that the plots were limited to showing admirable socialist behavior. Not surprisingly, they never became very popular. In 1976 Mao died and Jiang Qing was removed from power. Traditional Peking opera re-emerged but never regained its earlier vitality.[25]

The socialist realism of Mao and Jiang Qing was a twentieth-century invention, but Chinese thought had long held that art should show people engaged in morally desirable behavior. The idea was that by presenting the ideal, one would encourage people to try to live up to it. This perspective raises questions about both leadership and art. One question is whether this idealistic aim for art should be endorsed: Should one restrict oneself to portraying images of what one wants to see emulated? Should music be allowed to express antisocial sentiments, or should only wholesome and sociable ones be tolerated?

Another question concerns effectiveness: Even if one wants to promote only the behavior becoming to good citizens, is artistic presentation of the ideal the best strategy? Socialist realist art, such as reformed Peking opera tends to be very heavy-handed and tedious. Simone Weil contends,

> Imaginary evil is romantic and varied; real evil is gloomy, monotonous, barren, boring. Imaginary good is boring; real good is always new, marvellous, intoxicating. Therefore "imaginative literature" is either boring or immoral (or a mixture of both). It only escapes from this alternative if in some way it passes over to the side of reality through the power of art—and only genius can do that.[26]

If Weil is right, the aesthetics of socialist realism is doomed to failure. Art cannot depict only "good" behavior and still be sufficiently interesting to motivate its audiences. Nevertheless, some art has managed to be both excellent and idealistic. Traditional Indian drama, which aimed to present dharmic characters, that is, those who lived up to their morally prescribed roles, also faced the challenge of how to make such presentations interesting. The solution to this challenge was to combine many arts into an extravaganza and to offer moving presentations of deep and basic human emotions.[27] The aesthetic richness of classical Indian drama suggests that artistic rendering of the ideal is not incompatible with high quality art. Most socialist realist art is very blatant in presenting its message. The aesthetic failure of such art suggests that more subtle tactics may be more motivating. Thus, both artists and political leaders with the agenda of inspiring good behavior need to ask themselves how blunt they should be in this effort.

MUSICAL AROUSAL

Another reason ancient Greek thinkers considered music an important means of moral education was that music *arouses* emotions. Plato's Socrates argues that behavior is contagious. Theater productions with characters acting like buffoons or tricksters could result in audience members behaving the same way. Consequently, he suggests that behavior that is presented should be seriously restricted. The same kind of reasoning is used in the current argument that music videos encourage sadistic behavior and unrestrained sexual activity on the part of young people. Not all popular music, of course, is consumed in connection with videos. But we hear the same complaint that the lyrics of some music promotes violence, and that the rhythms of the music underscore the words.

If music can promote violence and sexual promiscuity, presumably leaders within society should be concerned. Exactly how leaders might promote certain kinds of music and discourage other kinds becomes a question. Should lyrical content of music albums be rated, for example? Should some kinds of music be banned outright? Again we confront the issue of musical censorship.

Plato's Socrates is not exclusively interested in the sort of musical productions that exert bad influence. He also stresses the kind of music that is conducive to socially desirable behavior. So does the Confucian tradition. Living at a time when uncontrolled warlords amassed territory and social order was undependable, Confucius contended that ritual and music were important means for restoring social harmony. The period of turmoil during which he lived had led to a breakdown of trust and cooperation within society. According to Confucius, ritual and music were complementary means by which people could interactively attune themselves to other members of the community.

The cohesion of a society depends on people comfortably interacting in a certain way of life, in which some gestures and procedures become customary. A leader should promote organized circumstances in which traditional music and dances are employed in a ritual function. Such means help to create the circumstances in which citizens will become inclined to participate in cooperative endeavors. Ritual and music could teach people to harmonize themselves without coercion. According to the *Analects* (or *Lun Yu*), Confucius said,

> Govern the people by regulations, keep order among them by chastisements, and they will flee from you, and lose all self-respect. Govern them by moral force, keep order among them by ritual and they will keep their self-respect and come to you of their own accord.[28]

Confucius draws attention to the fact that music creates bonds among individuals. The leader who wants to promote solidarity among the populations does well to use music for this purpose. We share music even in a physical sense. As Hanslick observes, "The other arts persuade, but music *invades* us."[29] The same music physically enters the ears and thus the bodies of everyone who can hear the music, and as we listen we are aware that the same music is within and outside us. Those who listen together synchronize the pace of their movements and their biorhythms, such as respiration and heartbeat, which follow the timing of the music. Music also entrains us, that is, we adjust the pace of our own activities to the rhythms of the music. We tend to do this without paying conscious attention, as we sometimes notice when we have discovered that we are tapping a foot to the music. We go for a walk with a companion and soon find ourselves coordinating our steps. Working songs are useful precisely because they set a rhythm to which workers entrain.

Camaraderie among musical participants also develops because they share a deeply felt common experience. Phenomenologist Alfred Schutz observes that solidarity is "founded upon the partaking in common of the different dimensions of time simultaneously lived through by the participants." [30] He points out that when we make music together we each recreate the music, step-by-step, in the inner time of our subjective experience, while also sharing an event in external time. Making music, accordingly, brings the flows of inner and outer time together. But the same is true of those who listen to music together, a condition that is rather like an inwardly "singing along," as Donald Callen puts it.[31]

Music affects even our basic sense of connection with other people. Daniel Stern points out that we first learn to recognize other human beings through what he calls "vitality affects." These are the quasi-musical dynamic and kinetic aspects of a caregiver's behavior that allow an infant to first recognize a specific other being. Stern characterizes them as "those dynamic, kinetic qualities of feeling that distinguish animate from inanimate and that correspond to the momentary changes in feeling states involved in the organic process of being alive." [32] Rather than using our usual emotional terminology, Stern suggests that the vitality affects "are better captured" by words that themselves seem appropriate to music, "dynamic, kinetic terms, such as 'surging,' 'fading away,' 'fleeting,' 'explosive,' 'crescendo,' 'decrescendo,' 'bursting,' 'drawn out,' and so on." [33] Stern contends that infants and their caregivers attune to each other in the timing and contours of their acts of expression. Such proto-musical interactions allow infants to learn what it is to be "with" another person, an ability that is crucial for interpersonal relationships down the line.

The feelings of solidarity that music provokes can result in cooperative action even in the absence of a leader's direction. The 1914 Christmas truce during World War I is a case in point. At certain points along the front line between France and Germany, Allied and German combatants put down their arms and celebrated Christmas together. Song was a central catalyst in this remarkable development. Stanley Weintraub, in his book about the Christmas truce, observes,

> Yuletide carols initiated a tentative courtship that further developed through physical contact and ultimately the sharing of the soldiers' most valued commodities—food and tobacco and such souvenirs as uniform buttons and insignia. . . . Everywhere, Christmas ritual—especially song—eased the anxiety and fear of initial contact.[34]

The case of the Christmas truce suggests that the ancient Chinese thinkers were right in their belief that music could engender spontaneous, noncoercive cooperation. Obviously, military leaders did not encourage this development, for they could hardly have been sanguine about their troops collaborating with the enemy. In this case, song among the troops themselves led to tentative gestures of trust for the occasion.

This in itself raises questions about the extent to which official leaders should aim to actively direct their subordinates. Most schools of Chinese thought encourage the notion of *wuwei* (nonaction or nonassertive action) as an ideal for leaders as for others. According to the *Dao De Jing*, for example, [35]

> *The best of all rulers is but a shadowy presence to his subjects. . . .*
> *When his task is accomplished and his work is all done*
> *The people all say, "It happened to us naturally."*

This ideal of nonassertiveness raises questions in the philosophy of leadership. Should one aim to "make one's mark" by leading? Or should one focus more on stability in the way the system functions? Should one aim to improve the way it functions, and if so in what respect(s)? The relevance of these questions is not uniquely evident in policies regarding music, but instead extends across the range of how leaders conduct themselves. But adoption of the *wuwei* ideal would certainly have implications for how leaders use music. For example, a leader who consistently aimed to lead nonassertively would not suppress dissident music. Such a leader might well think that such music is a peaceful means by which discontented people express themselves. As Confucian philosopher Xunzi observes, music is a means of channeling emotion. Noninterference with people's musical practices, therefore, can itself promote social stability, and thus be in the ruler's own interests.

Indeed, allowing music to run its natural course might be a good way for a leader to encourage feelings of well-being within the populace. The leader who aims at *wuwei* might also recognize that participation in musical activities promotes feelings of security. This is not to say that all instances of music are reassuring. But music in familiar styles and "old favorite" songs do encourage comfort in one's situation. Indeed, the German philosopher and sociologist Theodor Adorno argues that music is too comforting, encouraging complacency with the status quo when change is what is really needed. He contends that society needs music that will push people beyond their comfort zone and inspire them to take action. I think that underestimates the social value of a basic sense of security, but Adorno correctly recognizes that music helps establish it.

Music induces a sense of security in part because it is remarkably conservative, in the sense that it is built on pattern repetition at every level to a much greater degree than is the case in other arts. Notes, measures, phrases, sections, and whole pieces of music are reiterated, enabling listeners to commit these patterns to memory. As a result, listeners recognize the recurrence of the familiar, which itself is comforting.

Ethnomusicologist Alan Lomax contends that music plays a central role in helping a child become a member of a society in the first place, and music is able to do this because it develops a sense of security in the listener.

> The child begins to learn the musical style of his culture as he acquires the language and the emotional patterns of his people. This style is thus an important link between an individual and his culture, and later in life brings back to the adult unconscious the emotional texture of the world which formed his personality.
>
> . . . from the point of view of its social function, the primary effect of music is to give the listener a feeling of security, for it symbolizes the place where he was born, his earliest childhood satisfactions, his religious experience, his pleasure in community doings, his courtship and his work—any or all of these personality-shaping experiences. As soon as the familiar sound pattern is established, he is prepared to laugh, to weep, to dance, to fight, to worship. His heart is opened.[36]

The repetition of the same pieces of music over time also yields a sense of connection with other people who share the music even when they are distant in both time and space. Members of different generations feel intimately connected when they share the same music. Even the gap between the living and the dead is traversed through musical experience. We can rightly feel that we "hear Mozart" when we perform or listen to his music. The 1991 virtual duet of "Unforgettable" sung by Natalie Cole and her deceased father Nat King Cole, a feat of modern recording technology, is electrifyingly moving because it is so obvious that this music enables connection with the departed. Music also intimates connection with the future. Alan Merriam claims that music's confident flow toward the future assures us that the future may turn out well. Music, he says, is "a normal and solid activity which assures the members of society that the world continues in its proper path."[37]

Leaders, then, may expect that the simple presence of musical activity within society, especially music that is well known and loved, will help to instill a sense of social equanimity. More proactive leaders, however, may be inclined to do more than tolerate music. They may do what they can to stimulate musical activity, aware that music can help to motivate good human interaction.

Music makes us aware of our capacity for social harmony by providing us with a direct experience of mutual coordination with others. Dance, which is closely related to music, is a physical expression of the interpersonal coordination that is stimulated by music. Xunzi describes music's ability to arouse social attunement.

> When music is performed in the ancestral temple of the ruler, and the ruler and his ministers, superiors and inferiors, listen to it together, there are none who are not filled with a spirit of harmonious reverence. When it is performed within the household, and father and sons, elder and younger brothers listen to it together, there are none who are not filled with a spirit of harmonious kinship. And when it is performed in the community, and old people and young together listen to it, there are none who are not filled with a spirit of harmonious obedience. Hence music brings about complete unity and induces harmony.[38]

The coordination of multiple individuals' sense of time in an experience that the entire audience finds deeply satisfying, to all the aspects of their persons, encourages the conviction that one's own interests are not inherently at odds with the interests of others. This conviction, utilitarian philosopher John Stuart Mill reminds us, is crucial to the social feeling on which morality depends.

> . . . a person in whom the social feeling is at all developed cannot bring himself to think of the rest of his fellow creatures as struggling rivals with him for the means of happiness, whom he must desire to see defeated in their object in order that he may succeed in his. The deeply rooted conception which every individual even now has of himself as a social being tends to make him feel it [is] one of his natural wants that there should be harmony between his feelings and aims and those of his fellow creatures. If differences of opinion and of mental culture make it impossible for him to share many of their actual feelings . . . he still needs to be conscious that his real aim and theirs do not conflict.[39]

The German philosopher Friedrich Schiller concludes that the arts are crucial means for enabling people to recognize that they are not sacrificing their own satisfaction when they promote that of others. Our experience of the arts demonstrates that we can share enjoyment without diminishing it. Music, in particular, offers people the opportunity to experience the satisfaction of interacting amicably with others. As members of a musical audience, we experience ourselves as part of a harmonious social world, in which mutual attunement emerges without coercion. Leaders eager to encourage a stronger sense of social harmony can make use of music in this effort by providing musical accompaniment to important events of state.

This reasoning also suggests a rationale for leaders to encourage education that would involve everyone in some form of musical performance, for performance provides practice in mutual cooperation as well as the ability to recognize the sense of fulfillment that comes from it.[40] Beyond the general sense of solidarity that it promotes, musical practice involves the attempt to harmonize with other musical voices. As the "Record of Music" puts it, "The blending together without any mutual injuriousness (of the sentiments and the airs on different instruments) forms the essence of music." [41] This aspect of musicianship accords with the Confucian ideal of allowing others opportunities to rise to the occasion, for it illustrates the self-restraint required if the musician is to avoid interfering with either the articulation or the expressive character of other voices.

Moreover, musicians must structure the temporal unfolding of their performance in a way that is psychologically coherent and inviting, again a form of practice that develops skill in interacting with others. Daniel Barenboim, in one of his 2006 Raith lectures, compared the shaping of time in a musical performance with timing in international politics. He described discussing with his friend Edward Said the peace negotiations between the Palestinians and the Israelis in Oslo in the mid-1990s. Barenboim concluded that the process was not going to work. He reports telling Said,

> The preparation for the beginning of the Oslo discussions was practically non-existent, much too quick. And the process itself, once the discussion started, was very slow, and then it was interrupted, and then they said they would meet next Tuesday, and then it was cancelled on Monday, and then they met again a month later, and everything. It had no chance. And I sat down at the piano and I showed to him what I meant.

Barenboim demonstrated by playing a few bars of Beethoven's "Pathetique" sonata and then stopping. "And I said to him, 'Oslo, the equivalent of Oslo would be if I would play the introduction very fast and without any preparation of anything. . . . You would not understand anything what I am doing. And then I would get to the main allegro and I will play' "—and he demonstrated by playing a single note.[42] In order to demonstrate a serious willingness to treat each other as partners, it is important that the parties to negotiations mutually adjust the timing of their interactions, like musicians or dancers in concert.

A third aspect of musical performance that cultivates skill in personal interactions is the need for musicians to listen carefully to other musical participants. Jazz saxophonist Steve Lacy describes the tremendous insight he gained into the nature of performing music when Thelonious Monk told him to make the drummer sound good. Up to that point, he had been trying to show off with his playing. Lacy reports,

> I learned . . . to play with the other musicians and not get all wrapped up in my own thing and not just play interesting notes just to be interesting. . . . He got me out of the thing of trying to be too hip. . . . And Monk told me, "No, make the drummer sound good." And that was an enormous help to me, really. It stopped me cold, really, and changed my focus.[43]

William Day points out that this was "not exclusively a musical confusion; it is also a moral confusion. . . . One might characterize it as the false conviction that my identity (musical or otherwise) is, since mine, best pursued in isolation." [44] This description of what Lacy learned is akin to Confucius's characterization of personal virtue in terms of supporting others.

> [The Master:] Authoritative persons establish others in seeking to establish themselves and promote others in seeking to get there themselves. Correlating one's conduct with those near at hand can be said to be the method of becoming an authoritative person. [45]

If leaders encourage widespread musical interaction, they will nurture their citizens' ability to listen and attune to one another.

MUSIC AS IMAGE OF SOCIAL IDEALS

Music helps listeners and participants to develop interpersonal skills, but it also provides models for social interaction, including the interaction of leader and society. [46] Ethnomusicologist Alan Lomax suggests that cultural differences in preferred vocal style reflect different conceptions of how individuals should interact and different styles of leadership. He argues that a society's social structure correlates with its basic song style. Lomax developed cantometrics, a coding of generic style that features characteristics of the music of particular societies. [47] Cantometrics considers both "the phenomena described by European music notation—melody, rhythm, harmony interval size, and so on," and other factors, such as the size, social structure, leadership roles, integration of the music-making group, the kinds of embellishments employed, and the vocal tone quality typically adopted. [48] Lomax contends, "musical styles may be symbols of basic human value systems which function at the unconscious level and evolve with glacial slowness because the basic social patterns which produce them also evolve slowly."

Lomax considers the presence or absence of a dominating leader in a musical style to reflect a society's ideals for social organization, hierarchical or otherwise. Western Europe folk song is mainly organized with a leader dominating a passive audience (as are symphony orchestras, where the conductor gets extreme compliance from the orchestra as well as the audience). This is the same region's normative ideal for society:

> Dominance-subordination, with a deep sense of moral obligation, is the fundamental form of role-taking in the Protestant West. . . . Ultimately, this leader-follower pattern is rooted in the past, e.g., in the European concept of lifelong fealty to the king or the lord. [49]

By contrast, the Pygmy and Bushmen of Africa, have a musical style that reflects their idyllically cooperative and tolerant lifestyle.

> This extraordinary degree of vocal relaxation, which occurs rarely in the world as an over-all vocal style, seems to be a psycho-physiological set, which

symbolizes openness, nonrepressiveness, and an unconstricted approach to the communication of emotion. . . .

These stone-age hunters normally express themselves in a complex, perfectly blended, contrapuntal singing at a level of integration that a Western choir can achieve only after extensive rehearsal. . . . Even their melodies are shared pleasures, just as are all tasks, all property, and all social responsibilities.[50]

If Lomax is right that societies organize their basic singing style in accordance with their ideals of social organization, hearing such music from infancy amounts to an education in how society and its leaders should operate.

Some music also offers models and vicarious experiences of the individual or a minority group harmonizing with the larger group. The jazz solo provides an especially good illustration of a strong individual or minority voice within a larger texture.[51] This is the case especially in progressive jazz, where the solo instrument often displays extreme independence, at times seeming to ignore the ensemble. John Coltrane and Ornette Coleman's solos sometimes have this character.

The jazz solo is particularly valuable in modeling the tensions of human interactions realistically. The solo can be in considerable dissonance with the rest of the ensemble. When such a solo seamlessly rejoins the group, it demonstrates that strong individual expression does not necessarily compromise rapport. The aesthetic satisfaction that comes from experiencing such a solo reveals that we can take pleasure in adjudicating among various elements in tension with one another, a lesson that can be applied to societal experience as well. The progressive jazz solo demonstrates that individual expression need not compromise either its own integrity or that of the larger social whole. It offers us grounds for confidence that strong minority expression within society is an available option without the larger whole being undermined.

CONCLUSION

Music is effective for many purposes related to human motivation and its effects: it indicates emotional conditions within society, develops moral and political skills, conveys highly charged content, and displays and instills confidence in societal ideals. It also brings people together, facilitating a sense of connection and reinforcing relationships that already exist. Leaders aim to direct the actions their societies take, and to do this effectively leaders must inspire cooperation among citizens and motivate them to work together toward common ends. Music is so deeply involved with human motivation and feelings of solidarity that leaders cannot afford to ignore it.

NOTES

1. Friedrich Nietzsche, *The Gay Science: With a Prelude of Rhymes and an Appendix of Songs,* trans. Walter Kaufmann (New York: Random House, 1974), #84, 138–140.

2. "Guitars in the Classroom" is a current program that promotes memorization of many of the staples of elementary school through song. See http://www.guitarsintheclassroom.com/

3. Men who were skilled in mimicking natural sounds were sometimes used in ancient China to confuse the enemy. The bagpipe was used by Scottish troops to terrify opponents who had never heard it before. A United States soldier in Iraq describes in Michael Moore's *Fahrenheit 9/11* (2004) how he and his fellow soldiers prime themselves for battle by playing rock music with a driving beat.

4. Scientific investigators debate how the term "emotion" should be used, with some emphasizing the neurophysiological processes involved, often termed collectively "the affect program" of an emotion, more than the phenomenology, i.e., the experience of having an emotion. See, for example, Paul Ekman, *Emotions in the Human Face* (New York: Pergamom Press, 1972). I will not enter this debate here. Instead I will use the term in its ordinary sense as a multifaceted phenomenon that we paradigmatically *feel*.

5. See Nico H. Frijda, *The Emotions, Studies in Emotion and Social Interaction* (Cambridge: Cambridge University Press, 1986), 69–73.

6. Aristotle, *Politics,* trans. Benjamin Jowett, in *The Basic Works of Aristotle,* ed. Richard McKeon (New York: Random House, 1941), bk. VIII, l. 1340, 1311.

7. Eduard Hanslick, *On the Beautiful in Music,* trans. Geoffray Payzant (Indianapolis, IN: Hackett, 1986), 29.

8. Ibid., 10. Hanslick focuses in this discussion on absolute music, i.e., music without words, since these cases reveal what music can represent through its own resources, without the cues provided by texts. Many commentators since Hanslick have followed this strategy as well. See, for example, Stephen Davies, *Musical Meaning and Expression* (Ithaca, NY: Cornell University Press, 1994), xi. Recently, Aaron Ridley has objected to this approach, which he admits he once followed. See Aaron Ridley, *The Philosophy of Music: Theme and Variations* (Edinburgh: Edinburgh University Press, 2004), 2–3 and 76–83.

9. *The Analects of Confucius,* trans. Arthur Waley (New York: Vintage, 1938/1989), 8/8, 134.

10. Aristotle, *Politics,* trans. Jowett, in *The Basic Works of Aristotle,* ed. McKeon, bk. VIII, chap. 5, 1340b, 1312.

11. Plato, *Republic,* translated by G. M. A. Grube, revised by C. D. C. Reeve, in *Complete Works,* ed. John M. Cooper, with associate ed. D. S. Hutchinson (Indianapolis, IN: Hackett Publishing Company, 1997), II, l. 201d, 1038.

12. Actually, this probably differs from what the ancient Athenians would have known as Dorian. Europeans in the Medieval Era and the Renaissance used the Greek names for their own modes, even though scholars now think they were mistaken in they were using the same ones the Greeks had used. One challenge for researchers into ancient music is to determine exactly what sounds the ancients associated with what is left of their notation.

13. See Plato, *Republic,* III.

14. See Aristotle, *Politics,* 1341a, l.20–26.

15. See *Analects,* trans. Waley, 15/10, 195–196

16. For further discussion of the historical contingency of the associations between major keys with happy feelings and minor keys with sad feelings, see Kathleen Marie Higgins, *Suspended Harmony: Our Musical Nature and Its Global Potential* [forthcoming].

17. The *Shi Jing,* or *Book of Songs,* along with the *Shu Jing,* or *Book of Documents,* the *Yi Jing,* or *Book of Changes,* the *Zhun Zhiu,* or *Spring and Autumn Annals,* and the *Li Ji,* or *Book of Rituals,* is among The Five Classics that were the basis on which examinations for officials were based from the Han until the Song dynasties. Its influence, accordingly, is hard to overestimate. While the text itself includes only the poetry, the poetry comes literally from songs.

18. *The Shee King, or the Book of Poetry,* trans. by James Legge, in *The Chinese Classics,* 5 vols. (Hong Kong: Hong Kong University Press, 1960), Vol. 4, 34.

19. Kenneth DeWoskin, *A Song for One or Two: Music and the Concept of Art in Early China* (Ann Arbor: Center for Chinese Studies, the University of Michigan, 1982), 29.

20. The film *Yellow Earth* (directed by Chen Kaige, cinematography and screenplay by Zhang Yimou, 1993) offers a glimpse of this practice.

21. Cf. Stephen Davies, "The Expression of Emotion in Music," *Mind* 89/353 (1980): 67–86.

22. Typically music with political messages is not "absolute music" (music without words), but instead incorporates lyrics. This does not mean that music without texts is politically neutral. As we have noted, political identity can be flagged with means such as melody or instrumentation. Moreover, as we will consider below, musical forms reflect social organization and ideals for human interaction.

23. Cf. *Republic,* X, l. 607c, 1211.

24. I also discuss this example in Kathleen Marie Higgins, "Musical Education for Peace," in *Educations and Their Purposes: A Conversation among Cultures,* ed. Roger T. Ames and Peter D. Hershock (Honolulu: University of Hawaii Press, 2007), 392–393.

25. For an excellent account of the recent fate of Peking opera, see Timothy Lane Brace, *Modernization and Music in Contemporary China: Crisis, Identity, and the Politics of Style,* Ph.D. dissertation, The University of Texas at Austin, 1992, chap. 2. My discussion is largely drawn from this work.

26. Simone Weil, "Evil," in *Gravity and Grace* (New York: G. P. Putnam's Sons, 1952), 120. My thanks to Nicholas Partridge for drawing my attention to this passage.

27. See Kathleen Marie Higgins, "An Alchemy of Emotion: *Rasa* and Aesthetic Breakthroughs," *Journal of Aesthetics and Art Criticism,* Special Issue: *Global Theories of the Arts and Aesthetics* 65/1 (2007): 43–54.

28. *Analects,* 2/3, trans. Waley, 88.

29. Eduard Hanslick, *On the Musically Beautiful,* trans. Geoffrey Payzant (Indianapolis, IN: Hackett Publications, 1986), 50.

30. Alfred Schutz, "Making Music Together: A Study in Social Relationship," in *Symbolic Anthropology: A Reader in the Study of Symbols and Meanings,* ed. Janet L. Dolgin, David S. Kemnitzer, and David M. Schneider (New York: Columbia University Press, 1977), 114. Originally in *Social Research* 18, no. 2 (1951): 1951/1977: 76–97.

31. See Donald Callen, "Transfiguring Emotions in Music," *Grazer Philosphische Studien* 19 (1983): 88. See also Roger Scruton, "Musical Understanding and Musical Culture," in *What Is Music? An Introduction to the Philosophy of Music*, ed. Philip Alperson (New York: Haven, 1988), 357, where Scruton refers to the listener's "inner dancing."

32. Daniel N. Stern, *The Interpersonal World of the Infant: A View from Psychoanalysis and Developmental Psychology*, with a new introduction by the author (New York: Basic Books, 1985; introduction 2000).

33. Ibid., 54.

34. Stanley Weintraub, *Silent Night: The Story of the WWI Christmas Truce* (New York: The Free Press, 2002), 26–27 and 30. My thanks to Marilyn Maxwell for drawing my attention to this book. I discuss this case also in "Musical Education for Peace," 389.

35. Lao Tzu, *Tao Te Ching*, trans. D. C. Lao (New York: Penguin Books, 1963), 17, 31.

36. Alan Lomax, "Folk Song Style," in *The Garland Library of Readings in Ethnomusicology*, 7 vols., ed. Kay Kaufman Shelemay (New York: Garland Publishing, 1990), Vol. 3, 61; originally in *American Anthropologist* 61 (1959): 929.

37. Alan P. Merriam, *The Anthropology of Music* (Evanston, IL: Northwestern University Press, 1964), 225.

38. Hsün Tzu, *Basic Writings*, trans. Burton Watson (New York: Columbia University Press, 1963), 113.

39. John Stuart Mill, *Utilitarianism*, ed. Oskar Piest (Indianapolis, IN: Bobbs-Merrill, 1957), 42–43.

40. Portions of the following discussion appear also in Kathleen Marie Higgins, "Rising to the Occasion: The Implication of Confucian Musical Virtue for Global Community," presented at the International Symposium on "Confucianism in the Postmodern Era" (sponsored by Center for Chinese Studies, University of Hawai'i at Manoa, Honolulu, and College of Humanities, Beijing Language and Culture University, Beijing), Beijing, October 31, 2006.

41. "Yo Ki, or Record of Music," in *The Sacred Books of China*, 6 vols., in *The Sacred Books of the East*, 50 vols., ed. F. Max Müller, Vol. XXVIII, trans. James Legge. *The Texts of Confucianism*, Part IV: *The Li Ki* (Delhi: Motilal Banarsidass, 1885; reprinted by Clarendon, 1966), 101.

42. Daniel Barenboim, Reith Lectures 2006, Lecture 1: "In the Beginning was Sound," Cadogan Hall, London, April 7, 2006, BBC Radio transcript available at http://www.bbc.co.uk/radio4/reith2006/lecture1.shtml

43. Steve Lacy, interview by Terry Gross, Fresh Air, produced by WHYY-FEM/Philadelphia, distributed by National Public Radio, November 20, 1997, cited in William Day, "Knowing as Instancing: Jazz Improvisation and Moral Perfectionism," *Journal of Aesthetics and Art Criticism* 58 (Spring 2000): 108. Day points out that Lacy tells essentially the same story in Thomas Fitterling, *Thelonious Monk: His Life and Music*, trans. Robert Dobbins, a foreword by Steve Lacy (Albany, CA: Berkeley Hills Books, 1997), 13–14.

44. Day, "Knowing as Instancing," 110.

45. *The Analects of Confucius: A Philosophical Translation*, trans. Roger T. Ames and Henry Rosemont Jr. (New York: Ballantine, 1998); *Analects* 6/30, 110.

46. A version of the following discussion also appears in *Suspended Harmony,* chap. 4.

47. See Alan Lomax, *Cantometrics: An Approach to the Anthropology of Music* (Berkeley: University of California Extension Media Center, 1976). Lomax considered more than 3,000 songs from 233 cultures. He coded the songs on the basis of 37 features.

48. Alan Lomax, "Song Structure and Social Structure," in *Readings in Ethnomusicology,* ed. David P. McAllester (New York: Johnson Reprint Corporation, 1971), 228–229; originally in *Ethnology* 1 (1962): 425–451.

49. Lomax, "Song Structure and Social Structure," 241.

50. Ibid., 237 and 239–240.

51. A version of this discussion of the jazz solo as modeling the interaction of individual and group, and of minority and majority groups within society, also appears in Kathleen Marie Higgins, *The Music of Our Lives* (Philadelphia: Temple University Press, 1991), 175–182 [forthcoming in a reissued edition by Lexington Press].

9

Leadership through Music and Laughter: How Henry Carey Reinvented English Music and Song

JENNIFER CABLE

Of all the Toasts, that Brittain boasts; the Gim, the Gent, the Jolly,
the Brown, the Fair, the Debonnair, there's none cry'd up like Polly;
She's charm'd the Town, has quite cut down the Opera of Rolli:
Go where you will, the subject still, is pretty, pretty Polly.

Polly refers to Miss Polly Peachum, a character in John Gay's *The Beggar's Opera* of 1728 (January). Henry Carey (1687–1743) set this verse (1728) to his famous tune *Sally in our Alley*, which Gay had used in the opera. Carey's verse about Polly Peachum became so popular that it was eventually incorporated into *The Beggar's Opera* libretto, beginning with the third edition.[1] Even in this short example, we can detect Carey's delight that Polly had overtaken "the Opera of Rolli," alluding to Italian opera in general by referring specifically to the Italian poet and librettist who adapted libretti for several *opera seria* composers whilst they were in London. Though this particular victory celebration for English opera would not last long, Polly's triumph was one of the indicators that the period of significant success for Italian opera in London was growing short—a situation that surely would have pleased Henry Carey. Poet, composer, librettist, singer, teacher, and Englishman to the core, Carey was on the frontlines of the battle between the theatres presenting ballad opera and English opera, and the theatres presenting the Italian operas of

Handel, Bononcini, Ariosti, Porpora, Hasse, and Broschi. Through studying Carey's innovative songs and poems one immediately discerns Carey's nationalistic sentiments, expressed during a time when the English musical arts were set aside in favor of Italian musical forms and performers.[2] Carey was in the forefront of those seeking to change English attitudes towards their own music (in particular English opera) and musicians. Carey also wrote pieces of political and social satire, taking the lead in producing wickedly humorous social commentary. This discussion of Carey's creative output, referencing songs and poems dating from the 1720s and 1730s, will demonstrate the distinctive ways in which artists use their work to lead.

THE MUSIC SCENE IN ENGLAND

In order to place Henry Carey's leadership role in perspective, it is helpful to review the position of importance that Italian music, and especially Italian vocal music, could claim in England during the first few decades of the 1700s, when Carey was most active. By the end of the first decade of the eighteenth century, Italian opera had seized the attention of English audiences, replacing English stage works and discouraging further attempts by English composers to try their hand in the operatic genre. In 1713, Daniel Purcell wrote: "The introducing [of] Italian Operas upon the English stage, has so altered the Taste of the nation, as to MUSICK, that scarce any thing, but what bears some Resemblance to the Italian Style and Manner, is received with Favour or heard with Patience." He further states: "This is indeed a Calamity to be lamented, but hard to be redress'd unless the Composing Opera's in our own language was promoted, which would very probably answer any Encouragement that should be given to such Undertakings."[3]

Despite Purcell's plea for support and encouragement for the development of English opera, strategies were instead devised to support Italian opera. In late 1718, under the patronage of George I, the Royal Academy of Music was established with the charge to produce Italian opera that would rival the great opera houses on the Continent. John Jacob Heidegger was named as the company manager, the aforementioned Paolo Antonio Rolli was the secretary and librettist, and George Frederic Handel was given the post of music director. In May 1719, Handel was instructed to hire singers for the company, and the castrato Senesino was specifically mentioned as a singer whom Handel should attempt to secure for the King's Theatre. Incorporated by royal warrant, which included a stock agreement of £10,000, the academy was bankrolled by 63 individuals, the majority of whom purchased a single share at 200 guineas, which entitled them to season tickets.[4] Once all of the pledged funds were tallied, the founding members had provided the society with a £16,000 base, far exceeding the £10,000 that the agreement required.[5]

Yet the costs of producing Italian opera were much higher than the directors expected and the money on hand was quickly spent. The academy directors frequently called upon subscribers during the 1720s, attempting to recover the costs incurred by the opera company; at times, even lawsuits and finally, appeals to the gentleman's honor were attempted so subscribers would "pay the call." [6]

USING LAUGHTER TO BRING CHANGE

By 1727, it was apparent that Handel's Royal Academy was in jeopardy, and within ten years London audiences began to turn their backs on *opera seria*. Several factors contributed to the downfall, beginning with the onstage contretemps in 1727 between Francesca Cuzzoni and Faustina Bordoni, two notable Italian singers. The infamous dispute, which took place before a royal family member, Princess Caroline, was preceded by a long period during which the press compared Cuzzoni and Faustina, continually alluding to an enormous rivalry between the two (each diva had her strong and stalwart band of supporters who would not hesitate to boo when the rival appeared on the stage.) Following the public debacle, commentaries appeared intending to mock the event. Two examples are Scriblerian John Arbuthnot's "The devil to pay at St. James's: or, A full and true account of a most horrid and bloody battle between Madame Faustina and Madam Cuzzoni. . . . Moreover, how Senesino has taken snuff, is going to leave the opera, and sing psalms at Henley's oratory" and "The contre temps: of, Rival queans: a small farce. As it was lately acted, with great applause, at Heidegger's private theater near the Hay Market," printed for A. Moore. Both commentaries appeared in 1727.

Henry Carey, active in the London theater scene by 1727, made reference to the rivalry between the two singers in his 1730 version of *The Beau Monde or The Pleasure of St. James's*. After beginning with the chorus that speaks of the lovely St. James, and the balls and operas that take place there, he tells us:

> There's little Lady Cuzzoni,
> And bouncing Dame Faustina,
> The Duce a Bit will either Sing
> Unless they're each a Queen-a.[7]
> And when we've ek'd out History,
> And make them Rival Queens,
> They'll warble sweetly on the Stage,
> And scold behind the Scenes.

The onstage brawl was just the beginning of Handel's woes. During the 1728–1729 season, no Royal Academy operas took place due to high production costs and the inconvenient departure of several significant Italian singers, namely Cuzzoni, Faustina, and Senesino. This absence of Italian singers (in particular the castrati Senesino, who left London again in 1736, and Farinelli, who departed London for Spain in 1737) also impacted the production of Italian opera in the 1730s. Ever alert to locating areas ripe in potential for social satire, either in music or in prose, Henry Carey wrote several songs lampooning these famous singers (two, "The Lady's Lamentation" and "The Beau's Lamentation" directly address their departure from England), one of which, "The Musical Hodge Podge," serves as a musical parody, incorporating the signature melodies of the popular castrati.

The excessive salary demands made by the Italian singers throughout the 1720s and 1730s crippled the companies that were attempting to produce Italian opera in England. Again, from *The Beau Monde* (1730) Carey writes,

> *When having fill'd their Pockets full,*
> *No longer can they stay;*
> *But turn their Backs upon the Town,*
> *And scamper all away.*
> *The Belles and Beaux cry after them,*
> *With all their might and main;*
> *And Heidegger is sent in haste*
> *To fetch 'em back again.*[8]

And a final blow to the success of Italian opera in England concerns the simple equation of too many opera companies and inadequate funding. By the 1730s, two companies were producing Italian opera (Handel's company and Giovanni Bononcini's company, the Opera of the Nobility) while "English" companies were producing popular English ballad opera and burlesque, or attempting English opera (for example, ballad operas such as John Gay's very popular *The Beggar's Opera*, first produced in 1728, and Carey's *The Honest Yorkshireman* of 1735; burlesques such as *The Dragon of Wantley* [1737]; Carey's comic opera *The Contrivances* [1729]; and English operas *Amelia* and *Teraminta*, both with libretti by Carey).

Carey embraced the role of social commentator and satirist, revealing a facile wit in song and verse. The rivals and scandals of the Italian opera proved to be excellent material, and Carey was quick to exploit each of them in order to produce a wickedly clever commentary. Always maintaining his sense of humor, "Carey chose to expose the foibles of the fashionable society which patronized the opera, highlighting the fickle taste of the town in preferring foreign artists and entertainments at the expense of native performers and performances."[9] In *Faustina, or The Roman Songstress. A Satire on the Luxury and Effeminacy of the Age*, first published in 1726, Carey speaks to the problem of preferring Italian singers to English ones, referring to the castrati as "Foreign Ox of monstrous size" and the Italian female singers as "foreign strumpets" who are imported from the Italian shore at great expense.[10] He asks, "Can then our British Syrens charm no more," surely referring to, amongst others, the English alto Anastasia Robinson, mentioned by Carey earlier in the poem. Carey raises the question, "And are we now so despicable Grown, that Foreigners must reign in Arts alone, and Britain boast no Genius of its own?" The final four lines highlight Carey's razor sharp sarcasm:

> Let's to our pristine State return once more,
> And leave these foreign Minstrells all our store;
> And when we've learn'd to speak Italian, then,
> If they so please, we may come Home again.[11]

LEADING THROUGH POETRY AND SONG

In his early professional life, Henry Carey was recognized as a poet and translator (initially French, then later Italian and Latin), and his first published poems appeared in 1710 in the periodical "The Records of Love, or Weekly amusement for the Fair Sex." Carey published his first collection of poetry in 1713 (two others appeared in 1720 and 1729). In 1715 Carey began to set his own poems to music, an activity that would continue throughout his life. Two of Carey's earliest songs, "Flocks are sporting" and "Sally in our Alley" appeared in 1715 and 1716/17, respectively.[12] Carey's early musical training most likely comprised singing and composition lessons with John Reading. Carey wrote of Reading in glowing terms during these early years while Reading appeared to serve in a mentorship capacity to the young composer. Additional evidence of the connection between Carey and Reading is found in Reading's *A Book of New Songs, Compos'd (after the Italian Manner)*, published c. 1710. Carey was the only poet to be credited for the use of his texts, three of which appear in the collection.[13]

Carey's career mentors and supporters can also be found on the literary front. Though I have not yet located evidence that Carey was a member of the Scriblerus Club, a literary club founded in 1714 and described by one member as including some of the "greatest wits of the age," it is clear that Carey had connections with several Scriblerians, most notably John Gay and Alexander Pope. Gay surely knew of Carey, as he used Carey's tune "Sally in our Alley" in *The Beggar's Opera* and later incorporated the Polly Peachum text into the libretto. Carey wrote *A Lilliputian Ode on their Majesties' Accession* for George II's coronation on October 11, 1727: a work most assuredly inspired by Scriblerian Jonathan Swift's book *Gulliver's Travels*, published the previous year (1726). An anonymous work published in 1725, entitled *Namby pamby; a panegyric on the new versification addressed to A——P——, esq.,* was thought to be by Scriblerians Swift or Pope, a misconception that continued long after the poem's publication. An advertisement from 1726 tells of the true author: it states that *Namby Pamby* was by the author of *Mocking Is Catching,* a work irrefutably penned by Carey.[14] Also, *Namby Pamby* was published in Carey's *Poems* of 1729. Carey mentions his work *Namby Pamby* in another work, *Of Stage Tyrants,* written in 1735, and there he thanks Alexander Pope for defending him when all others thought that, since the piece *Namby Pamby* was clever, it had to have been written by someone else.[15] *Namby Pamby* is a satire of various odes by Ambrose Philips, many of which were written to children of nobles with the intention of bettering Philips's standing, thus propelling his career. In *Namby Pamby* Carey ingeniously uses similar language to that used by Philips; however, one cannot miss his deriding tone. Carey also employed the same seven-syllable line as did Philips in his flattering verse. One of the most damning points of Carey's *Namby Pamby* are his references throughout the piece to Philips's second childhood, implying perhaps that Philips had reached senility, thus reducing him to a second childhood of sorts.[16]

> Namby Pamby's *doubly Mild,*
> *Once a Man, and twice a Child;*[17]

and later,

> *Second Childhood gone and past,*
> *Shou'd he prove a Man at last,*
> *What must Second manhood be,*
> *In a Child so Bright as he!*[18]

Carey suggests that Philips had difficulties with drink by the statement "Now he acts the Grenadier, Calling for a Pot of Beer: 'Where's his Monday? He's forgot; Get him gone, a Drunken Sot.' "[19] Carey's *Namby Pamby* was so popular that Philips was called "Namby Pamby" not only in public, but also by Pope in his work *The Dunciad* of 1727.[20]

A final example of Carey's talent for penning innovative and thoughtful political satire consists of two anonymous pieces of prose printed as pamphlets. The first is entitled *A Learned Dissertation on Dumpling; Its Dignity, Antiquity, etc.* This pamphlet appeared in 1726, the author clearly possessing a knowledge of cooking as well as an understanding of the political situation of the day. Consisting of 25 pages with a two-page preface, this decidedly anti-Whig work takes aim at several political and social targets, Robert

Walpole and John Churchill Marlborough among them, who had an appetite for dumpling, i.e., bribery and under-the-table monetary gifts. *Dumpling* continued to be published as late as 1770, an exceptionally long printing life, especially for a satirical pamphlet.[21] Authorship of the pamphlet has long been contested amongst scholars of Henry Carey's literary works; however, the first seven printings of *Dumpling* contain verses from *Namby Pamby* and, if more evidence is needed, a version of Carey's song *Mocking Is Catching* contains an advertisement for *Dumpling* at the bottom of the folio sheet, announcing that the pamphlet had recently been published.[22] A second pamphlet appeared in 1727, also anonymous yet also by Carey, entitled *Pudding and Dumpling Burnt to Pot or, a Compleat Key to the Dissertation on Dumpling*. This second text denounces Swift (whose "Wit has out run his Judgment")[23] for meeting privately with Walpole, suggesting Walpole's possible return to the Whig party in exchange for dumpling.[24] In sum, *Dumpling* and a *Compleat Key* allow

> Carey to attack by indirection a complete spectrum of traditional eighteenth-century targets. Like the musician and the satirist that he is, he builds up to a magnificent crescendo which results in one of the finest displays of sustained virtuosity in early eighteenth-century pamphlet writing.[25]

REVIVING THE ENGLISH VOICE

Henry Carey was possessed of a vast talent, as few of his contemporaries were as versatile as Carey so that they could succeed in the realms of music and theatre as readily as in the areas of satire and social commentary. Possibly as early as 1714, Carey appeared as a singer at Stationers' Hall in a benefit concert (documents exist from this period stating "sung by Mr. Carey at the Dury Lane theatre").[26] His efforts as composer and librettist for that theater spanned from 1723 to 1734. He also published collections of ballads and cantatas during the same period (the vast majority of the texts in those collections were by Carey). Carey began to write cantata texts as early as 1713, including a set of six cantata texts, after the Italian manner, modeled on those in the Johann Christoph Pepusch / John Hughes cantata publication of 1710. When considering Carey's English cantata composition, mention must be made that his output in that genre during the 1720s and 1730s served to connect the early English cantata of John Eccles to the further development of that form by John Stanley, William Boyce, and others later in the eighteenth century. Carey was the most prominent composer during this period to return to the mad song form, his efforts resulting in an innovative eighteenth-century vocal compositional style, which built upon an English seventeenth-century vocal tradition. Carey also published cantatas that took the form of mad songs, modeled after those of Henry Purcell. Briefly described, *mad songs* are multisectional song forms in which the protagonist incrementally loses touch with reality. Carey was the only composer during this period to return to the mad song form, thereby creating an innovative eighteenth-century vocal compositional style through building on an English seventeenth-century vocal tradition.

By 1723, Carey had entered a period rich in composition, creativity, and intermittent commercial acceptance that would sustain him until the early 1740s. Continuing to write of the flaws and fetishes of those who supported Italian opera, Carey created very popular songs, which to this day continue to delight and amuse. A brief study of three such compositions spotlights Carey's strengths as poet and satirist. The first, a "The Lady's Lamentation," was published June 11, 1726, as "Mocking Is Catching, or a Pastoral lamentation for the Loss of a Man and no Man in the simple style." In the poem, a young woman is making her "moan," for her favorite, Senesino, has left London. His actual departure was June 7, 1726, and Carey's poem appeared only four days later. "The Lady's Lamentation" was very well received. Following Senesino's second departure from London in 1736, Carey set "The Lady's Lamentation" to music. The musical version was performed by Mrs. Clive, better known as Kitty Clive, the actress and singer who, as it happened, was also a voice student and friend of Carey's.[27] In this humorous poem, a gentleman observes a lady, weeping and wandering alone in the meads. When asked what was causing her upset, she replied that Senesino had flown. The questioner, having no idea who Senesino was, thought that he was a cruel man for leaving so lovely a woman and refers to him as a "Monster." The word "monster" serves as a double entendre with the first meaning a "terrible person"; the second was more onerous, as castrati such as Senesino were often referred to as either "monster" or having a "monstrous" size or shape. The lovely lady then states that Senesino is neither man nor woman, saying

> *Tis neither for Man or for Woman said she,*
> *That thus in lamenting I water the Lee,*
> *My Warbler celestial sweet Darling of Fame,*
> *Is a Shadow of something a Sex without Name.*

The gentleman, still not understanding, now assumes that she has lost a bird and can easily replace it with a linnet, blackbird, or lark. She ends the poem by saying that she will never again return to the opera, now that Senesino has "flown."

> *Adieu Farinelli, Cuzzoni likewise,*
> *Whom Stars and whom Garters extol to the Skies*

Adieu to the Op'ra, adieu to the Ball,
My Darling is gone and a Fig for 'em all.

With the success of "The Lady's Lamentation" in mind, Carey revised the poem to address Farinelli's departure from London in 1737, made the mournful figure a man rather than a woman, and set it too to music. "The Beau's Lamentation for the Loss of Farinelli" is set to the same tune as "The Lady's Lamentation," with only slight alterations to the melody and the continuo line. Carey also changed the key. Still, one could sing the melody from first with the bass line from the second or vice versa (in the same key, of course) and the lines would fit together nicely, though we would miss Carey's subtle musical turns, which reflect each text so beautifully.

In "The Beau's Lamentation" Carey references contemporary English singers John Beard, Thomas Salway, and Kitty Clive when suggesting that the beau, clearly cast in the role of "dandy," consider English singers instead:

Come never lament for a singer said I,
Can't English Performers his Absence supply,
There's Beard and there's Salway and smart Kitty Clive,
The pleasantest merriest Mortal alive.
Let's go to the Dragon, good Company's there,
There's Marg'ry & Maucy & Signor Laguerre.[28]

The beau responds with great disdain, allowing Carey the opportunity to satirize those who prefer Italian music to English:

Oh talk not of horrible English said he,
I tell you Italian's the Language for me,
Tis better than Latin, 'tis better than Greek,
'Tis what all our Nobles and Gentry should speak,
Plain English may serve for the Cit or the Clown,
But not at the Elegant End of the Town.

It was said that Farinelli departed England because money was owed to him. Carey lampoons the perceived greed of the Italian singers in a later stanza when the beau suggests giving money (what would appear to be an enormous amount) to Farinelli in order to entice him to return to England:

A Curse upon silver, a Curse upon Gold,
That could not my favourite songster withhold,
'Tis Gold that has tempted him over to Spain,
'Tis nothing but Gold can allure him again,
Let's pay the 7 hundred & 7 hundred more,
Nay 7 times 7 Thousand & 10 times 10 score.

The third song can be found in Carey's second play, a farce entitled *Hanging and Marriage, or The Dead Man's Wedding*, which was produced in March 1722. Regrettably, the play was not a success and had only one performance. At the end of the play, a song is called for and immediately a performer sings in Italian. Once finished, a second song is quickly requested, this one in English if you please, so that all might understand. What follows is the wonderful "A Touch on the Times," which later appears in score in Carey's *Cantatas for a Voice*, published in 1724. Aspects of "A Touch on the Times" reveal a true social commentary, as Carey addresses the state of politics at the time, hinting in the text that he was neither Whig nor Tory, but stood somewhere in between. Carey makes no effort to mask his disdain about the politicians of the day and sets the tone of the work at the outset. The song contains five stanzas, of which the first, third, and final follows:

> *A Merry Land by this Light,*
> *We Laugh at our own undoing,*
> *And Labour with all of our Might,*
> *For Slavery and ruin.*
> *New factions we daily raise,*
> *New Maxims we're ever instilling,*
> *And him that today we Praise,*
> *To Morrow's a Rogue and a Villain.*
> *The Statesmen rail at each other,*
> *And tickle the Mob with a Story.*
> *They make a most Horrible Pother*
> *Of National Int'rest and Glory.*
> *Their Hearts they are bitter as Gall,*
> *Tho' their Tongues are sweeter than Honey.*
> *They don't care a Figg for us all,*
> *But only to finger our Money.*
> *Too long have they had their Ends,*
> *In setting us one against t'other,*
> *And sowing such Strife among Friends,*
> *That Brother hated Brother.*
> *But we'll for the future be wise,*
> *Grow sociable, honest and hearty.*
> *We'll all their Arts despise,*
> *And laugh at the Name of a Party.*

In 1732, Carey, along with composers Thomas Arne, John Frederick Lampe, and John Christopher Smith, formed the English Opera Company with the intention of reviving serious opera in English. With the establishment of the English Opera Company, Carey was aligned with some of the most notable English musical figures of the age. He wrote two libretti for this venture,

Amelia, which was produced at The Haymarket and *Teraminta,* produced at Lincoln's Inn Fields. Despite the failure of the company, Carey "emerged as the leading fixture" of this group whose goal it was to reestablish English serious opera.[29] "Throughout his career, Carey had been an ardent campaigner for native music, and native talent."[30]

CAREY'S LEGACY

Though Carey's early contributions to establishing an English opera did not reach the goal of establishing an audience for that genre, his later theatrical efforts experienced significant commercial success. By 1737 Carey's ballad opera *The Honest Yorkshireman* (1735) was playing at Lincoln's Inn Fields at the beginning of the year, and *The Dragon of Wantley* was produced at Covent Garden, then being run by John Rich, in October. The revised version of *The Dragon of Wantley,* with the libretto by Carey and music by his good friend John Frederick Lampe (Carey first became acquainted with Lampe in the mid-1720s) was very well received by London audiences. Originally intended to lampoon Handel's oratorio (such as *Esther, Deborah,* and *Athalia*), the revised version of *Dragon* burlesqued the numerous traditions, musical and otherwise, found in Italian opera. How the tables had turned: now an English burlesque was playing in the fashionable theatre of Covent Garden while Handel, in the two opera seasons that followed, at times had to settle for the lesser theatre of Lincoln's Inn Fields. With the success of *Dragon,* Carey was finally able to have a hand in the decline of continued demand for Italian opera in London.

It merits mention that Carey's barbs and satires were never directed toward Handel, an enormously important and influential musical figure whom Carey held in high esteem. In a poem addressed "To Mr. Handel on his Admetus" published in 1729, Carey describes Handel as an "unexhausted Source of Harmony, Thou glorious Chief of Phoebus' tuneful Sons! In whom the Knowledge of all Magick Numbers, Or sound melodious does concentrated dwell." As additional evidence of Carey's respect and admiration for Handel's compositional skills, Carey's name could always be found on the subscriber lists of Handel's operas, beginning with *Rodelina* in 1725.[31] On the contrary, Carey's targets were the Italian *opera seria* genre, the Italian singers, particularly those who were commanding large salaries and exhibited enormous egos, and his English countrymen: those who believed that by glorifying any and all things Italian, and by denigrating all things English, they were, as a result, moving in a higher and more fashionable society. These people were the objects of Carey's scathing sarcasm and wit, as well as his disdain and scorn.

What must have been a season of extraordinary satisfaction for Carey, theater producer John Rich produced a number of works by Carey during the 1738–1739 season at Covent Garden: *The Dragon of Wantley*; the sequel, *The Dragoness*; *The Honest Yorkshireman* (performed over 100 times during Carey's lifetime); and *The Contrivances* (which remained popular until the end of the century).[32] Exhibiting leadership skills in yet another area, Carey became a founding member of the "Fund for the Support of Decay'd Musicians and their Families," an organization known today as the Musicians Benevolent Fund. Other founding members included Arne, Boyce, Galliard, Handel, Pepusch, and Stanley, an august and powerful group, to be sure.[33] The pace of Carey's career began to slow by 1740, and he wrote no new works for the theatre from 1741 to 1743. He published the set *Three Burlesque Cantatas* in 1741, though all three had been composed and published earlier. In 1742 he published some of the last songs that he was to compose in *A Choice Collection of Six Favourite Songs*. New trends were emerging, along with a new generation of composers, and Carey could not find a suitable outlet for his talents. In 1743 Carey completed not only the third edition of his substantial song collection *The Musical Century* (with subscribers a plenty) but also a complete edition of his theatrical works, entitled *The Dramatick Works of Mr. Carey*. Sadly, on October 4 of that year, having completed the editions, thus putting his affairs in order, Henry Carey proceeded to take his life by hanging himself in his home. He was 56 years old. Contemporary accounts call Carey's death a loss to the musical world (*The Daily Post*) and described him as the author of many excellent songs (*The Annals of Europe*).[34] Two additional happenings compound this tragedy: first, Carey's youngest son, still in infancy, died on the same day. Perhaps, this child's death was simply too much for Carey to bear. Second, soon after Carey's suicide, the demand for songs and ballads once again increased with the advent of the London pleasure gardens. Regretfully, we can only imagine what inventive, delightful, humorous, and satirical entertainments Carey would have created for those venues.

Henry Carey used his talents as an artist to bring about change in the music world and to criticize elements of his own society. Throughout his lifetime, his work as composer, poet, satirist, and performer allowed him access to venues and arenas from which to promote his nationalism and support for English music and musicians. He made innovative use of satire in text and music to advance his cause. He turned backward to older musical forms (such as those of Henry Purcell) yet continued to advance the development of the English cantata and English song through the 1720s and 1730s. Though his endeavor with the English Opera Company was not successful, Carey was recognized for his leadership and for his devotion to native music and musicians. During his lifetime Carey faced challenges and obstacles, spending his career in the neighborhood of Grub Street, which by name alone suggests something less than high society, noble intentions, and glorious opportunities. However, his Grub Street ties brought life and light to his creative work, permeating his characters and portrayals with experiences that occurred to the everyman, not to those few who lived only in elegance and wealth. His tragic suicide ensured that Carey would never know the full impact of his leadership, nor would he be able to appreciate the number of change that he had helped to initiate.

NOTES

1. Norman Gillespie, "The Life and Work of Henry Carey (1687–1743)" (Ph.D. dissertation, 2 vol., University of London, Royal Holloway College, 1982), 2:75.

2. Songs, prose, and poems discussed in this essay were located through archival research at the British Library (Printed music collection) and the Bodleian Library (Harding Collection). Additional materials were located at the Parsons Music Library, University of Richmond.

3. Daniel Purcell, *Six Cantatas for a Voice with a Through Bass, two of which are accompanied with a Violin; compos'd (after the Italian Manner) by Mr. Daniel Purcell none of which were ever before Publish't. By the Author;'s direction carefully Engrav'd on Copper Plates by Thomas Cross* (London: Printed for J. Cullen, 1713), 1.

4. Carole Taylor, "Italian operagoing in London, 1700–1745" (Ph.D. dissertation, Syracuse University, 1991), 110.

5. Ibid.

6. Ibid., 111. Carey, in his song "The Beau's Lamentation for the Loss of Farinelli" (1737) refers to the "call" or plea from Academy directors for funds, in the final line of the song. The singer is quite upset that the castrato Farinelli has left London and ends the song with "Without Farinelli the Opera must fall, So I'll fling up my tickets & not pay the Call." Henry Carey, *The Musical Century, volume II* (London: author, 1740), 5.

7. Carey is alluding to the Italian *opera seria* convention whereby the importance of the role determined the number of arias for the singer. Principle roles offered more arias than secondary roles. Faustina and Cuzzoni desired roles of equal dramatic importance, thus having an equal number of arias.

8. As company manager for Handel's opera company, John Jacob Heidegger was often asked to secure singers for the season. Here, Carey is poking fun at Heidegger for he is being sent to the continent in the hopes of returning with singers such as Senesino and Cuzzoni. For individuals such as Henry Carey who were seeking to promote English musicians, the high salaries commanded by the Italian singers must have been particularly galling.

9. Gillespie, "The Life and Work of Henry Carey," 1:73, 96.

10. The *Faustina* of the title is the Italian singer Faustina Bordoni.

11. Henry Carey, *Faustina or The Roman Songstress* (London: author, 1726).

12. Gillespie, "The Life and Work of Henry Carey," 1:59.

13. Ibid., 48–49.

14. Ibid., 206.

15. Ibid., 1:207.

16. Ibid., 1:209.

17. Henry Carey, *Namby Pamby: or, a Panegyric on the New Versification Address'd to A—P— Esq* (author, London, 1725; reprinted University of California, Los Angeles: The Augustan Reprint Society, 1970), 2.

18. Ibid., 4.

19. Ibid., 3–4.

20. Gillespie, "The Life and Work of Henry Carey," 1:207.

21. Henry Carey, *A Learned Dissertation on Dumpling* (London: author, 1726; reprint University of California, Los Angeles: The Augustan Reprint Society, 1970), i.

22. Ibid., ii.

23. Henry Carey, *Pudding and Dumpling Burnt To Pot. Or, A Compleat Key to the Dissertation on Dumpling* (London: author, 1727; reprint University of California, Los Angeles: The Augustan Reprint Society, 1970), 18.

24. Carey, *A Learned Dissertation on Dumpling*, iii.

25. Gillespie, "The Life and Work of Henry Carey," 55.

26. Ibid., v.

27. Kitty Clive continued to be a supportive presence and remained in close contact with Carey during his lifetime. She performed at benefit concerts intended to support his widow and children following Carey's death.

28. Here Carey is referring to his burlesque, *The Dragon of Wantley*, for which he wrote the libretto. The music was by Carey's good friend John Frederich Lampe. *Dragon* was intended to burlesque Italian vocal music traditions and was enormously popular with English audiences, beginning with its second incarnation in 1737. Margery and Mauxalinda (Maucy) are characters in the mock opera, while Signor Laguerre is John Laguerre, an English baritone who performed the role of Gaffer Gubbins.

29. Gillespie, "The Life and Work of Henry Carey," 1:96.

30. Ibid.

31. Ibid., 1:74.

32. Ibid., 140.

33. Ibid., 141.

34. Ibid., 1:216.

PART V

HOW ARTISTS AND ART LEAD

10

Art History and Leadership Studies

CHARLES JOHNSON

Art history is a valuable resource in the study of leadership. The core of the relationships between leaders and followers is reflected throughout the history of art. The history of art is, in effect, a history of leadership. Works of art have served many important functions in relationship to leaders. Leaders have commissioned art to define their power and stature, to proclaim their beliefs, to educate, inspire, and rally their followers, and to enrich the lives of their subordinates. Leaders, however, by their actions have also provoked outrage among their followers including artists. Artists, in certain situations, have created works to disturb the public and express contempt for leaders. We will examine the following three situations in broad historical contexts that illustrate the complex relationships between leaders and artists.

When Florence in the early Renaissance faced tremendous challenges with political, economic, and social crises that confronted the entire population, the concerns of chancellors, guilds, and artists over the fate of their society played a leading role in the emergence of the fundamentally new style of the visual arts called Renaissance. Leaders and artists combined talents to produce works of art that were crucial in inspiring the Florentines to overcome adversities. Between 1399 and 1427 a host of statues made their appearance in the center of Florence. In essence what the leaders and artists did was to populate the center of Florence with heroic statues that inspired Florentines to fight against enemies who threatened them with absorption and dictatorship.

When Martin Luther ignited the upheavals of the Reformation in the early sixteenth century, the ensuing religious controversies between Catholics and

Protestants were expressed and conveyed in the new forms of communication, the printing press and printmaking. Prints in particular provided a popular forum for Reformation polemics and, as Professor Craig Harbison points out, they also became the primary artistic medium that expressed the sixteenth-century longing for nonidolatrous religious imagery. Protestants became "people of the book" and their leaders became great pamphleteers. Between 1518 and 1523, Martin Luther with the help of artists authored nearly one-third of all the publications printed in Germany.[1]

When Honoré Daumier in the nineteenth century undertook a general examination of modern life, what he found was disturbing. One of his chief concerns was the abuse of power at the expense of the poor by the leaders of France. Yet the leader of France, King Louis-Philippe, the "Citizen King," during his reign from 1830 to 1848 did little to improve the marginal existence of the working class poor. To express and vent his frustration, Daumier created lithographs, one of which was the disturbing image of King Louis-Philippe depicted as *Gargantua* in 1831. Daumier paid a price for his unflattering rendering of the King. He was fined and spent time in prison. Daumier is part of a long history of artists who paid a price for being critical of leaders.

LEADERSHIP AND ART IN THE ITALIAN RENAISSANCE

The story of great leadership and art in the Italian Renaissance can begin with this important building, the Orsanmichele, rebuilt in the middle of the fourteenth century (Photo 10-1). The building originally functioned as a grain market, but because of a series of disasters that occurred in Florence and throughout Tuscany during the century, it was transformed into a church. Dictatorships, famines, floods, epidemics, and financial crashes had occurred. The worst disaster was the Black Plague, which struck with unbelievable intensity in 1348 and beyond, killing off more than half the population throughout Tuscany. People fell sick by the thousands and died untended without the comfort or the sacraments of the Church. Fear intensified the desire for religious solace and the need for people to expiate their overwhelming sense of guilt brought on by this disaster, which was likely attributed by many people to God's wrath and retribution for their sins. In the immediate aftermath of the plague, the confraternity of Orsanmichele found itself the recipient of an enormous sum of money, 350,000 gold florins in gifts and legacies, a sum that was more than the entire annual income of the Florentine state. Over the next decades, resources from this windfall were used to embellish this building, including the construction of a shrine with an elaborate tabernacle to frame a painting of the *Madonna and Child* that had been commissioned from Bernardo Daddi in 1346, only two years before the plague. Given the circumstances of an era of pain and death, this painting

Photo 10-1 *Orsanmichele*, Florence, showing sculptures of guild patron saints and tabernacles. Rebuilt 1337; arches closed, later fourteenth century; niches and sculptures, fourteenth to sixteenth centuries.

Credit: Alinari/Art Resource, New York.

became important; a fragmented culture could find solace in "Our Lady of Orsanmichele." Public pressure forced the cessation of mercantile activities in Orsanmichele, and by 1357, the decision was made to remove the grain market to another location. In 1365, Daddi's Virgin in the Orsanmichele was made *Special Protectress* of the city of Florence, and in 1366, the decision was made to close in the open arches on the building and add stained glass windows, thus transforming Orsanmichele into a church. In the post-plague years, the Orsanmichele, with Daddi's inspiring painting inside, was a great comfort to the people of Florence. Orsanmichele became the destination of numerous pilgrimages of people grateful for survival who yearned to find meaning in an era of death and chaos.[2]

Problems, however, did not cease. The plague reappeared periodically, there was proletarian unrest that caused trouble in Florence's important woolen industry, and there were also political problems that became increasingly ominous near the turn of the century. At the beginning of the fifteenth century, Florence was thrust into a rapidly changing world where awesome challenges called forth its every resource: economic, military, intellectual, and artistic. Since there was no single authoritative ruler in Italy during the

Renaissance, Florence, a city of some 40,000 to 50,000 people, was pitted against ambitious regional states. Independent enemy communes became breeding grounds for power-seeking tyrants. By the 1390s, every part of the Florentine community was affected by the threatening relations with Gianga- leazzo Visconti, Lord of Milan. Giangaleazzo was, reportedly, a cruel and ambitious man. By 1400, Florence and Milan were locked in a struggle for sur- vival. Giangaleazzo deliberately hit the vulnerable aspects of Florence's economy by causing damage to the cloth industry. And by exerting an astute combination of diplomatic and military pressure, this tyrant surrounded Flor- ence by 1402. His troops also occupied Bologna, Siena, and Pisa so that Florentine merchants could not utilize their ports for their trade. Thus Flor- ence, an artisan republic controlled by its guilds, was threatened by economic catastrophe and potential loss of freedom. To make matters worse, the Floren- tine Republic was no longer protected by membership in any league against the Visconti of Milan.

Florentines, however, had weathered many crises and, for the sake of their own survival, had developed a staunch character under adversity. This qual- ity of courage in difficult situations depended on fortitude, wit, energy, and strength of character. During the fifteenth century it was the marshalling of the city's strengths of character that served as a catalyst for what became one of the most dazzling and inventive periods in Western art. An era of astonishing creativity, fueled by the revival of classical learning, emerged in Florence. One of the greatest tools of inspired leadership during the period was art, which to this day defines Florence as the greatest city of the Renaissance.

Such was the importance of public art in inspiring Florentines to overcome the dangers threatening their freedom that between 1399 and 1427 no less than 32 over-life-size sculptured male figures made their appearance in the center of Florence, 18 on the Cathedral and 14 at Orsanmichele. The 14 Orsanmichele niches had originally been assigned to the leading guilds of Florence in 1339. By 1400, only three had been made and installed, but in the first decade of the fifteenth century, pressure on the guilds renewed, likely because of the political situation Florence was facing. All the statues, the saints at Orsanmichele and the prophets and evangelists at the Duomo, were destined for the exteriors of these two churches of predominately civic char- acter, and all were addressed to the imagination of people in the street. Some, in fact, were placed hardly above street level, as shown in the niche statues on the exterior of the Orsanmichele. Professor Frederick Hartt described these marble and bronze figures as "soldiers" and "the race of heroes that popu- lated the center of the city." By their expressions, the dignity and intensity of characterization, and the forcefulness of their poses and glances, these stat- ues betray a realization of the forces against which they must struggle and summon the full resources of their personalities. In the words of Chancellor Leonardo Bruni, who became a great apologist for freedom, "What greater thing could this commonwealth accomplish, or in what better way prove that the *virtus* of her forebears was still alive, than by her own efforts and resources to liberate the whole of Italy from the threat of servitude." Professor Hartt commented, "it is indeed, *virtus,* which might be defined not so much as virtue but as the kind of courage, resolution, character in short, that makes a man a man, which flashes from the eyes of these statues of marble and bronze." [3] In Florence, inspiring public statues had become recognized and valued as a civic and moral responsibility.

Giorgio Vasari, writing in the sixteenth century, singled out Ghiberti's *John the Baptist* (Photo 10-2) as "the beginning of a new style," and at the same time singled out Ghiberti's second set of bronze doors for the Florence Baptistry, "as the finest masterpiece ever created, in ancient or modern times." There are important ideas implied in Vasari's comments. One is the realization that there was a new style of sculpture emerging in the early fifteenth century. The concerns of leaders and artists over the fate of their society and its well-being were reflected and paralleled in the content and style of the new Renaissance art. Another significant idea implied in Vasari's comments is the conscious realization of Florence's glorious ancient past, which emerged with the recovery and study of the writings of the ancients from the Greco-Roman world, which was an important resource for the leaders of Florence in the fifteenth century.

Humanism—literally the study of mankind, its history, literature, and institutions—which was rooted in knowledge of ancient secular Latin authors, had begun to emerge in the Italian city-republics in the fourteenth century. It influenced the Latin Constitutions of Siena in the fourteenth century and was brilliantly furthered by Petrarch and Boccaccio. Humanism led a flourishing if somewhat rarified existence in Italian universities and courts during the last decades of the fourteenth century, but the Florentine contribution to humanism lay in bringing humanistic learning out of the contemplative sphere and giving it an important role in active life, making it particularly relevant to civic responsibility and moral duty. Taking their cue from the recently rediscovered letters of Cicero and the legacy of other writers who positioned themselves as ardent defenders of the late Roman Republic, Florentine intellectuals involved themselves in political affairs. To give moral force and authority to their diplomatic enterprises, humanists sought and found convincing analogies with ancient times, abstracting from history lessons to be applied to contemporary situations. With the development of a vernacular literature based on the Tuscan dialect, the audience for humanist writings was expanded. According to Chancellor Leonardo Bruni, Florence was the great home of writing in the vernacular, the *volgare,* and her Italian speech was the model for the peninsula. Bruni also praised Florence as being alone in calling back the forgotten knowledge of antiquity.

> Who, if not our Commonwealth, has brought to recognition, revived and rescued from the ruin the Latin letters, which previously had been abject, prostrate and almost dead? . . . Indeed, even the knowledge of the Greek letters, which for more than seven hundred years has fallen into disuse in Italy, has been recalled and brought back by our Commonwealth with the result that we have become able to see face to face, and no longer through the veil of absurd translations the greatest philosophers and admirable orators and all those other men distinguished by their learning.

(Leonardo Bruni, Chancellor of Florence)[4]

It was during Bruni's chancellorship that Florentines came to feel they had an historical affinity with the Athenians of ancient Greece, an affinity that was complementary to both Florence and her leaders. The ancient Greeks had dealt successfully with their Persian enemies, under the able leadership of Pericles, as now the Florentines had repulsed their enemies, the dukes and lords of Milan and Naples, under the able leadership of their chancellors.

Ghiberti's statue of *St. John the Baptist*, the patron saint of Florence, was cast in one piece, a tour de force, which introduced wholly new possibilities into the realm of techniques of sculpture at the time (Photo 10-2). No bronze figure on this scale—more than eight feet tall—had been cast for centuries in Italy. And given its size, the viewer at street level is in the presence of a work of inspiring heroic proportions.[5]

Donatello's statue of *David* (Photo 10-3) depicts the Old Testament hero who was victorious over his enemy Goliath, a theme relevant to Florence at the time because of the obvious connection between a triumphant Scriptural victor and the contemporary political circumstances. In the Old Testament, David, the youthful champion of the chosen people, defeated the tyrant, Goliath. The wreath above the head of Donatello's *David* has been identified as amaranth, a purplish plant whose name in Greek means "nonfading." It was considered the fitting crown for the undying memory of heroes. In the New Testament, the amaranth crown is held out as the ultimate reward of the faithful. Originally, there was an inscription in Latin engraved on a bronze strap in David's right hand (the slingshot that David used to kill Goliath), which read: "To those who bravely fight for the fatherland the gods will lend aid even against the most terrible foes."[6]

The relevance of this rendering of the hero David to Florence and its political and military situation can be judged by the fact that there were no statues of the youthful, victorious David (as distinguished from the adult King David) before this time, and from this time on, they became legion in Florence; Donatello, Castagno, Verrocchio, and Michelangelo all created images

Photo 10-2 Lorenzo Ghiberti. *St. John the Baptist* **and inlaid marble tabernacle. 1405–1417. Bronze figure, height 8 feet 4 inches. Commissioned by the Arte di Calimala for their niche on Orsanmichele.**

Credit: The Image Works.

of David. Florence became, in effect, the city of David. As Professor Hartt points out, lest anything be lacking to reinforce its significance, in 1416, two years after the overthrow of Ladislaus, the Signoria demanded Donatello's statue of *David* urgently and without delay from the *Arte della Lana*, so that it could be set up in the Palazzo Vecchio in the council halls of the Republic where it stood for many years. The same thing happened again in Florence almost a century later when the *David* of Michelangelo, also intended for a buttress of the cathedral in 1502, was set up after its completion in 1504 as a kind of symbol of the embattled republic under Piero Soderini, then engaged in the last and tragic phase of its struggle for survival against tyranny.[7] It is noteworthy that in terms of the politics in Florence, Donatello's *David* of

**Photo 10-3 Donatello. *David*. 1408–1409; reworked 1416. Marble, height
6 feet 3 inches. Originally commissioned by the Opera del Duomo for one
of the buttresses of the Duomo, the Cathedral of Florence.**
Credit: The Image Works.

1408 and Michelangelo's *David* in the early sixteenth century mark the
parameters of the history of Florentine freedom.

Donatello's statue of *St. Mark* (Photo 10-4) is a stately and formidable figure
with a serious noble face expressing severe determination. The Italian term
terribile, which is what the Renaissance would use to describe the face, has
been described as a symbolic portrait of the ideal Florentine under stress as
identified at the time by humanist propagandists for the Republic. In other
words, Donatello's figure of *St. Mark* is a summation of the virtues demanded
in a crisis. Had the Visconti of Milan succeeded in conquering Florence a decade before when this work was first commissioned, Florentines would have
been subjected to the rule of a tyrant. But in the hot summer of 1402, the
plague reappeared and, after sweeping through the northern regions of

Photo 10-4 Donatello. *St. Mark.* **1411–1416. Marble figure, height 7 feet 10 inches. Commissioned by the** *Arte dei Linaioli e Rigattieri* **(the linen weavers and peddlers) for their niche on Orsanmichele.**

Credit: Alinari / Art Resource, New York.

Lombardy, it carried off Giangaleazzo Visconti. In a short time, the Milanese empire collapsed, and Florence was saved. People believed the duke's death had been heralded by the appearance of a comet. In their joy, the Florentines repeated the verses from Psalm 124: 7–8: "We have escaped as a bird from the snares of the fowlers; the snare is broken, and we have escaped. Our help is in the name of the Lord, who made heaven and earth." [8]

Divine intervention or not, the Florentines had been ready for the battle, and prominent leaders of the time, who cast the conflict as a struggle between "tyranny" and "liberty," credited victory to the character of the Florentine people, the very attributes celebrated in Donatello's *David* and *St. Mark* sculptures. Almost immediately after the defeat of the Visconte, Leonardo Bruni, the great Chancellor of Florence, wrote *The Laudatio of the City of Florence*, which was the most vigorous and complete expression of the ideas that inspired Florence during the struggle with Milan. In the section entitled *Why Florence Is to be Admired*, Bruni claimed that Florentine citizens were ennobled by their descent from the ancient Roman people and that Florence, founded before the Caesars, had all the virtue necessary to resist tyrants. Bruni extolled the patriotism and love of liberty that he argued had been inherited from ancient Rome and that had inspired the Florentine people in the defense of their city against Milan:

> There is no place on earth in which justice is fairer to all. For nowhere does such liberty flourish . . . There are in this city the most talented men, who easily surpass the limits of other men in whatever they do. Whether they follow the military profession, or devote themselves to the task of governing the commonwealth, or to certain studies or to the pursuit of knowledge, or to commerce—in everything they undertake and in every activity they far surpass all other mortals, nor do they yield first place in any field or to any other nation. They are patient in the labor, ready to meet danger, ambitious for glory, strong in counsel, industrious, generous, elegant, pleasant, affable, and above all, urbane.[9]

Donatello's statue of *St. Mark* the Evangelist also reveals notions about the subject, St. Mark. Although the old and venerable symbol of St. Mark, the winged lion, was omitted from the statue, it is shown below on the ledge of the niche and is associated with several ideas. The lion, St. Mark's main attribute, refers to John the Baptist's prediction: "Behold, I send my messenger before thy face, who shall prepare thy way; the voice of one crying in the wilderness" (Mark 1:3), identified with the roaring of the lion. The relationship to a lion, the king of beasts, and to Christ the King was not casual. It reflected the contemporary concern with interpreting physiognomy and character in humans by reference to the animal world, which was often done in art. In this circumstance, Donatello and Florence were "leonine" in character, a quality not unrelated to the concept of the virtue of courage.

Ghiberti's and Donatello's sculptures were, in essence, allegories of esteemed virtues drawn from venerable sources, both Christian and ancient classical. Their presence was important in Florence where leaders of the Republic could use them to help shape and influence contemporary events. What is also significant about these searching estimates of the resources of human character is that they differ profoundly from the medieval longing for divine deliverance. By the time of the installation of the statues on Orsanmichele, deliverance or salvation in the temporal world was now up to the individual, based upon his character. These inspiring statues reflect men of character who took charge of their civic and moral responsibilities. They are a tribute to the great artists who created them and leaders who inspired and supported the artists, leaving a legacy that lives on.

REFORMATION PRINTS: PROBLEMS OF LEADERSHIP IN THE EARLY SIXTEENTH CENTURY

In the early sixteenth century, leaders and artists combined their talents in the context of the emerging Protestant Reformation. Art, specifically print-making, which transformed communication, became a vital medium for the articulation of Reformation ideas.

By the dawn of the sixteenth century, there were serious problems in leadership in both the church and the courts that would have enormous consequences for all of Europe and beyond. Machiavellian leadership—that is, the application of conscious systematic realism to political affairs in a manner that separated political practices from Christian ideals—had emerged full force. This period in history produced striking examples of "Machiavellian" leaders, whose ends justified whatever their means. Emperor Charles V, patron of the Roman Catholic Church, who threatened the life of the pope, had the capital of Christendom destroyed in the horrific Sack of Rome in 1527. His son, King Philip II of Spain, sent 10,000 troops into the Netherlands to quell Protestant uprisings "with fire and sword." Even Martin Luther betrayed the common people when he urged the nobility to feel no compunction in adopting any form of violence to dampen the Peasant Revolt of 1525, in which more than 100,000 lives were lost.[10] Luther's response to the revolt was a pamphlet, written hurriedly in 1525, entitled *Against the Rapacious and Murdering Peasants: Smite, Strangle, and Stab*. The pamphlet went through 20 editions.[11]

To pretend that Christian love and ethics governed men's lives was, to Machiavelli, a contemptible hypocrisy that must have seemed especially hypocritical with regard to the leadership of the Roman Catholic Church. Italians and other reformers since Dante had lamented that the nearer one came to Rome, the wider the gap between Christian teaching and practice. By the early fourteenth century, while most people still believed in the divine foundation of the medieval church, strong antipapal sentiments had begun to emerge and criticism of the papacy was mounting.

By the late fourteenth century, there were loud calls for papal and church reform; the English theologian John Wycliffe (c. 1324–1384) at Oxford and Jan Huss (c. 1372–1415) at the University of Prague were two of the most outspoken critics of popes. With the condemnation of his views by Pope Gregory XI in May 1377, Wycliffe began using Antichrist rhetoric against the papacy. As Professor Steven Ozment points out, the thrust of his incessant attacks was to see the papacy itself, not just any individual pope, as the culmination of the power of Satan. Jan Huss, who was influenced by Wycliffe, also had a keen sense of the corruption of the papacy. Antichrist language against the papacy was widely used during the course of the Hussite movement. After he was excommunicated by Pope John XXIII in 1411, Huss remained defiantly outspoken against the church, expressing his ideas in a major treatise written in 1413, *On the Church,* which led to his being burned as a heretic on July 6, 1415.

Huss's follower, Nicolas of Dresden, issued a work in 1412 called *The Old Color and the New,* in which the symbolic opposition between Christ and Antichrist took on a new form in relation to the contrasts between the poor and humble Christ of the Gospels and the wealth and power of the popes who were then claiming the throne of St. Peter in the waning years of the Great Schism. Nicolas's treatise, contrasting the "old color" of the apostolic church with the "new color" of papal Christendom was intended for the learned as well as for popular consumption. A century later, Nicolas's treatise would influence Martin Luther during the Protestant Reformation.[12]

At the end of the fifteenth century, the best known prophetic voice of doom was that of Girolamo Savonarola (1452–1498), the powerful and influential Dominican preacher of Florence who dominated the city from 1494 until he was finally hanged and burnt in 1498. Crowds thronged to hear his sermons, which became ever more daring, especially against Pope Alexander VI, whom Sidney Alexander described as one of the most corrupt popes in the history of the church, *Pontifex Maximus Corruptus.*[13] Savonarola used the word "whore" publicly in his Lenten sermons delivered from the pulpit of the Florence Cathedral in the late 1490s in reference to the corruption of the Church.

> Turn back O wicked Church; I have given you, sayeth the Lord, rich vestments and you have made idols of them. Rich vessels give rise to pride, sacraments to simony; in your abominations you have become a shameless prostitute . . .
>   . . . You have made of the church a public place; you have constructed a brothel open to all . . . And thus O Whorish Church you have shown your ugliness to all the world and your stink rises to heaven. You have multiplied your fornication in Italy, in France, in Spain, everywhere.[14]

Savonarola preached not only about the corruption within the church, but also about a variety of issues he felt were corrupting the culture. He persuaded people to cast out of their homes vulgar and lascivious things, and all statues and all kinds of paintings that might incite persons to bad and indecent thoughts. Iacopo Nardi, an observer, describes the 1497 bonfire of vanities in which art and other decorative objects were burned:

> Hence, the children went, sometimes alone and sometimes accompanied by their elders, to all the houses of the citizens in their quarter and gently asked that

all objects of anathema be cast out of the houses as dirty things, cursed by God and by the Canons of the Holy Church . . . And on Carnival day all these unclean things were brought to the Piazza della Signoria where a special wooden pyramid, with seven steps for the seven deadly sins, had been erected . . . And on the last day of the Carnival . . . all our Florentines thronged to the Piazza to see this second Bonfire of Vanities, and it was greater than the year before.[15]

Savonarola also attacked artists. He preached sermons addressed to artists in which he accused them of painting their mistresses and whores in the guise of the Madonna. A number of artists were swept by his fervor, including Michelangelo, who all his life carried around with him a book of Savonarola's sermons, and especially Botticelli whose painting, *Calumny of Apelles*, 1497–1498(?) quite possibly makes reference to Fra Girolamo's tragedy.[16] What finally destroyed Savonarola was his conflict with Pope Alexander VI. The Pope ordered Savonarola to cease preaching, forbidding him to exercise his ecclesiastical duties. Savonarola simply dispatched other members of his order to preach sermons he had written. Under torture Savonarola was charged with having sent letters to all the crowned heads in Christendom calling for a new council to depose the Pope. Exasperated, the Pope finally placed the entire city of Florence under interdict; Florentines found themselves excommunicated, which turned people against Savonarola. After being excommunicated, arrested, and tortured, Savonarola was publicly burned as a heretic in Florence in the Piazza Signoria on May 23, 1498. In retrospect, it is perhaps ironic that Savonarola never once projected the notion of another church outside the See of St. Peter. His passion was the purification of the Church, the vessel of salvation that had been tarnished. For a time, Savonarola no doubt was an effective leader and gifted preacher. Early on he even gained a reputation among followers as a prophet, but his rigid methods of trying to achieve goals and his unwillingness to exercise diplomacy with superiors ended his life in tragedy. Apparently, what Savonarola did achieve was the fulfillment of his thirst for martyrdom, his Christ identification, an *Imitatione Christi* that was to culminate in the spectacular parallels of his death to Christ's death at Calvary.[17]

On the eve of the Reformation, at a time when strong leadership was needed, the Catholic Church had become trapped in a hierarchical structure headed by a dissolute and outrageously extravagant papacy that required huge sums of money to support its gigantic building program (St. Peter's Basilica in Rome was in the early stages of reconstruction) and maintain lavish living standards for its high clergy. The leadership of the Catholic Church had abdicated its responsibilities; bishoprics had become the special refuge of nobility, the majority of whom were appointed to their ecclesiastical offices on the basis of economic or political considerations, not because of religious preparation or aptitude. There were widespread abuses of fiscal responsibilities, the practice of simony, the buying and selling of ecclesiastical pardons and offices, and many of the clergy violated their vows of celibacy by keeping concubines.

As a young monk in Wittenberg, Luther had become painfully aware of the moral and financial abuses in the Church. In 1510, Luther made a pilgrimage to Rome where he saw, first hand, the splendor of the Roman Church, which reinforced his mounting distrust of the Catholic hierarchy. By 1517, Luther, a member of the Augustinian order and doctor of theology and professor at the University of Wittenberg, had become so offended by practices in the Church that on the Vigil of All Saints, October 31, 1517, he posted his 95 theses on the door of the Wittenberg church challenging his colleagues to debate issues of Roman Catholic doctrines and practices. The particular issue that prompted Luther to post his theses was the sale of indulgences, collected in Germany at the time by a Dominican priest, Johann Tetzel, who became the immediate object of Luther's protest. A veteran indulgence salesman who would receive a certain percentage of the amount collected, Tetzel made outrageous claims about the benefits indulgences could provide for those penitents who purchased them.

A contemporary account in Friedrich Myconius's *Historia reformationis* describes the outlandish behavior of Tetzel:

> His preaching raised enormous amounts of money which were sent to Rome . . . the claims of this uneducated and shameful monk were unbelievable. Thus he said that even if someone had slept with Christ's dear Mother, the Pope had power in heaven and on earth to forgive as long as money was put into the indulgence coffer. And if the Pope would forgive, God also had to forgive.[18]

In 1517, Tetzel stated in his Sermon on Indulgences:

> You may obtain letters of safe-conduct from the vicar of our Lord Jesus Christ [the pope], by means of which you are able to liberate your soul from the hands of the enemy, and convey it by means of contrition and confession, safe and secure from all pains of Purgatory, into the happy kingdom.[19]

Luther not only objected to the idea of people having their sins forgiven by purchasing "Letters of indulgence" dispensed by the pope, but he was also outraged by Tetzel taking money from his poor German countrymen to be used by the young German archbishop, Albrecht von Brandenburg, who needed to pay off a huge debt to the pope in return for papal favors. Luther's response to the sale of indulgences was to post his 95 theses, which included the following:

> No. 5. The pope has neither the will nor the power to remit any penalties . . .
>
> No. 6. The pope has no power to remit any guilt, except by declaring and warranting it to have been remitted by God . . .

No. 21. Those preachers of indulgences are in error who say that by the indulgences of the pope a man is free and saved from all punishment.[20]

A copy of Luther's *Theses* was sent to Pope Leo X by Cardinal Brandenberg, and on April 17, 1521, Martin Luther had become a condemned heretic under the pope's ban. On that day Luther, wearing his doctoral cap, stood in the presence of the newly elected Holy Roman Emperor, Charles V, and refused to recant his alleged errors and made his famous declaration. He declared:

> Unless I am convinced by the testimony of Scripture or by clear reason, for I do not trust either the pope or in councils alone, since it is well known that they have often erred and contradicted themselves, I am bound by Scriptures I have quoted and my conscience is captive to the Word of God. I cannot and will not retract anything, for it is neither safe nor right to go against conscience. I cannot do otherwise, here I stand, may God help me, Amen.[21]

The religious upheaval instigated by Luther was greatly aided by both printing and printmaking. With the invention of the printing press, prints became the ideal medium for communicating messages, since multiple copies could be reproduced for dissemination to wide audiences. Moreover, the starkness of a black-and-white print was likely more appropriate for controversial messages than the sensuousness of colors in paintings that conveyed traditional Catholic orthodoxy. Printmaking became the primary medium that expressed the sixteenth century longing for nonidolatrous religious imagery. It is perhaps no coincidence that there is a complicity in the vocabulary of printmaking technique—the "acid" and "bite" in an etching, or the "cut" in a woodblock—that matches the intent of artists who wished to express their polemical ideas during the Reformation period. The significance of illustrated printed books during the period was extraordinary. Within a few decades of one of the first books printed on a press with moveable type, the Latin Bible issued by Johann Gutenberg in Mainz, circa 1455, printing had spread from Germany to all the countries of Europe. By the end of the fifteenth century, printing presses existed in over 200 cities and towns, and an estimated 6 million books had been printed with more than half of them on religious subjects. More books were printed in the 40 years between 1460 and 1500 than had been produced by scribes and monks during the entire Middle Ages.[22]

In the sixteenth century, it was the polemical tract, a short printed pamphlet 14 to 40 pages in length, with decorated pages, that became the vehicle for the spread of Reformation theology. Luther, with the help of artists like Lucas Cranach the Elder, produced about 30 of these tracts, which were distributed in editions of up to 300,000 copies, some of which went into as many as 19 editions. Woodcuts and prints became a powerful medium for supporting Reformation polemics.

Cranach's woodcuts were inspired by Nicolas of Dresden's work of 1412 called *The Old Color and the New,* in which the symbolic opposition between Christ and Antichrist contrasted the poor and humble Christ of the Gospels and the wealth and power of the popes. These woodcuts were published shortly after the Edict of Worms, issued in May 1521, which condemned Luther for heresy and insurrection and decreed that "his books are to be eradicated from the memory of man." Having been excommunicated, Luther issued his attack on the bull of excommunication, entitled *Against the Execrable Bull of Antichrist,* which contained a strong denunciation of the papacy as the seat of the Final Enemy (Antichrist).[23]

Cranach's prints depict the contrast between Christ and the papal Antichrist in 13 sets of aptly captioned double pictures. In set No. 11 (Photo 10-5), on the left, we see the humble Christ driving the money changers from the Temple, and on the right, the pompous and prosperous pope receiving the gold of indulgence money at the altar. Other polemical

Photo 10-5 Lucas Cranach the Elder (German, 1472–1553) Set No. 11:
Christ Expelling the Money-Changers from the Temple **and** *The Pope Giving Out Indulgences for Money.* **Woodcuts, each 4-1/2 inches by 3-5/8 inches.**

Source: Print Collection, Miriam and Ira D. Wallach Division of Art, Prints and Photographs, The New York Public Library, Astor, Lenox, and Tilden Foundations.

examples included: *Christ Washing the Feet of the Apostles* and *The Pope Sitting on an Imperial Throne Having His feet Kissed by the Emperor; Christ Crowned with Thorns* and *The Pope Crowned with the Triple Tiara; Christ Healing Cripples and Lepers* and *The Pope Watching a Tournament; Christ and Peter Walking Barefoot Along a Path* and *The Pope Being Carried in a Litter.* Cranach's book closes with illustrations adopted from late medieval portrayals of *Christ's Ascension* opposite to the *Antichrist's Demise.* On one side Christ ascends to heaven from the Mount of Olives, while on the opposite side the papal Antichrist is dragged down into the fires of hell by a host of devils. This book is one of many works produced by Luther and his colleagues who were quick to see the value of the print medium to spread their views. While didactic prints were routinely used by all parties in the Reformation controversy, the artists who supported Martin Luther were an illustrious group. In addition to Cranach, there was Dürer, Grünewald, and Holbein, to name a few.

Cranach's portrait of *Martin Luther in Profile with Doctoral Cap,* is one of several admirable portraits of Luther made during the emerging Reformation. This particular portrait was done for the occasion of Luther's defense at Worms. Cranach shows him wearing the headpiece of a university doctor, which gives a strong impression of Luther's learning and authority. The inscription below the portrait reads: "Lucas' work is this picture of Luther's mortal form; but he himself expressed his spirit's eternal form." By this date, Luther had, indeed, expressed himself through his writings. After he posted his 95 theses, Luther's fame had spread and by 1520 many people were curious to know the appearance of the man who had challenged the Catholic Church. There was likely a market for Luther's portraits.

The Catholic Church responded to Luther's attacks by trying to stem the flow of propaganda. In 1521 the Edict of Worms tried to censor the press and explicitly forbade the publication of satirical matter. The Diets of Nuremberg (1524) and Augsburg (1530) also confirmed and strengthened censorship laws. In spite of these efforts, political and religious literature and prints persisted, as did the Reformation, which would have enormous consequences for both Catholics and Protestants.

In the final analysis, it was art that played such an important role in conveying the most important ideas of the Reformation crisis. And subsequent to the Reformation, art remained a powerful tool for leaders in both the Catholic and Protestant worlds. Baroque art, "the marble megaphone of papal dogma" according to art critic Robert Hughes, emerged with full force in the Catholic world during the seventeenth century.

In the Protestant world, art evolved in different directions in Holland, in England, and eventually in America. In these locations, art would reflect the emerging secular world of science, exploration, industry, and wealth.

Religion had its place in the scheme of things in the Protestant world, but that place was clearly defined and circumscribed.

DAUMIER AND THE PROBLEM OF LEADERSHIP IN NINETEENTH CENTURY FRANCE

Daumier's work represents an unhappy relationship between an artist and a leader, which in no way reduces the significance of his art. To the contrary, many artists throughout history have depicted leaders in critical and highly controversial works using unconventional means by which to reveal truths about leadership that are painful and sometimes outrageous. The function of such art has not been to please, but to disturb, or more strongly, to prick the conscious of viewers with the hope of improving or rectifying situations that are intolerable. Daumier's work depicts an intolerable situation in nineteenth century France in which the leader was not only inept but morally bankrupt. In such situations, the work of art, in effect, leads and ultimately is of greater significance and value than the leader who provoked the artist's frustration and anger. Often, artists who challenge leaders pay a price. Daumier never achieved wealth or fame in his lifetime, but posthumously he is remembered with likely greater affection and acclaim than Louis-Philippe, Citizen King of France.

While the July Revolution of 1830 in France may have been a triumph for the bourgeoisie, it was a disaster for the vast majority of Frenchmen, especially the rapidly growing and increasingly restless working classes. After the revolution Louis-Philippe, the new "citizen king," was committed to the bourgeoisie who were coming into full possession and awareness of their power. His advisors, confidants, and supporters wanted freedom to build their fortunes unhampered by governmental restrictions or by pressures from worker or peasant movements. During this postrevolutionary era, railways and roads were built, cities grew in size, and industrialization took great strides. But with these developments came social antagonisms between rich industrial capitalists and the working-class poor.[24]

Through the Industrial Revolution of the eighteenth and nineteenth centuries, the working masses in France and in England were plagued by long hours (many worked more than 12 hours a day), poor wages, and the deplorable consequences of poverty, hunger, disease, and unsanitary housing. With the July Revolution of 1830 they had hoped for an improvement in their marginal existence and a relief from the haunting specter of unemployment, but the inactivity of Louis-Philippe and his ministers in the face of the critical needs of the poor made turmoil inevitable. In 1831, weavers and other workers in the silk industry in Lyon (who worked an average of 16 hours a day) revolted. The government, with troops, crushed the uprising of these workers who wanted to negotiate wage increases with their employers. This event in turn led to laws that forbade striking and unionization. For nearly two decades following the July Revolution, working class people were severely circumscribed by the policies of Louis-Philippe.

The disparity and polarization between social classes engendered responses in art and literature. Outraged by the excesses of industrialization, an avant-garde emerged among artists and writers that developed into the critical and increasingly combative conscience of bourgeois civilization. As art critic Hilton Kramer pointed out, the avant-garde was, from the start, a vital coefficient of bourgeois culture. The cultural history of the bourgeoisie is the history of its gradual and painful adjustment to this conscience—an adjustment that made the bourgeoisie, despite its own worst inclinations, the moral and aesthetic beneficiary of the avant-garde's heroic labors.[25]

In France, artists with a polemical bent, united by their dislike and frustration with the government and its allies, used art as a political weapon. Artists had both the weapons and means to express their ideas. One very effective weapon was the relatively new technique of lithography whereby artists could produce images of sarcastic caricatures in a very powerful medium. The means to publish this kind of expression for the public was the two newspapers edited and published by the caricaturist Charles Philipon, who was to wage editorial war for 30 years against the French government, chronicling the repressive activities of Louis-Phillipe. Philipon launched *La Caricature* as a political weekly in 1830, and two years later he added *Le Charivari*. These publications from the outset were planned as both a graphic as well as a written attack on government leadership. Philipon had an extraordinary range of talents from which to draw. Writers like Honoré de Balzac wrote polemics at *Le Caricature*, and leading satirical artists pilloried political leaders. One of the most gifted artists was the young Honoré Daumier (1808–1879), who was powerful enough in his use of biting imagery to attempt to dethrone Louis-Philippe and the established order.[26]

Daumier, from the July Monarchy of 1830 on through the Second Empire of Napoleon III, used art to chronicle Parisian life, drawing images from the corrupt and pompous behavior of judges and deputies and the broad spectacle of city dwellers. Perhaps Daumier's most important use of art was to champion the causes of the masses disinherited by industrialization. In 40 years, he would produce 4,000 lithographs—an average of two a week—which must have provided him with a sense of satisfaction at boldly striking out against those issues that disturbed him. Out of a total population of nearly 31 million people there were approximately 26 million Frenchmen who lived at a poverty level. It was these people who became Daumier's concern. He made the poor working class his subject over and over again in various seemingly unplanned poses and arrangements—the modern city dweller in the hubbub of expanding city life, anonymous, insignificant, and often patient with a lot they could not change. Daumier's work is testimony to his integrity and obstinate belief in a republic, in economic and political equality, in the right of all Frenchmen to determine who should best represent them, and in full freedom of written and spoken opinion. He lived in a world, however, where the leadership did not allow such equality, and that is why Daumier became an indignant eye, a man of enormous moral conviction, who used art to express his views in a clear and powerful way.

One of Daumier's most disturbing lithographs was his image of 1831 entitled *Garguntua.*

By the time Daumier submitted the lithograph in Photo 10-6 of Louis-Philippe as *Gargantua* on December 16, 1831, to the publishing business run by Charles Philipon (1800–1862), the king of France had become among the avant-garde a symbol of dashed hopes, mediocrity, and materialism, the leader of a detested form of government. Press attacks against royal authority and especially against the person of the king had already become outlawed, punishable by fines and imprisonment or both. Caricature was suppressed because of political instability and commotion, which ultimately resulted in the so-called "September Laws," which represented a virtual reestablishment

Photo 10-6 Honoré Daumier (French 1808–1889), *Gargantua,* **1831 Lithograph.**

Source: Fine Arts Museum of San Francisco, Museum purchase, Herman Michaels Collection, Vera Michaels Bequest Fund, 1993.48.1.

of press censorship. Daumier's print *Gargantua,* in other words, was an act of courage for which he would be imprisoned and fined. In late December, the police seized the print. They had orders to destroy the original lithograph stone and all remaining proofs. The extreme rarity of impressions today suggest that the police were largely successful in achieving their goal.

It is not hard to understand why the lithograph was suppressed. Daumier's image is a grotesque and scathing representation of the king as the ugly and obese giant *Gargantua,* a character from François Rabelais's *Gargantua et Pantagruel,* originally published in 1532–1535.

As Elizabeth Childs explains, the monumental king lounges in a large *chaise percée,* or toilet, with a huge plank descending from his mouth like a grotesque extended tongue. On the lower right, cripples, emaciated mothers, and tattered workers gather in front of the Parisian skyline, identified by towers that may include Notre Dame. The poor are dropping coins into the baskets of ministers, who march up the gangplank to dump the tribute, and apparently themselves, into the gaping maw of the waiting monarch. As stray coins fall from overloaded baskets, obsequious ministers huddle at the feet of the king grabbing for riches. And as Louise-Philippe feeds, he excretes a fresh load of rewards to the miniature officials over on the far left gathered beneath his toilet-throne in front of the National Assembly. These officials eagerly flock to receive the shower of decorated crosses and papers having to do with "nomination of peers" and "military commissions." [27]

There were several strong reasons why this print was so offensive. *Gargantua,* a mythic giant in French folklore in the late middle ages, was chronicled in a burlesque epic by François Rabelais. Rabelais's work enjoyed wide popularity during the first half of the nineteenth century; his complete writings were published in Paris in at least nine editions between 1820 and 1840. The character of *Garguntua* appeared in passing reference in the works of such novelists as Victor Hugo and Balzac as the archetypal glutton and the embodiment of material excess. Daumier connected the image of *Garguntua* to important issues in Louis-Phillip's administration and leadership. Daumier's image raised serious and provocative issues that intensified the direct opposition between the powerful and the powerless, between the leader and his followers. The grotesque and gluttonous body of *Gargantua* exemplifies the imbalance of the leader devouring and consuming far too much of the world's resources at the expense of the laboring poor who can ill afford to supply his meal. *Gargantua* depicts the king and his administration as greedy and self-serving, using power for personal gain.

As Mikhail Bakhtin points out, in attacking Louis-Philippe's literal seat of power, Daumier has transformed the throne room into the bathroom. Consequently, the cycle of feeding in Daumier's lithograph is self-perpetuating but perverse—the baskets of coins poured into the giant king's mouth resemble turds more than money. Money metamorphoses into food/feces, and feces metamorphose (through defecation) back into paper symbolic of wealth and position. Such reversals of nature are consistent with Bakhtin's analysis of Rabelais's humor of the burlesque, in which a logic of inversion rules in a topsy-turvy world. Perhaps the real issue with regard to money had to do with the growing mood of political disillusionment that swept through France in 1831. The national economy had been severely depressed in the months following the revolution of 1830, resulting in widespread bankruptcies and staggering unemployment among the working class.

Yet, the current inflated national budget included extravagant funding for the king's selfish needs. In an article published in *La Caricature*, which undoubtedly inspired Daumier, Balzac blasted the government's proposal to spend 12 to 18 million francs on the monarch's support. Balzac was especially cynical in his account of the inflated budget for heating, wine, cuisine, the royal stable, and other miscellaneous pleasures. Daumier refers to these expenses by inscribing the numbers 12 and 18 on the second of the baskets the ministers carry up the gangplank. Daumier extends the inversion with the infantilized king being fed by others. Daumier's Louis-Philippe rules not in the spheres of politics, power, and philosophy, but in the lower spheres of food, fat, and feces. The use of excrement can be a powerful means of expressing profound disgust in a nonviolent way. Excrement is, as Bakhtin has observed, one of the best substances for the degrading of all that is exalted.[28]

Perhaps the most infuriating aspect of Daumier's violation of the king's person was not simply his gluttony, obesity, and defecation, but his transformation into the shape of a pear (*la poire*), which came from a metamorphic satire developed by Philipon. The comparison was a clever insult, since *poire* means "fathead" or "simpleton" or "dullard" in French slang. Although the sign of the pear soon evolved into a satirical emblem of the entire political regime of Louis-Philippe, it was closely linked in its early days to the specific identity and physiognomy of the king.[29]

For taking such liberties with the king's person, Daumier was tried, convicted, and sentenced to six months in prison and fined 500 francs in August 1832. His conviction for *Gargantua*, however, did little to alter his commitment to political caricature. He continued to draw biting political satires, but these were submitted to less overtly political journals and generally his attacks on political leaders took a more subtle and covert form. Once the September Laws of 1835 imposed rigid and explicit press censorship, French caricaturists were forced to abandon overtly political subjects until after the revolutions of 1848, which ended the reign of Louis-Philippe.

Daumier was hardly alone in his role as a social and critical observer. All through the nineteenth century, modernist artists chronicled what could be described as moral outrages caused by the actions and policies of leaders they disdained. From Géricault to Picasso and beyond, events prompted artists to respond courageously in ways that were often detrimental to their own well-being. Daumier's lithographs no doubt satisfied his strong moral convictions, but they also resulted in fines and imprisonment, and they provided him with only a meager living, keeping him constantly on the verge of poverty.

Daumier, a kind and generous person who was a highly gifted draftsman, created a body of work that fired an early volley in what became a long history of artistic attacks against leadership. He died of a stroke on February 10, 1879, at the age of 71 years. Only posthumously has he received the recognition he deserved.

CONCLUSION

In conclusion, it is my hope that the foregoing examples of the complex relationships between leadership and art, as shown in the Florentine Renaissance, in the Reformation period of the sixteenth century, and in nineteenth century France, offer evidence that the combined study of leadership and art history can be enormously beneficial. Throughout history, art has inescapably reflected the way that leaders have embodied their values and the integrity of their commitments. When leaders have failed, artists have focused on the consequences of their choices, often producing works of art that become the indelible legacies of leaders. Some years ago, art historian Vincent Scully wrote: "For me, the history of art is a delight and a wonder because it teaches me more human history than I can learn in any other way." In view of Professor Scully's comments, I would suggest that the study of leadership in any period of history that excludes the art of the times, is incomplete. Likewise, the art of any period studied without consideration of the leadership of the period is also incomplete. As mentioned at the beginning of this brief discourse, the history of art is, in effect, a history of leadership.

NOTES

1. Cited in *Religion and Politics: The Renaissance Print in Social Context.* Exhibition Catalogue, Marsh Art Gallery, University of Richmond, 33.

2. Nancy Rash Fabbri and Nina Rutenburg, "The Tabernacle of Orsanmichele in Context," *The Art Bulletin* LXIII, no. 3 (September 1981): 388–390.

3. Frederick Hartt, "Art and Freedom in Quattrocento Florence," in *Modern Perspectives in Western Art History,* ed. W. Eugene Kleinbauer (Toronto: University of Toronto Press, 1989).

4. Ibid., 304.

5. Frederick Hartt and David Wilkins, *History of Italian Renaissance Art* (Upper Saddle River, NJ: Prentice-Hall, 2006), 184.

6. Ibid., 185.

7. Hartt, "Art History, Society, and Culture," 301.

8. Ibid., 298.

9. Leonardo Bruni, "The Laudatio of the City of Florence," in *Perspectives on Western Art,* Vol. 2, ed. Linnea Wren (Boulder, CO: Westview Press, 1994), 2–4.

10. Arnold Hauser, *The Social History of Art* (New York: Vintage Press, 1985), Vol. 2, 118–119.

11. Martin Luther, "Martin Luther, Against the Rapacious and Murdering Peasants, Smite, Strangle, and Stab," in *Perspectives on Western Art,* ed. Wren, 108–109.

12. Cited in *The Renaissance Print in Social Context.* Exhibition Catalogue, Marsh Art Gallery, 28.

13. Sidney Alexander, *Lions and Foxes: Men and Ideas of the Italian Renaissance* (New York: Macmillan, 1974), p. 171.

14. Ibid., 180–181.

15. Cited in ibid., 183–184.

16. Hartt and Wilkins, *History of Italian Renaissance Art,* 349–351.

17. Alexander, *Lions and Foxes,* 187–188.

18. Ibid., 250.

19. Johann Tetzel, "Sermon on Indulgences," in *Perspectives on Western Art,* ed. Wren, 103.

20. Martin Luther, "Ninety-Five Theses," in *Perspectives on Western Art,* ed. Wren, 104–105.

21. Cited in *The Renaissance Print in Social Context.* Exhibition Catalogue, 33, 36.

22. *The Renaissance Print in Social Context,* 17.

23. Ibid., 36.

24. Ralph E. Shikes, *The Indignant Eye* (Boston: Beacon Press, 1969), 148.

25. Hilton Kramer, *The Age of the Avant-Garde* (New York: Farrar, Straus and Giroux, 1973), 6.

26. Shikes, *The Indignant Eye,* 150.

27. Elizabeth Childs, "Big Trouble, Daumier, Gargantua, and the Censorship of Political Caricature," *Art Journal* (Spring 1992): 26–31.

28. Ibid., 31.

29. Ibid., 33.

11

Establishing Regimes of Truth: A Study of the Relationship Between Leaders, Power, and Artistic Expression

SCOTT BOYLSTON

Each society has its regime of truth, its general politics of truth: that is, the types of discourse which it accepts and makes function as true; the mechanisms and instances which enable one to distinguish true and false statements, the means by which each is sanctioned; the techniques and procedures accorded value in the acquisition of truth; the status of those who are charged with saying what counts as true.

—Michel Foucault[1]

Whoever reads bourgeois newspapers becomes blind and deaf. Away with the stultifying bandages!

—John Heartfield, caption from Photo 11-1, 1930

In his book *The Selfish Gene,* the evolutionary biologist Richard Dawkins coined the term *meme* to define the building blocks of human coexistence. He argues, "Just as genes propagate themselves in the gene pool by leaping from body to body via sperm and eggs, so memes propagate themselves by leaping from brain to brain."[2] Memes are attractive ideas that spread through a culture with the efficiency of a virus. Whether defining an acceptable mode of transportation or the belief that *might makes right,* the most successful memes become foundations for unassailable societal norms. Even as they are defined by a culture, they transform it, and within their perceived

Photo 11-1 Goebbels's Recipe against the Food Shortage in Germany (1930) by John Heartfield.

"naturalness" they generate de facto refutations of alternative concepts. While the primary goal of a leader's rhetoric is to define linguistic memes that are attractive to the populace, artists attempt to define memes by way of visual rhetoric.

The separate acts of artistic creation and leadership are more intimately related than one might first imagine. Art can help leaders emerge and lead by creating visual frameworks to disseminate their core values to an intended audience in a meaningful fashion. Conversely, art can construct visual frameworks that challenge inconsistencies between leaders' rhetoric and their actions. In both instances, one might consider art a vessel, yet such a conclusion is incomplete. It neglects to account for a fundamental attribute shared by the majority of artists who create it, that of independent vision. While art is merely a vessel, the creator of that art is an active consumer, digester, and transformer of social and political ideology.

Artists are critical thinkers who possess the ability to sift through vast and sometimes contradictory volumes of information. More importantly, they possess the ability to synthesize such information into cogent declarations that make use of symbolic codes that, by design, are understood and appreciated by the cultural milieu. In this manner, artists performing in the public arena attempt to construct viable memes as a means to legitimize the arguments of the leaders they support.

Those artists who commit to engaging public opinion do so because they are either aligned with or in opposition to the policies of those in power. A common fate of artists willing to speak out against leadership can be appreciated by studying historic examples. They are demonized, ostracized, jailed, banished, and sometimes murdered for their actions. They can be subjected to such treatment even at the same time they are idolized by a large segment of a population. The fate of artists who contribute their talents to the cause of emerging and established leaders, however, is not as well documented. While not nearly as vulnerable to abuses of power against them as artistic dissenters, these artists are somewhat less secure in the new establishment than one might assume. In fact, it is not uncommon for the most creative artists in service to leaders to be deemed unhealthy to the new order once it is firmly established. In such situations, it is often at the moment of victory and consolidation of power that the instincts of the artist and the leader begin to diverge. Innovative artists generally remain committed to exploration and experimentation, even as they mature in life. Leaders, on the other hand, as innovative as they may have been during their rise to power, embrace protectionist and stabilizing tendencies once they are established. While many forms of stasis are favored by established leaders, stasis in any form is anathema to most artists. Furthermore, while many artists explore creativity for its intrinsic qualities, leaders tend to embrace creativity as a means to an end. Once that end is reached, the leaders must reassess their needs and methods, even if it means dispensing with or silencing artists who have contributed to their rise. It is here, then—at the pinnacle of achievement—that fundamental personality traits of artists and leaders create the potential for discord.

Artists who act against leaders, on the other hand, will sometimes do so for the benefit of oppositional political groups, but more often they act out of personal motivations. Even when designing works of art for organizations, they tend to do so only because they share the same enemies. Alain le Quernec, the famous French poster designer, has put it this way:

> And so it's by the negative: why are you from the left in France? Because I think it's impossible to be from the right. I never wanted to belong to a party. I wanted to be free. Even while I did a lot of work for the Socialist party it was because I had a friend there. But I never belonged to this party because I never wanted to be obliged to follow. I'm not property.[3]

Finally, there is the relationship between business leaders and artists as commercial agents, which is quite different from the relationship between leaders and artists in a public arena. Because the worlds of advertising and design embody the most commonly occurring nexus of art and leadership in Western culture, however, it is a fitting place to begin our examination.

THE PRODUCTION OF ART AS A SERVICE TO BUSINESS LEADERSHIP

Businesses require competitive branding, and to attain it they exchange money for the services of graphic artists and brand specialists. These creative experts have a professional obligation to create art (in the form of advertisements, commercials, and various print and multimedia objects) that is geared toward their client's clearly articulated needs. This collaboration between leaders and artists has a singularly defined objective: to create a unified public vision for the benefit of the company in question.

Maud Lavin, in her book *Clean New World,* calls graphic design a "bizarre form of hamstrung power." She states:

> Many of its corporate clients' practitioners are instructed to provide order and clarity, to give their clients' companies the look, sheen and promise of a clean new world. It's a fairly neurotic expectation, since designers can't really clean—they just cover up, wrap, accent, or put into a clean envelope some messy realities. In corporate service—design's most common function—it is implicated in both cultural stasis and change, but with only partial control.

This acknowledges the discomfort that some designers feel when promoting a product or service that they personally consider harmful to the public interest. The contradiction is embodied in "someone who has tremendous power to communicate visually and no power whatsoever to influence the content." [4] Artists in service to business, then, subjugate personal ideology for the sake of their client's needs. Sociologist Robert Jackall, in his book *Moral Mazes,* compares business hierarchies to fiefdoms of the Middle Ages, where loyalty to the cause of the "king's" edicts (the demands of the CEO) are the sole measure of what is acceptable and unacceptable. [5] Commercial artists, while not a part of these kingdoms, enter into them, if only temporarily, with the constant risk of falling prey to the values and memes declared unassailable by their rulers. In the end, they must also reconcile their own sense of morality with the company's desire to create a public presence that may or may not be an accurate reflection of reality.

A brand, as Marty Neumeier explains in his book *The Brand Gap,* is "a person's gut feeling about a product, service, or company. It's a gut feeling because we're all emotional, intuitive beings, despite our efforts to be rational." A brand, then, is "not what you (as a business leader) says it is. It's what they (the public at large) say it is." [6] Neumeier uses Plato's example of a *horse* to further define this. When the word *horse* is heard, most people conjure an immediate iconic form: a majestic stead. Horse, in this sense, is branded. In this sense, too, horse represents a meme. This does not mean the company is powerless to define itself in the public realm. Quite the contrary, corporations spend millions of dollars to create a presence that guides public perception toward a very specific form of their "horse." A majority of that money is spent on visual presentations of the key corporate memes.

While advertising is blamed for the ubiquity of useless products, it is rarely seen as anything more than a minor nuisance. It has been deemed "normal" by our culture (*Shop 'til you drop*, for instance, is a securely entrenched meme), and it is generally assumed to be nothing more than a benign offshoot of Western ideology. Its role in maintaining the present power structure is rarely considered, let alone challenged. Yet, as John Berger argues in his book *Ways of Seeing*, "(Advertising) turns consumption into a substitute for democracy. The choice of what one eats (or wears or drives) takes the place of significant political choice." [7] Berger further claims that advertising formulates a "philosophical system" which "explains everything in its own terms," and "interprets the world," in a way that decontextualizes meaning for the sake of unrelenting consumption. Berger sees advertising as "a political phenomenon of great importance" that "recognizes nothing except the power to acquire." Ultimately, Berger believes, advertising is "imposing a false standard of what is and what is not desirable," within a culture.

Notice we have shifted the focus of leadership from CEOs and other business leaders to a more amorphous and elusive entity that frames the power structures of a commercially oriented society. The philosopher Michel Foucault proposed that power was not enforced upon people as much as through them. His focus on the mechanisms of power provided him the opportunity to study the role of knowledge and truth in their varied manifestations within the realm of power. In his book *Power/Knowledge*, Foucault states, "We are subjected to the production of truth through power and we cannot exercise power except through the production of truth." [8] His focus on the organic systems of power, however, was never intended to "minimize the importance and effectiveness of State power" (and hence, the more traditional institutions accessible to leaders). Instead, he believed that, "excessive insistence on (state power) playing an exclusive role leads to the risk of overlooking all the mechanisms and efforts of power which don't pass directly via the State apparatus, yet often sustain the State more effectively than its own institutions." [9] The social formation of knowledge (and therefore truth) leads to widely held belief systems, and these systems subsequently lend credibility to emergent power structures that, in turn, lead to newer forms of truth.

Truths that lose favor in this cultural evolution become "subjugated knowl-edge," which are deemed deviant, dangerous, or unworthy of further acknowledgement. In this manner, certain ways of perceiving the world become ingrained in cultures. The society itself, then, wittingly or otherwise, defines those character attributes that will be most prized in their authority figures through an ongoing process of value judgments as defined by shifting cultural norms. Followership, by its own design, is a form of leadership.

In his book *Captains of Consciousness,* the social critic Stuart Ewen unearths some of the underlying principles that led to the formation of our present consumer model. As early as the 1920s, specialists were hired by industry giants to promote overconsumption as a means of keeping pace with their phenomenal growth in production capabilities. One expert warned that, "Sat-isfied customers are not as profitable as discontented ones," and promised that, "Advertising helps to keep the masses dissatisfied with their mode of life." [10] It was accepted as fact that consumers had to be manufactured as a means to keep up with production, and those citizens who insisted on more thrifty lifestyles were publicly disparaged as engaging in the destructive act of "puritanism in consumption." [11] Insecurities were actively targeted as a means to sell products, and the self-proclaimed ad men and commercial artists of the day bragged about the creative ability to turn the straw of human self-consciousness into an abundant heyday for manufacturers of all ilks. Business economist Paul Nystrom claimed that those unwilling to go along with the emerging consumptive paradigm would be sufficiently ostra-cized: "There will be quizzical looks, doubtful stares and critical estimates. He will be judged as lacking the brain power and, perhaps, as an undesirable person. If he persists (in violating norms of consumption) . . . He will lose all of his friends." [12] Edward Bernays, a nephew of Sigmund Freud and an indi-vidual integral to the establishment of modern commercial public relations, claimed, "it is now possible to control and regiment the masses according to our will without their knowing it." [13]

Elmo Calkins, perhaps the best known consumer specialist of the time, claimed that there were two kinds of goods: "Those we use, such as cars or razors, and those we use up, such as toothpaste or soda biscuit. *Consumer engineering* must see to it that we use up the kinds of goods we now merely use" (italics added). He then famously asked, "Can artificial obsolescence be created?" [14] The ever-changing face of style as a reflection of what is "in" and what is not—rather than functional need—has in great part dictated con-sumer demand ever since. The production of style—an art form in itself—provides a means of cultural leadership.

While most people in our culture accept the present rate of consumption, and the present methods of stimulating it as "naturally" occurring phenom-ena, and as phrases such as *buy your own happiness* and *money is not everything, it is the only thing* become more deeply embedded cultural memes, individuals become less tolerant of alternative views and less capable of assessing the actual influence of such behavior on the well-being of society. Although it presently exists as a self-perpetuating social norm, consumerism, as it was envisioned by individuals like those quoted above, is the result of an engineered effort on the part and behalf of industrial leaders. As Ewen concludes,

> The cultural displacement effected by consumerism has provided a mode of perception that has both confronted the question of human need and at the same time restricted its possibilities. Social change cannot come about in a context where objects are invested with human subjective capacities. It cannot come about where commodities contain the limits of social betterment. It requires that people never concede the issues of who shall define and control the social realm.[15]

Even art forms that claim no role in social manipulation often do so indirectly. The linguist Roland Barthes wrote extensively about cultural myths that define a certain manner of behaving and a specific regiment of appreciating what was to be considered right and proper in a culture. In his book *Mythologies,* he explores the meme-centric effects of such cultural artifacts as *Toys, Wine and Milk,* the art of *Striptease,* and other everyday objects and rituals that express power and influence within them. Stemming from the field of semiotics (the study of signs and sign systems), and similar in many ways to the theories of Foucault, these essays were attempts at critiquing "the language of so-called mass-culture." The objects and rituals we surround ourselves with are designed not only for specific purposes, but with specific cultural values in mind, and in his writing Barthes was reacting to his own feelings of "impatience at the sight of the 'naturalness' with which newspapers, art and common sense constantly dress up a reality"[16] that was fabricated by contrived social imperatives.

Barthes's proposition that "myth is a language" explains how systems of signs come to define realities that are only so within the context of the needs of those who generate and perpetuate them. By these standards, individuals who paint seemingly benign pictures of rural life are engaged in defining cultural norms; they are creating an unchanging model by which the "real" and evolving reality will be judge. The ubiquitous watercolor depictions of seaside leisure activities adorning the walls of beach houses around the country are another form of this "normalizing" effect in that they codify lifestyles that are coveted by those who can afford only a glimpse of such a life (one week a year, for example). This manufacturing of expected means and methods of existence creates a societal tunnel vision; it generates an atmosphere in which citizens are expected to strive for a specific set of so-called needs.

Within the realm of successful advertising, we can observe that consumers react to the influence of business leaders by becoming facilitators of the business leader's ideas, so as we further explore the relationship between artists and leaders, we can expect to see the phenomenon of effective leadership convincing followers to do more than simply follow, but to lead in their own right by becoming ardent acolytes who are as convinced of accepting the leader's values as they are of rejecting those values perceived as contradictory to them.

There is a distinct difference between artists in service to business and those in service to public leaders. The former are usually driven purely by financial incentives, while the latter are more often driven by ideological concerns. Despite this disparity, the dynamics can be considered similar due to the leader's need for control over public perception, and his or her understanding that these perceptions can be successfully manipulated by visual messages.

THE PRODUCTION OF ART AS A SERVICE TO POLITICAL LEADERSHIP

Aspiring leaders require certain tools in order to attain positions of power, and we have seen how artwork that inspires the fervent support of followers is one of them. As individuals capable of visually representing a political leader's set of values, artists are invaluable in establishing legitimacy for the leader's rhetorical positioning. When public leaders have successfully achieved their ultimate leadership position, however, artists who have helped these leaders achieve such status rarely survive fully intact. They are often treated in one of several ways: they are labeled dangerous to the survival of the state; they are exiled or murdered; or they are forcefully transformed into mouthpieces of state-sponsored propaganda. Of course, there are always exceptions, and we will take a brief look at two of those before examining other cases similar to that of Gustav Klutsis.

By the early 1930s, Klutsis had risen to the stature of "the master of photomontage in Stalinist propaganda." In 1938 he was executed at Joseph Stalin's command.[17] During those few intervening years, the content of Klutsis's work had not changed, neither had the prevailing ideology of the Soviet state. There was one clear distinction between Soviet Russia in the early 1930s and the late 1930s, and that was the level of political stability within the country. While Stalin had gained full control over the government by 1927, the volatility of earlier power struggles had left the economy in shambles. Stalin's first Five-Year Plan (begun in 1928) was designed to transform Russia into an industrial and agricultural world leader, and many policies—while touted by the party apparatus as widely popular—were heavily resisted by the country's mostly rural population. Artists such as Klutsis were needed to convince Russian citizens to make substantial personal sacrifices for the greater benefit of the Communist experiment. By the late 1930s many of these objectives had been met, and Russia—despite (or perhaps because of) the brutal coercion that systematically followed behind the barrage of visual propaganda—established itself as a world power with which to be reckoned. Once established, the Communist Party no longer required a cultural catalyst in the form of artistic agitation. In fact, they feared such catalysts, and artistic experimentation was soon deemed a threat to the Soviet state; only state-sanctioned Socialist Realism was acceptable, and innovative artists like Klutsis were silenced.

Two prominent historical exceptions to the general rule of eventual abandonment of innovative artists by leaders are Francisco de Goya of Spain and Ludwig Hohlwein of Germany. Francisco de Goya (1746–1828), considered to be the Father of Modern Art by many, was a well-known portrait painter and printmaker at a time of great turmoil in Spain. Goya's relationship with

Photo 11-2 *The Family of Charles IV* (1800) by Francisco Goya.
Source: The Yorck Project.

Spanish royalty was ambivalent and tenuous. His royal portrait *The Family of Charles IV* (1800) (Photo 11-2) treats the King's family with visible disdain. They are not shown in some idealized form, as was the norm for court portraiture of the time, but instead as a "collection of ghosts: the frightened children, the bloated king, and—in a master stroke of sardonic humor—the grotesquely vulgar queen." [18] It is difficult to determine how Goya was able to get away with such subversion. It has been suggested that Goya was simply blessed with dim-witted and self-absorbed benefactors who were incapable of perceiving his actions as anything other than humble service.

The international power struggles that led to the creation of *The Third of May, 1808* (1815) provide insight into the general political instability that artists are confronted with when they engage leaders as patrons. Charles IV of Spain was a corrupt and callous leader, and Goya agreed with many Spaniards who believed that Ferdinand VII, the son of Charles, would make a more reform-minded ruler. Ferdinand VII enlisted the aid of Napoleon Bonaparte, who, once granted the opportunity to send French troops into Spain, forcefully installed his brother Joseph Bonaparte on the throne.[19] The painting, which depicts the slaughter of Spanish peasants at the hands of Napoleon's invading forces, was created for Ferdinand VII seven years after the event it depicts, and only after Spain reestablished its independence from France. Unfortunately, the hopes of a more democratic rule under Ferdinand once he regained the throne never materialized, and Goya found himself painting this scene of power's tendency toward violent repression for the benefit of a ruler who himself abused power.

Goya's *Disasters of War,* a series of 80 prints created during the 1810s, were not published until 1863—35 years after his death—due to their provocative nature. With such titles as *And We Are Like Wild Beasts, Bury Them and Keep Quiet, Great Deeds! Against the Dead!,* and *Perhaps They Are of a Different Breed,* these aquatints revealed the day-to-day horrors of war that common people suffered. They stand as a historically unprecedented antiwar statement by an artist, let alone by one considered a "court" painter with allegiances to the ruling class. Within the context of epic power struggles played out at the expense of Europe's peasantry, Goya's œuvre can be seen as an attempt to bear witness to aristocratic hypocrisy and greed, and to the societal price paid for such avarice. Even as he served the ruling class, he performed as a voice of dissent. Goya, disillusioned by the slow rate of social change in his native home even as it proudly considered him an important part of its cultural legacy, chose to spend his later life in France.

Ludwig Hohlwein (1874–1948) was a sought-after painter and poster designer long before Germany succumbed to Nazism. During a period of time when the flat colors and simplified silhouettes of the German *sachplakat* (object poster) were of international renown, Hohlwein offered an original and compelling alternative in the form of his vividly rendered anecdotal realism. While his commercial clients ranged from chocolatiers to clothiers, he also produced memorable work for veteran's relief efforts after World War I. Hohlwein was often considered a court painter in his own right, only the aristocracy he catered to were the "kings and princes of business and industry."[20]

An ardent believer in the sanctity of the Germany "fatherland," Hohlwein's work through the 1920s became increasingly nationalistic. In 1933, when Hitler became Chancellor, Hohlwein urged fellow artists to use their skills for the glory of the fatherland:

> Today, art, as a cultural factor, is more than ever called upon to take a leading place in the building and conserving cultural values ... May the best among us realize fully the significance of what is at stake and their own responsibility, and may we labor creatively and with conviction at the preservation of our cultural civilization and its restoration to perfectly healthy conditions.[21]

Hohlwein was a member of the Nazi party and worked directly with Goebbels's Ministry of Propaganda and Enlightenment. In his work for the Nazi government, Hohlwein resisted portraying negative stereotypes of German "enemies"—a cornerstone of most other Nazi propaganda—in favor of depicting the heroic and monumental beauty of the Aryan race. He did so by glorifying the power and grace of the German physique, and within these physical attributes he expressed the supposed superiority of Nazi identity. In this sense, his work is equal in its disturbing beauty to the movies of Leni Riefenstahl in its glorification of extreme racism.

While Hohlwein is used here as an example of an artist who served the needs of an emerging leader and survived, it is impossible to tell what would have become of him had Adolf Hitler remained in power. The sudden defeat of the Third Reich at the end of World War II may have actually saved Hohlwein from an unbecoming end. Of course, it is also possible that Hohlwein could have survived a longer Nazi reign. His ardent support of the party platform could have kept him in good stead with Hitler. When his house and studio were destroyed by bombs as late as 1944, he was granted residence at Hitler's Berchtesgaden estate. Still, we should not forget the fate of Klutsis, who remained true to Soviet ideology to the very day he was murdered by its guardians.

One general observation that could be made when considering the dangers of performing as a "court" artist would be that the overall decency of a leader is a good indicator of how those artists will be treated. Klutsis, for instance, was not alone in being betrayed by the Soviet political machine. The shift in the interpretation of socialist ideology that occurred in Russia from the time of the Bolshevik Revolution of 1917 to the reign of Stalin was so extreme that its historical record is littered with the abuse of brilliant artistic innovators that were at the forefront of the revolution. For this reason, twentieth-century Russia is a fitting case study of a leader's propensity to destroy artists that once aided him in his rise.

In her book, *Iconography of Power*, Victoria Bonnell claims, "The critical issue facing the Bolsheviks in 1917 was not merely the seizure of power but the seizure of meaning."[22] The impressive capabilities of the Bolshevik propaganda apparatus effectively altered the population's appreciation for "reality," so much so that these new meanings—Foucault's knowledge and truth—effectively overthrew the old meanings. The Bolshevik's visual propaganda took two distinctly different forms: domestic propaganda for the consumption of the peasant masses (Photo 11-3), which appropriated the old iconography of the church and state—iconography that had been used by the Tsarist regime as a means to suppress and exploit the working class —and reformulated it to glorify a new hierarchy of power; and international propaganda, which defined a new and highly abstracted visual language best expressed through the work of the Constructivists. The Constructivists, as young artists, were a part of an international avant-garde movement determined to generate a revolutionary form of communication. Although they were convinced of the need for world revolution just as the Bolshevik leaders were, they believed such a movement required new art—a never-before-seen and universal form of communication—yet their pursuit of that art was so truly innovative that its results often alienated the working class it sought to proselytize. The Russian peasantry had long been accustomed to the iconic religious paintings of the Russian Orthodox Church and traditional folk art, so the task of creating effective domestic propaganda was assigned primarily to experienced iconic painters and *lubki* illustrators (a term for peasant wood-cut posters, or broadsides).

Lazar el Lissitsky, Vladimir Mayakovsky, and Alexander Rodchenko were three of the more prolific Constructivists. Lissitsky's *Beat the Whites with the Red Wedge* (Photo 11-4) is one of the most frequently reproduced examples of modern graphic design due to its revolutionary application of abstraction. His other work ranged from international exhibit design, poster design, book design, and "constructed" paintings. Mayakovsky was both an illustrator and a poet. His book of poems *For the Voice*, a patriotic peon to the October Revolution, made him a national hero (the book was designed by Lissitsky). His "ROSTA" illustrations could be seen in most every window in Moscow immediately after the civil war. And Rodchenko, who worked closely with both of these artists, was also world renowned for his artistic skills.

By 1930, one of these internationally acclaimed artists had committed suicide, while the other two were creating outlandish propaganda for the Soviet Union. Lissitsky oversaw the development of the most dramatically

СМЕРТЬ МИРОВОМУ ИМПЕРИАЛИЗМУ

Photo 11-3 *Death to World Imperialism* (1919) by D. S. Moor. Reproduced from Stephen White, *The Bolshevik Poster* (1988: Yale University Press) with the author's permission.

misleading editions of an international magazine called *USSR in Construction*. Even as Stalin's regime routinely brutalized its own populace with massive arrests, purges, and murders, the state-sponsored magazine remained true to the cause of glorifying the social experiment of the Soviet state to the outside world. In 1940, *USSR in Construction* dedicated a full issue to the "liberation" of eastern Poland by Russian forces. By all accounts this act represented a forced occupation of these territories, yet the magazine's representation of the event was one of selfless Russian sacrifice for the sake of the Polish people. The cover of this special issue, designed by Lissitsky, went so far as

Photo 11-4 *Beat the Whites with the Red Wedge* **(1920) by Lazar el Lissitsky.**
Source: U.S. Library of Congress.

showing a Polish citizen so filled with gratitude for his "liberation" that he kisses a Soviet soldier[23] (Photo 11-5).

In the same year, Rodchenko, who worked with Lissitsky on *USSR in Construction,* oversaw the production of another special issue of the magazine. The subject matter for this issue was none other than Mayakovsky, and he was represented as a shining example of an artist who had dedicated his life to the Soviet cause, despite that fact that he had grown so distraught with the regime that he committed suicide. So, within the course of a single year —and within the pages of the same journal—two of the most important avant-garde artists of the twentieth century, who were celebrated for their creativity in service to the ideals of human equality, were used by an oppressive regime to perpetuate lies to the world.

There is a special irony in this example that is helpful when considering the changing relationship between artists and leaders as the leaders become more secure in their positions of power. Marxist ideology, especially as interpreted by Leon Trotsky, encouraged the notion of "permanent" revolution as a means of achieving true autonomy for the working class. Such an ongoing evolution toward social equity would require constant agitation, and in such an environment, the services of dynamic artists would surely have been welcome. Trotsky's theory, however, was condemned by Stalin (and Trotsky himself was exiled) for the sake of a more autocratic rule that essentially froze any hope for a permanent revolution at a point that was most advantageous to Stalin, at the point of his uncontested acquisition of control.

Photo 11-5 Cover image of *USSR in Construction, Polish Peasant Welcomes Russian Forces* (1940) by Lazar el Lissitsky.

Confronted with so much talk of a continual change in government, it seems natural that an egotistical and power-hungry Stalin would do his best to silence any artist who had formerly displayed a penchant for revolutionary artistic expression. It is no wonder, then, that the Soviet experiment represents the extremes to which an established leader will go to obliterate creative expression. While it is an especially severe example, it is by no means an isolated tendency.

THE PRODUCTION OF ART AS A SERVICE TO SOCIAL JUSTICE

As an introduction to this section, it must be stated that the blame for a society's human injustices cannot always be placed solely at the feet of its leaders.

As mentioned earlier, societies evolve according to a continual interplay of ideas, events, and influences, and unless the culture in question is dominated by a powerful dictator, the causes of any social injustices are usually varied and complex. Some common causes include the intractable quarrels between two (or more) factions within a culture, systemic corruption within the culture's power structures, and the resilience of outmoded traditions and the resulting tendency to accord injustices a certain legitimacy due to these traditions.

Of course, not one of the above examples can be discussed without acknowledging its connection to the others. Apartheid, Jim Crow, gender inequalities, and caste systems are just a few examples of injustices that transcend one single cause. The most difficult common trait to surmount in all of these is the strength of the memes that legitimize, establish, and maintain them. Challenging these memes, therefore, becomes a primary objective of any artist interested in fighting against entrenched social injustices. This action constitutes a form of leadership in and of itself in that the artist must be willing to thrust unpopular ideas (Foucault's subjugated knowledge) continually back into the public limelight in the hope of convincing individuals these ideas hold more merit than the society has hence accorded them.

In cases of extreme enforcement of social control, as was often the case in colonial Europe when the absolute power of kings and queens was slowly being undermined by the establishment of parliaments and other forms of representative governance, dissenting artists were seen as heroes of the common people. The Industrial Revolution helped drive the massive social changes during this period, and the invention of the printing press in the mid-fifteenth century transformed the control of knowledge and public opinion in unprecedented fashion. Before this, scribes hand-copied texts, books were reserved for churches and royalty, and the content and tone of all public documents were tightly controlled by those in power. With the advent of mass-publication technologies, broadsides (posters) could be printed and distributed widely through villages without permission from those in power. In this manner, artists began disseminating satirical caricatures of leading figures of the day that mocked their human shortcomings, and revealed their hypocrisies and abuses of power.

By the 1800s, magazines were considered one of the most dangerous forms of subversion; their short articles were unsparing in their criticism of those in power, and for any individual who could not read, the illustrations clearly defined the crux of the accusations. Many of these magazines were quickly confiscated by the government, and the publishers jailed. Lithography, which was invented just before 1800, also provided artists with the ability to create more high-quality illustrations for these publications.

Honoré Daumier (1808–1879) was a prolific artist who was jailed and intimidated by the French government for his unending stream of political caricatures. He created "thousands of iconic dissenting images—both symbolic and realistic, comic and tragic—that continue to have resonance" today.[24] Some of his most pointed satire was created for two magazines of the times: *La Caricature,* which was forcefully shut down by the government, and *Le Charivari* (Disturbance), which also came under state sanction and censorship. Both of these were founded by caricature artist Charles Philipon. Daumier's acerbic commentaries were aimed at the ruling class and even at the king himself. Louis-Philippe, the self-proclaimed "Citizen King," who had been brought to power by the revolution of 1830, was renowned for his empty promises of free speech and democratic process.[25]

One of Daumier's most famous lithographs, *The Massacre of the rue Transnonain* (1834) depicts a family brutally murdered in their own bedroom. The painting provides a haunting parallel to the massacre in Haditha, Iraq, in 2005 when an American soldier was killed in a roadside bomb explosion. In response to the attack, the rest of the unit went door to door in the village and killed 24 innocent Iraqis, including 11 women and children. The title of Daumier's painting refers to a street in Lyon "where an unknown sniper killed a civilian guard, part of a government force trying to repress a worker demonstration. Because the fatal shot had come from a worker's housing block, the remaining guards immediately stormed the building and massacred all of its inhabitants."[26]

Daumier's *Gargantua* (1832) led to a six-month prison sentence and the forceful closing down of *La Caricature.* In the lithograph, the king is represented as an obese giant sitting on a chamber pot with a large plank leading from the ground to his mouth so that peasants could feed him their money and the fruits of their labor. From this nourishment, the king "produced" edicts and decrees. This image of a corpulent monster requiring ceremonial offerings of the toil of the masses has become a recurring motif for satirical artists around the world. By 1835, the French king had become so frustrated with such caricatures that a censorship law banned the publication of political caricatures of any kind. Daumier continued generating images of biting satire, focusing instead on the societal repercussions of corrupt leadership without openly implicating the political leaders. Because of the admiration and respect that the French population held for him, Daumier enjoyed a long life of artistic expression relatively free of state-sponsored retribution. In fact, history has shown that artists or writers who are well known in their country of origin can sometimes elude harsh treatment from their government, as their own notoriety acts as a shield against retaliation.

Regardless of the level of censorship and intimidation, artists attempting to uproot the power structures that define or control a society must determine the tone of their messages, and this is most often done while considering the desired effect on the intended audience. Daumier was equally comfortable with shocking imagery as he was with humor. While shock can be an effective catalyst in extreme situations, it can often backfire in more egalitarian and democratic societies. In the case of many social injustices within cultures that are not dominated by overtly oppressive regimes, there are three general categories of public attitude: those who are in ardent support of the dominant memes, those who are opposed to them, and those who are not quite sure what to believe. Those in the third category lend their support to the status quo by default, often in the form of a passive majority. It could be argued that such demographics exist even within totalitarian states, only the categories are more firmly entrenched, with those ruling elite who have been granted the favor of the regime in full support of the status quo, the underground dissenters as the vocal opposition to the regime, and the oppressed population living in fear as the passive majority.

If a designer is trying to reach the second category—that category composed of individuals who already agree with the artist's point of view—tone matters little because the audience is predisposed to supporting the message, and little can be done to alienate them. While provocation can often ignite support of those in favor of the artist's viewpoint, however, such provocation is often used by the opposition as an example of how "extreme" that specific ideology is. Humor, on the other hand, can evoke strong support without alienating the undecided. Either method requires a willingness to present to the public the formerly unpresentable. Taboos are excavated as a means of framing the concepts behind them in a "new" context. Icons, as visual representations of memes, are powerful reminders of the predominance of the manner of thinking that is prevalent in a culture. The appropriation and subversion of iconic forms, therefore, can be a compelling form of dissent.

We have looked briefly at Ludwig Hohlwein's Nazi propaganda, so it is only fitting that for our second example of art in the service of social justice, we take a look at an individual who was creating art in direct opposition to fascism's rise. Helmut Herzefeld (1891–1968) changed his name to John Heartfield in reaction to the hysteria of German nationalism during and after World War I, and in celebration of American values. Heartfield, along with his brother Wieland and the painter George Grosz, created, edited, and designed some of the most stridently antimilitary and antifascist publications in Germany between the wars, and they did so partly by turning the popular iconography of Nazism on its head. All three were members of the Berlin Dada group. Their early forays into polemic discourse pronounced the moral imperative of artists to give up "pure art" in order to engage in the political struggle. As set forth in the publication *Art Is in Danger:* "Either he is an architect, engineer or commercial artist in the army ... which develops industrial power and exploits the world; or . . . he finds a place in the army of the suppressed who fight for their just share of the world." [27]

Heartfield's publishing house, Malik Verlag, printed several magazines through the 1920s that were quickly banned by the Weimar Republic due to their provocative antiestablishment content. Even while the trial against one of those publications was still taking place, they began publishing yet another controversial magazine.

In 1925, as an offshoot for an international charity organization funded by the International Communist Party, the magazine *AIZ* (*Arbeiter-Illustrierte Zeitung* or *Worker's Illustrated Paper*) began publication. Heartfield started contributing to the magazine in 1930 with satirical photomontages of Hitler, Göering, and the Germany industrialists who funded their rise. "New political problems demand new means of propaganda," he declared. "For this task, photography has the greatest persuasive power." [28] Heartfield was credited with reinventing political satire by developing a highly sophisticated method of photomontage.

Heartfield's beliefs that Stalin had successfully eliminated class struggle—in hindsight, his gullibility to the international propaganda that artist's such as Rodchenko and Lissitsky were creating—drove him to praise the Bolshevik Revolution in some of his photomontages. His best work, however, was that which shed light on the harsher realities of Nazi cruelty and hypocrisy. *AIZ* features Heartfield's most biting satirical photomontages, with Germany's military-industrial complex and the rising Nazi regime its primary targets. The magazine was forced to flee Germany when Hitler became chancellor and enforced strict rules against freedom of the press. It moved to Prague, and changed names to *Volks Illustrierte* or *VI* (*People's Illustrated*). In 1938, with the Gestapo actively enforcing their will in Czechoslovakia, the magazine moved to Paris where it was published one last issue before closing down permanently. Before France fell to Germany, Heartfield moved to England where he was interned due to his German ancestry, despite the overwhelming evidence of his resistance to Nazi ideology. After the war, he returned to the newly formed East Germany, where he was temporarily considered to have "treasonable connections" to Western powers before finally being allowed to live in peace. It was not until 1964—at 73 years of age, four years before his death and half a century after he changed his name—that this "new" name was officially recognized.

CONCLUSION

If it is true that a picture is worth a thousand words, then visual artists are well equipped to successfully distill the complexities of a leader's ideas into a form that communicates most effectively to an audience. Memes can be formed and legitimated by visuals alone. Yet memes devised by other means—the phrasing of jingles and catchphrases, for instance—are also creative acts, and they are imbued with more communicative power by visual reiterations of their key concepts.

In the public realm, emerging leaders require a catalyst for galvanizing public support if they hope to succeed in their endeavor. The quality of their own charisma will certainly play a role, but they are also dependent upon competent manipulation of the contemporary forms of mass media at their disposal. Regardless of the era, creative individuals, as masters of mass media, offer the most effective form of public persuasion. Whether it be the Web designers, radio personalities, or multimedia directors of today, or the poster artists, muralists, or poets of a past era, artists are actively sought by campaigning leaders to help frame their messages. There is also a clear understanding on the part of leaders that artists expressing opposition to them can prove to be very damaging to their potential leadership.

Emerging leaders aim to proselytize among those who would support them—to create a vision of what the world could be like if only they were granted control. Such a performance requires a strongly defined emotional appeal. At this point in the process, the artist and the leader often find themselves well suited to one another. The creative passion of one feeds the creative passion of the other, and they work in tandem to generate an illuminating message capable of galvanizing wide support. It is at the point that this wide support is secured that artists and leaders find themselves somewhat at odds. Leaders aim to convert, and then to normalize those they have converted, which requires the introduction of stability. Artists, however, are driven from the beginning by a quest for novelty—a tendency toward change, even rebellion. An artist's desire to create art that communicates in a visceral and immediate manner, after all, is not a passing fancy. Instead, it exists at the very core of the artist's personality. And so, with the onset of political stability comes a fear from those who have achieved this stability of the artist as a force with the potential to challenge the newly established memes and destabilize the new power structure. The tendency for leaders to condemn new creative ideas as subversive and dangerous to the newly established status quo often proves irresistible.

While the relationship between leaders and supporting artists requires a fair degree of collaboration, artists who challenge leaders often work alone or within small groups of like-minded individuals. The tendency for these artists to reject the ideas of the ruling hierarchy can also manifest itself in their relationships with political organizations of any ideological stance, even those possessing values similar to their own. It is not uncommon for socially active artists to treat larger organizations with a degree of skepticism simply because they are uncomfortable with the tendency within large organizations to make compromises and shift allegiances, as well as their vulnerability to corruption and factional infighting.

Individuals striving to create art as critical commentary must have the intellectual capacity to weigh the deeper truths of the issues that inform it. Because artists are not always articulate in discussing their own work, their intellectual abilities are often overlooked or minimized. The inability to verbally articulate a premise with finesse can be confused with a shortcoming in intellectual capacity. Contrary to this perception, many artists explore nonverbal means of expression as their method of critical thought. The most successful artists are those with significant intellectual curiosity and capacity. While intellectual vigor is a shared trait of many artists, it is important to acknowledge that this does not always translate into accurate assessments of social dynamics on the artist's part. Deeply ingrained biases and moral inconsistencies are as much a part of an artist's genetic makeup as that of any other human being.

It is important also to consider that the potential weakness of such an act resides in its very power. Framing, after all, is a form of simplification, and simplification can be dangerous in its refusal of nuanced consideration. Art can simplify complex ideas into concise expressions—into memes. In this sense, artists engage in the hard work of critical thought so that their audiences do not necessarily have to. Yet, simplification as an end in itself—rather than a means of expressing the logic of a desired end—is one of the most common causes of human strife. Bigotry, for instance, is a form of simplification, as is xenophobia and any other expressions of hatred and intolerance. It was Josef Goebbels, the Nazi Minister for Public Enlightenment and Propaganda, after all, who proclaimed, "In the long run only he will achieve basic results in influencing public opinion who is able to reduce problems to the simplest terms and who has the courage to keep repeating them in this simplified form despite the objection of intellectuals."[29] If the simplification of an idea is used as a rationalization to reject a more nuanced understanding of that idea's complexity, far greater damage may be perpetuated than if the idea had remained inchoate.

If leadership scholars concern themselves with the definition of good leadership, and attempt to define it as both good in a moral sense and good in a goal-oriented sense, scholars exploring the relationship between artists and leaders would do well to consider the same criteria. Ludwig Hohlwein, by any standard was a technically good—if not great—artist. Yet, if much of his work was in service to Nazism, how, then, can we even consider the word *good* when discussing his work?

Art, in and of itself, is an act void of any ethical value. Art is merely an expression, as powerful as it might be, that requires both an audience and a setting. Art, then, despite the artist's best intentions, is often interpreted not by the measure of the artist himself, but by the measure of the times and conditions with which that art is experienced. Art requires followers as much as leaders, in both senses of the phrase.

NOTES

1. Michel Foucault, *Power/Knowledge; Selected Interviews and Other Writings, 1972–1977* (New York: Random House, 1980), 131.

2. Michael Dawkins, *The Selfish Gene* (New York: Oxford University Press, 1990), 192.

3. Personal interview, Savannah, Georgia, 2004.

4. Maud Lavin, *Clean New World: Culture, Politics and Graphic Design* (Cambridge, MA: MIT Press, 2002), 2.

5. Robert Jackall, *Moral Mazes: The World of Corporate Managers* (New York: Oxford University Press, 1989).

6. Marty Neumeier, *The Brand Gap: How to Bridge the Distance Between Business Strategy and Design* (Berkeley, CA: New Riders Publishing, 2003), 2.

7. John Berger, *Ways of Seeing* (London, England: British Broadcasting Corporation, 1972), 149.

8. Foucault, *Power/Knowledge*, 93

9. Ibid., 72

10. Stuart Ewen, *Captains of Consciousness: Advertising and the Social Roots of the Consumer Culture* (New York: McGraw-Hill, 1977), 39.

11. Ibid., 57.

12. Ibid., 95.

13. Ibid., 83.

14. Stuart Ewen, *All Consuming Images: The Politics of Style in Contemporary Culture* (New York: Basic Books, Inc., 1988), 52.

15. Ewen, *Captains of Consciousness*, 220.

16. Roland Barthes, *Mythologies* (New York: Farrar, Straus & Giroux, 1972), 11.

17. Victoria E. Bonnell, *Iconography of Power: Soviet Political Posters Under Lenin and Stalin* (Berkeley, CA: University of California Press, 1999), 144.

18. H. W. Janson, *History of Art*, 5th ed. (New York: Harry N. Abrams, Inc., 1995), 660.

19. Fred Kleiner, *Gardner's Art Through the Ages*, 12th ed. (Belmont, CA: Wadsworth, 2005), 830.

20. Steven Heller, Ed., *Design Literacy (continued): Understanding Graphic Design* (New York: Allworth Press, 1999), 248.

21. Ibid., 250.

22. Bonnell, *Iconography of Power*, 1.

23. Victor Margolin, *The Struggle for Utopia: Rodchenko, Lissitsky, Moholy Nagy, 1917–1946* (Chicago, IL: The University of Chicago Press, 1997), 207.

24. Steven Heller, *Merz to Emigre and Beyond: Avant Garde Magazine Design of the Twentieth Century* (London, England: Phaidon Press Limited, 2003), 14.

25. Robert Philippe, *Political Graphics: Art as a Weapon* (New York: Abbeville Press, Inc., 1980), 146.

26. Kleiner, *Gardner's Art Through the Ages*, 858.

27. Heller, *Merz to Emigre and Beyond*, 75.

28. David Evans, *John Heartfield: AIZ/VI, 1930–38* (New York: Abbeville Press, Inc., 1980), 12.

29. Matthew Hughes and Chris Mann, *Inside Hitler's Germany* (New York: MJF Books, 2000).

About the Editor and Contributors

THE EDITOR

Joanne B. Ciulla is Professor and Coston Family Chair in Leadership and Ethics at the Jepson School of Leadership Studies, University of Richmond. She has also held the UNESCO Chair in Leadership Studies at the United Nations International Leadership Academy and academic appointments at La Salle University, the Harvard Business School, Oxford University, and The Wharton School. Her B.A., M.A., and Ph.D. are in philosophy. She has published numerous books and articles on leadership ethics, business ethics, and philosophy of work. She edited the Praeger *Leadership at the Crossroads* three-volume set.

THE CONTRIBUTORS

Scott Boylston is a designer and writer exploring the nexus of visual communication and social dynamics. His third and upcoming book is on sustainable package design. He has published numerous short stories and participated in various poster exhibitions on social themes. He is presently a professor of graphic design at the Savannah College of Art and Design, and speaks widely on ethical considerations of the practice.

Jennifer Cable earned her D.M.A. and M.M. degrees from the Eastman School of Music in Rochester, New York, and her B.M. degree from Oberlin College. The study of eighteenth-century English song is the primary focus of her research work, with recent papers and lecture recitals presented on the cantatas of Johann Christoph Pepusch, the early eighteenth-century English cantata, and the solo vocal music of Henry Carey. She is Associate Professor of Music at the University of Richmond, Richmond, Virginia, where she directs the Vocal Program.

Ruth Capriles was born in Venezuela. She graduated with a degree in history and a Ph.D. in political science. Professor of Venezuelan Political and Economic History at the Catholic University Andrés Bello, she also coordinates the Center for Information and Documentation on Economic Crime. She teaches ethics and democracy at the Metropolitan University and business ethics and leadership at postgraduate programs in several universities in Venezuela. Among her publications are several works on corruption, Venezuelan economic behavior, and ethics. She is also a regular contributor to the newspaper *El Universal*.

George R. Goethals holds the E. Claiborne Robins Distinguished Professorship in Leadership Studies at the University of Richmond. Previously at Williams College, he served as chair of the Program in Leadership Studies and Provost. With Georgia Sorenson and James MacGregor Burns, he edited the *Encyclopedia of Leadership* (2004) and with Sorenson, *The Quest for a General Theory of Leadership* (2006). A psychologist, Goethals's recent scholarship explores rooting for the underdog, image making in presidential debates, and the presidency of Ulysses S. Grant.

Michael Harvey is Senior Scholar at the James MacGregor Burns Academy of Leadership at the University of Maryland, and Chair of the Department of Business Management at Washington College (Chestertown, Maryland). He has a Ph.D. in government from Cornell University, a Master's in international business from the University of Wisconsin–Milwaukee, and a B.A. in English from the University of Maryland. His work focuses on exploring leadership in literature. He has published articles and presented conference papers on Machiavelli and literary approaches to leadership. He is the author of *The Nuts and Bolts of College Writing* (Hackett, 2003).

Aurora Hermida-Ruiz is associate professor of Spanish at the University of Richmond. She received her bachelor's degree in Spanish literature from the University of Seville and her doctorate in Spanish literature from the University of Virginia. Hermida-Ruiz's current book project analyzes the critical construction of Garcilaso de la Vega (1503–1536) in contemporary Spanish historiography. Together with Ignacio Navarrete, she is the editor of *Garcilaso Studies: A New Trajectory*, a special issue of *Caliope: Journal of the Society for*

Renaissance and Baroque Hispanic Poetry. She has published on Castilian Cancionero poetry and Petrarchan poetics, as well as on the work of some influential literary critics and historians, such as Rafael Lapesa and Jose Antonio Maravall.

Kathleen Marie Higgins is Professor of Philosophy at the University of Texas at Austin, as well as a frequent visitor to the University of Auckland in New Zealand. In addition to numerous articles, she has published books on the history of philosophy, Nietzsche, and music, and edited books on such topics as Nietzsche, German Idealism, aesthetics, ethics, erotic love, and non-Western philosophy. Among her works on music are *The Music of Our Lives* (Temple 1991, reissue by Lexington) and a book on music and human nature, entitled *Suspended Harmony: Our Musical Nature and Its Global Potential* [forthcoming].

Charles Johnson is a senior fellow at the Jepson School and professor of art history, emeritus, at the University of Richmond. He was educated at Westminster College, Union Theological Seminary in New York, and Ohio University, and received his Ph.D. in comparative arts. At Jepson he co-taught several courses on leadership and art. He has traveled widely, lectured in various countries, and received numerous teaching awards.

Antonio Marturano is an adjunct professor of Business Ethics on the Faculty of Economics, at the Sacred Heart Catholic University of Rome. Marturano has held academic positions in Italy, the United Kingdom, and the United States. He was the first European to teach a course at the Jepson School of Leadership Studies. Marturano was awarded a Marie Curie Fellowship. Marturano received his M.A. in philosophy at the University of Rome "La Sapienza" and his Ph.D. in analytical philosophy and philosophy of law at the State University of Milan. He has published extensively on computer ethics, leadership ethics, and deontic logic.

Nicholas O. Warner received his B.A. from Stanford and his Ph.D. in English from Berkeley. After a visiting appointment at Oberlin, he came to Claremont McKenna College, where he is Professor of Literature and a Faculty Associate at the Kravis Leadership Institute. His publications include *Spirits of America: Intoxication in 19th-Century American Literature* (a *Choice* Outstanding Academic Book in 1999), and articles on British, American, and Russian literature. More recently, his scholarship has focused on leadership in literature and film.

Index